College Writing

by Joe Giampalmi, EdD

for
dummies®
A Wiley Brand

College Writing For Dummies®

Published by: **John Wiley & Sons, Inc.,** 111 River Street, Hoboken, NJ 07030-5774, www.wiley.com

Copyright © 2022 by John Wiley & Sons, Inc., Hoboken, New Jersey

Published simultaneously in Canada

For general information on our other products and services, please contact our Customer Care Department within the U.S. at 877-762-2974, outside the U.S. at 317-572-3993, or fax 317-572-4002. For technical support, please visit https://hub.wiley.com/community/support/dummies.

Wiley publishes in a variety of print and electronic formats and by print-on-demand. Some material included with standard print versions of this book may not be included in e-books or in print-on-demand. If this book refers to media such as a CD or DVD that is not included in the version you purchased, you may download this material at http://booksupport.wiley.com. For more information about Wiley products, visit www.wiley.com.

Library of Congress Control Number: 2022941665

ISBN: 978-1-119-89503-9 (pbk); ISBN 978-1-119-89509-1 (epdf); ISBN 978-1-119-89505-3 (epub)

SKY10035315_071522

Contents at a Glance

Table of Contents

CHAPTER 10: Showing Sensitivity: Language That Builds Better Societies

CHAPTER 11: Scrutinizing Your Paper for Sneaky Grammar Errors

Introduction

You have a dream, and I have a vision to help you achieve that dream. My vision is to help you earn your college degree by guiding you through your most challenging first-year course, Writing 101 (or whatever your institution calls it). You made the first commitment toward that goal by buying this book. You understand the importance of college writing to help you reach your dream.

I've been helping students like you achieve their dream by teaching writing for more than a half century, including more than three decades at the college level. I've evaluated more than 10,000 essays, research papers, reaction papers, and reports. I started helping students with their writing when papers were completed on artifacts called manual typewriters and pages were submitted on erasable bond paper. Ask Siri or Alexa to explain it to you.

For you to succeed, I am asking two things:

>> Commit your best effort.

>> Increase your book reading ten minutes a day.

Successful people make time for what's important to them, and reading is as important as your writing. The commitment, book reading, and earning a degree are difference makers for you and your family's future — especially if you'll be the first college graduate in the history of your family.

About This Book

College Writing For Dummies emerged from the need to help conscientious college writers like you improve their writing skills and progress to their sophomore year prepared and confident to write successfully throughout college and their careers. The highest college dropout rate occurs at the end of the first year when students don't pass their essay course.

In addition to this book based on my more than five decades teaching writing, it's also based on my four decades writing magazine articles, authoring books, and writing a twice-monthly newspaper article for 34 years.

As I was teaching, I was also writing and facing the same challenges as my students. I frequently used examples of my writing in the classroom and explained to students how I generated ideas, created openings, and revised at three levels. In other words, as I taught writing I was learning and practicing the craft I was teaching.

Those hands-on experiences bring you this book, and here are some of its unique features:

>> Defeating writer's delay by beginning your essay in the middle

>> Developing a college writing style with specific nouns, active verbs, and style-builders such as repetition, surprise, and figures of speech

>> Using the essay as a foundation for other writing requirements such as reaction papers, reports, reviews of literature, and research papers

>> Adapting the Writing 101 essay to essays required in other courses such as psychology, finance, the arts, and political science

>> Completing an essay portfolio

>> Incorporating student language to illustrate almost every skill in the book

Here's a quick sample of what I cover in this book:

>> Giving, receiving, and applying peer feedback

>> Choosing essay topics that build grades

>> Understanding a composition course syllabus

>> Writing an assignment in the sequence of the middle, ending, and beginning

>> Revising at three levels

>> Avoiding any hint of plagiarism

>> Writing a cover letter for an essay portfolio

>> Understanding how professors grade essays

>> Synthesizing evidence using language starters

>> Gaining grade advantages by analyzing assignments and surveying rubrics

Like your cellphone manual, this book wasn't designed to be read cover to cover. Here's a quick-start menu of topics you may need at the beginning of the semester:

>> Getting started with your first college essay

>> Completing a first draft

- » Exploring a typical Writing 101 course

- » Becoming acclimated to your new college environment

- » Learning the organization and structure of an essay

- » Writing reaction papers, reports, research papers, reviews of literature, and essays for other courses

- » Building a compelling argument

- » Documenting sources formally or informally

And here's a quick list of topics you may find helpful as the semester progresses:

- » Developing a college-level writing style

- » Writing sentences that vary in rhythm and structure

- » Addressing grammar errors that sneak up on you

- » Preparing to submit your writing projects

Foolish Assumptions

You have a busy life as a college student, not an assumption, but a fact. From my decades' experience teaching students like you and enjoying your academic energy in the classroom, I offer the following assumptions:

- » You're committed to earning good grades, preferably an A, but you're amenable to your best effort earning a B.

- » You recognize your family's role supporting you as a college student and sometimes a family emergency necessitates missing class.

- » You like the socialization of working in teams, but don't like the lack of effort by some team members.

- » First-year college is physically exhausting, and occasionally it may show in class.

- » First-year college on campus is a difficult adjustment if you never spent much time away from home.

In other words, you know the challenges and are ready to face them.

Icons Used in This Book

Icons are legendary in *For Dummies* books. They're like cell phone alerts of information that have special meaning. Here's an explanation of four icons used to this book to help you explore points of interest:

This icon is used to highlight information that deserves special attention.

Think of this icon as cautionary action that may be necessary.

This icon represents a brief digression from the flow of content. This information is interesting but not necessarily essential to being a good writer.

This icon reinforces an important point.

Beyond This Book

For additional information related to adjusting to college life and college essay writing, the *College Writing For Dummies* Cheat Sheet is available at www.dummies.com. Just search for "College Writing For Dummies Cheat Sheet."

Where to Go from Here

This book represents a course guide to parallel your classroom instruction. Use it to supplement the classroom when you're assigned an essay and other classroom writing projects, or use it as a tutor when you need focus.

This book also serves as a reference for the writing processes from idea generation to final submission. You can use it as an alternate source of instruction.

You can start reading wherever you want. Flip to the Table of Contents or index, find a topic that piques your interest, and head to that chapter or section. No matter where you start, you'll find this book chock-full of information to help you become a better writer.

1

Getting Started with College Writing

Examine the time-honored rite of passage of the essay, its storied history, and its role as the foundation of a variety of types of college assignments.

Compare the five-paragraph essay and the college essay and discover the role of the essay in college writing today.

See typical activities in a college composition course, such as warm-up writing assignments, reading and response assignments, portfolio preparation assignments, and team-building activities.

Recognize the opportunity to show writing improvement through the essay portfolio, arguing the success of writing with examples from essays.

Chapter **1**

Transitioning to Greater Expectations: College Writing

The signature activity of an educated person is reading books. Reading is the key to your college writing success and to seamlessly transitioning to college academics.

Congratulations on earning your college admission and your decision to read this book to improve your college writing, especially your essay writing. You've successfully fulfilled the requirements for 12 years of school, and you're entering a world that defies the math you've learned. Grade 12 isn't followed by Grade 13. It's followed by an opportunity to change your life and your family's life, and it begins with your first-year writing in college.

You can become one of almost a third of adults who earn college degrees. But capitalizing on that opportunity will require an academic commitment that exceeds your efforts in the past. Your immediate challenge requires conquering your Writing 101 essay course, a challenge that destroys the dreams of almost 40 percent of first-year students who never become sophomores.

In this chapter, I explain the demographics of students entering college today and the challenges they face transitioning from traditional and nontraditional venues.

I also debunk myths associated with writing and college degrees. Turn the page and take one giant step toward your college degree.

Full Steam Ahead — Entering College

The call to college occurs at different times in people's lives. A fortunate majority begin college as teenage high school graduates; a few determined adults begin after a quarter century experiencing life, and a few eager lifetime learners begin after 60. Colleges are ready at the convenience of students. The limitations of learning are a lifespan.

Here's a look at demographics of students entering college today:

>> 90 percent younger than 24

>> 10 percent between 25 to 39

>> 0.2 percent 55 years or older

>> 5 percent international students, average age 25

REMEMBER

The average age of undergraduates enrolled full time is 21, and the average of students enrolled part time is 27. In addition, almost half of college students enrolled are first-generation students, pursuing a goal to be the first in their families to earn a college degree.

Students enrolling in college today represent a variety of cultural, social, and economic backgrounds and a variety of purposes for earning a college education. Most entering students will participate in the most diverse population they'll have experienced in their lifetime. Classroom discussions will include ideas from people with diverse backgrounds and diverse thinking.

Your enthusiasm for learning will blend with the academic energy of other students as you immerse yourself in college life that includes the following:

>> Discussing readings in the classroom

>> Talking in small groups on campus about classroom topics

>> Researching on wireless networks in indoor, outdoor, and remote spaces

>> Celebrating academic accomplishments

>> Planning leisure activities around tight schedules of classes, study, and part-time work

SUCCEEDING AS FIRST-GENERATION COLLEGE STUDENTS

Do you think of yourself as an educational trailblazer? Do you want to change direction of future generations of your family? Do you want to immediately influence the educational goals of siblings, nieces, and nephews?

First-generation college students, students of parents who haven't earned college degrees, represent almost half of all students enrolled in college today. They're the dream makers and risk-takers who are determined to be the first in their families to earn degrees and change the financial dynamics of future generations of their families. They can achieve for their families what the Wright brothers achieved for flight.

The demographics of first-generation students is likely to be Black or Hispanic, between ages 24 to 30, a parent of dependent children, and employed full time earning slightly above the poverty threshold. They're likely to enroll in a two-year community college, commute to classes, and take part-time classes.

In addition to their determination to be first, they possess the following assets to help earn their degrees: pride in their family's future, foresight to see financial advantages for future family members, confidence, and grit.

A majority of first-generation students are also firstborn and engrained with attributes such as leadership, responsibility, and initiative. They're achievers who meet deadlines. During the admission process, they face challenges such as inexperience with the college selection and application process and inexperience with the financial aid process.

As first-year students they face the challenges of unfamiliarity with academic language and lack of confidence to ask professors and advisors for help, feeling socially isolated on campus like they don't belong academically.

Recommendations for first-generation students include the following:

- Master the advisory-registration process for taking courses required to graduate.
- Learn technology for your course management platform and for navigating academic life.
- Familiarize yourself with resources on campus, especially those related to literacy.
- Participate in campus activities.
- Get familiar with library resources and services available through reference librarians.

Understanding What to Expect in Your College Writing Course

Your admission to college entitles you to a classroom seat — anywhere in the classroom you choose to sit. You'll also receive a syllabus — your last reminder of assignments due throughout the semester. A *syllabus* is a contract between you and your professor (I explain in greater detail in Chapter 2).

On your first day of college class, you'll recognize that you're no longer in high school and your class size is most likely smaller than high school. Take a look around the room, and you'll see unfamiliar people who feel equally uncomfortable. You may feel similar to how you felt the first day in first grade, but you now have your cellphone for security.

The following sections identify what practices from high school English you won't expect to happen in college writing, including a comparison to your college writing class. You can also find information about what your professor will (and won't) do.

Realizing you're not in your high school English class anymore

Here are practices common to your high school English class that you'll no longer experience in your college classroom:

>> **Daily reminders:** Your high school teachers saw you daily and reminded you of upcoming assignments. Your college syllabus is your one-time reminder of everything due for the semester.

>> **Flexible deadlines:** High school deadlines for essays, text, and projects are carved in sand. College deadlines indelibly recorded in your syllabus are changed as often as a harvest moon during leap year.

>> **Grading with pity points:** College grades are based exclusively on academic performance with no consideration of how well you organized the community-wide blood drive or how many times you were student of the month.

>> **Five-days-a-week classes:** College writing classes generally meet for 75 minutes twice a week, maybe 50 minutes three times a week. Your college study day begins after classes end.

>> **Class interruptions:** You won't miss in-class announcements, calls to the office, late arrivals and early dismissals, assemblies, abbreviated schedules, and knocks on the door. Classes are the business of college, and the business is life-altering.

>> **Regular testing:** High school tests provide numerous opportunities to stabilize grades and raise grades over a period of time. College courses commonly include three or four graded assignments, each one covering four times the content of your high school tests.

>> **Unaccountable readings:** High school reading assignments frequently get lost in the wilderness and disappear from being required. College reading assignments have multiple lives, recurring in tests, writing assignments, class discussions, and final exams.

Table 1-1 compares some other areas so you can see how high school and college writing classes differ.

TABLE 1-1   ## Differentiating High School and College Writing

	High School	College
Assignments	Essays and research papers	Essays, research papers, reaction papers, reports, reviews of literature, and media presentations
Discipline	Primarily English class	Across disciplines
Evidence	Opinions and limited research	Primary and secondary sources, surveys, and observations
Length	400 to 500 words	650 to 700 words
Revision	Submitted as one daft	Submission process includes multi-drafts. Drafts and feedback usually required to be submitted with portfolio
Thesis	Broad thesis adaptable to multiple sources of supporting information	A thesis that identifies an arguable issue related to the assigned question

You'll never appreciate your high school teachers as much as you will when you walk into your first college class with the excitement of "Where do I start?" and walk out with the confusion of "How do I start?"

IDENTIFYING WHAT YOU'RE RESPONSIBLE FOR

Growing up isn't easy, and you've been longing for your independence since you first crossed the street alone. Congratulations, you're a fully responsible adult with some, not nearly all, of the obligations.

You were most likely a very responsible high school student, but more than likely you had a family support system that included providing food, shelter, and some clothing. Your responsibility will be tested in college as you exercise your new independence.

Here's a look at some of your new responsibilities as college student for all your courses, not just college writing:

- **Attend all classes.** Attending class is your number one priority as a college student. Professors design classes to follow a logical sequence and academic rhythm. When you miss a class, you break the rhythm. Classes are to college what the Internet is to your social life.

   Remember: Attending class also means arriving at least 5 minutes early and not leaving early or abusing restroom needs. You don't want your professor to associate your name with arrival and departure times. You're expected to remain grounded during class time.

- **Plan for your success.** Start planning completion of your degree by scheduling a meeting with your academic advisor to anticipate courses your first two years of college. You may not know your major, but you should determine a general field of study such as humanities, sciences, business, communications, and so forth (see Chapter 16).

- **Familiarize yourself with campus resources.** During the first week of school, search your school's website to determine locations and contact information for resources such as health services, writing center, career planning, academic skills center, recreation center, and public safety.

   Tip: Your independence also includes managing your finances. Responsible adults manage money by distinguishing needs from wants. Avoid the two financial disasters of many college students: unmanageable student loans and credit card abuse. Learn to say "no" and "I don't need it."

- **Meet deadlines.** Responsible people meet deadlines, sometimes a day early. Missing deadlines is the second easiest way to destroy your college dreams; missing classes and assignments is the first way.

- **Stay healthy.** A healthy lifestyle, including regular exercise, provides the stamina to meet the physical demands of classes and study. It's sometimes described as a strong mind through a strong body.

- **Begin career planning.** Almost every college campus has a career planning center. They guide you through career interest planning, resume building, and interview preparation. You will learn life-altering information such as the workplace has no spring break and you have no cut days.

Recognizing that college professors are nonnegotiable

You learned which teachers in high school you could manipulate for hall passes, assignment extensions, or full class discussions of your favorite music. That was high school. Save your negotiating skills for your career. Professors don't negotiate with terrorists or students. They only negotiate with their supervisors.

Your high school teachers and college professors are as different as synchronized swimming and ballroom dancing. Therefore, you face a greater chance of drowning in a college class.

Table 1–2 shows you differences between high school and college instructors; this information will help keep you afloat.

TABLE 1-2   **Differentiating between High School Teachers and College Professors**

	High School Teachers	College Professors
Availability	Available after school every day.	Availability two hours weekly and sometimes by email.
Homework	Almost every night.	"It's on the syllabus."
Submitting requirements	Will remind you, email you, track you down, tell friends to tell you an assignment is missing.	"It's on the syllabus."
Teaching style	Variety of styles to keep all level students interested. "I'm here afterschool every day to help you."	This is the content. You make sense out of it. "See me during office hours if you need help."
Testing	Every few weeks with minimal content.	Every few months with maximum content.
Training	Generalists in secondary topics in field.	Experts in field and nerds since birth.

EVERYONE HAS OTHER COURSES AND RESPONSIBILITIES

High school students regularly complain to their teachers that they're overwhelmed with work from other classes and that multiple tests fall on similar days. Say goodbye to the fantasy high school world and hello to the grown-up world where people you're responsible to expect you to fulfill your obligations. As a first-year college student, you're at the bottom of the food chain and responsible to everyone.

Everyday responsible adults fulfill work responsibilities with family members sick at home, transportation problems, relationship issues, financial complications, personal health concerns — and many more serious issues. That's the standard for responsible adults.

Successful college students are adults who find a way to fulfill their responsibilities and utilize resources available when they need help. High school students shed their training wheels when they enter college. Older nontraditional students already learned to manage complex adult lifestyles that include full-time employment and full-time family responsibilities.

Your college experience includes identifying your life's priorities and budgeting the time to fulfill those responsibilities. For example, because you're reading this book, academics is a priority in your life. And as a college student, academics requires a major time commitment of your allocated 24 daily hours.

Even though you'll be a lifetime learner, your academic commitment will never be as intense as it is during the 4 to 4.5 years to earn your degree. Approximately 4 million students, 18 percent of all students in college, earn degrees annually. Walt Disney said, "If you can dream it, you can do it." You have dreamed it, and you can do it.

Debunking Writing Myths

When first-year-college students become seniors, they thrive on telling comp course stories, such as being assigned to read James Michener's 868-page *Alaska* and write a 5,000-word reaction paper over the weekend.

The Michener assignment exemplifies a myth associated with first-year writing. Here's a look at other myths and their realities.

Myth No. 1: My professor doesn't like my writing style

Professors don't evaluate first-year writing primarily on style unless your interpretation of style includes faulty sentence structure, unintended fragments, inactive and weak verbs, vague nouns, and long sentences with delayed subjects and verbs (see Chapters 9 and 11). If that last sentence sounds like your style, your professor is correct and your writing needs a new wardrobe.

REMEMBER

As a general rule, professors accept any writing style that includes clear and somewhat concise writing. If you think a professor doesn't like your style, talk with your professor to clarify the meaning of "writing style," what the professor dislikes about the writing, and how you can fix it.

Myth No. 2: Writing is just too darn hard

Writing is difficult, but some students make it more difficult by not following what research shows are best practices for successful college writing. You've designed a plan to fail if you start writing assignments late, neglect to analyze the assignment, skip background reading and planning, and start to take the essay seriously two days before deadline. Chapter 12 explains how to avoid these problems.

That approach is like typing your assignment on your phone wearing mittens. You can make writing easier by following the process of writing: prewriting (see Chapter 12), drafting (see Chapter 13), revising (see Chapter 14), and preparing for presentation (see Chapter 15).

Here are the names of writers who found writing difficult and had classic works rejected: Agatha Christie, George Bernard Shaw, Beverly Cleary, Earnest Hemingway, Dr. Seuss, J.K. Rowling, Stephen King, F. Scott Fitzgerald, and John Grisham. If you're not familiar with any of these famous writers, you need to read more.

Writing doesn't come easy for most people, including most professional writers. But writing isn't an insurmountable task that only a few can master. Most people learn to write by following the practices of good writing, one of which is commitment. But it will never be as easy as skills you're more interested in and more motivated to learn. Check out Chapter 5.

Writing doesn't come easy for most writers, and neither do worthwhile accomplishments. That's why people climb mountains and not hills. That's why college degrees are earned and not awarded. The lesson is to work hard and believe in yourself. You'll find the more you practice, the easier it gets.

Myth No. 3: Only problem writers need feedback

All writers need feedback (read about feedback in Chapter 14) to tell them what works and what doesn't work. Classroom instructors at all levels provide opportunities for feedback. The rejections of the classic books was feedback that told the authors their books needed revising. Feedback is to writing what ice is to learning to skate. You can't move forward without it.

Myth No. 4: I suffer from the block

Picture this. You and your significant other are enjoying a romantic dinner at your favorite restaurant. You're waiting patiently for your dinner as your server appears at your table and says: "I'm sorry we can't serve you dinner. The chef is experiencing culinary block."

Being blocked, or the inability to perform creativity, has been attributed exclusively to the art of writing. Electricians, teachers, chefs, pilots, and so forth don't experience suffering from the block. Writers and creative innovators experience regular challenges that are addressed with problem solving and decision making. Chapter 13 explains techniques that help overcome writing procrastination and roadblocks. You can always do something to move your writing forward: read about the topic, question your organization, rethink your opening sentence, and so forth.

Writing requires completion of a series of complex processes that results in successful drafts. No student with a respectable work ethic can be blocked 360 degrees.

Myth No. 5: I can revise in ten minutes

Without feedback, writers wouldn't know if their writing is good or bad. A rejected novel tells Stephen King his book is unsuccessful. A Pulitzer Prize tells Ernest Hemingway his writing is good, and similarly academic writers who think they can revise in ten minutes not only confuse revising with editing, but also underestimate the influence of revising on improving writing.

Here's a quick overview how editing and revising differ (Chapter 14 explains these processes):

>> **Editing:** A form of revising, editing is usually associated with correcting. An editing session may be completed in ten minutes, but it's like the first step of a morning run.

>> **Revising:** Revising is the process where writers see the biggest improvements in their writing. It ranges from rethinking structure, organization, focus, development, and flow to correcting rules of grammar, usage, punctuation, and spelling. Revising isn't correcting writing, but clarifying the writing message. Good writers are good revisers.

Myth No. 6: Writers are born

Is anyone born with polished skills in any field? This line of thinking implies a fixed mindset (Chapter 5), the belief that you're either a college student or not or a confident person or not — and you can't do anything to improve. Education and self-fulfillment result from a growth mindset, the belief that improvement results from hard work.

REMEMBER

Writers become good when they work hard developing the skills needed to become a writer, such as information gathering, planning, organizing, drafting, and revising. First-year writing courses offer a venue to improve writing. Students who work hard at it, and get help when they need it, succeed.

Eyeing the Prize — Your Degree

Don't lose sight of the prize, earning your college degree. Keep your goal in mind with every class, study session, test, and assignment. Celebrate every successful semester as a major step forward. Expect minor setbacks such as a failed test or possibly a failed course. You can recover. Keep your eye on the prize, your belief in yourself, and the meaning of your degree to younger family members.

The economic return on the value of college — assuming control of student loans — remains as convincing as ever. Recent U.S. Census data shows that after the entry-level phase in the workplace, college degrees are worth approximately 2 million dollars over a lifetime, associate's two-year degree worth 1.5 million, and a high school diploma worth 1.2 million.

Another study examined salaries of workers age 23 to 60 over a cross-section of their career and found that bachelor's degrees earned approximately $43,000 annually, a high school diploma earned $30,000, and a non-degrees earned

$19,000. Those completing graduate school earned approximately $100,000 during the same period. A number of studies show the more you learn, the more you earn.

In addition, college grads are more likely to be employed full time compared with high school graduates. High school graduates are likely to be unemployed at twice the rate of college graduates.

The following sections identify the advantages of a college degree and the life adjustments required to transition into college and earn that degree.

Becoming a 33.3 percenter

Becoming one of the approximately one-third of adults with college degrees gives you the confidence that you can accomplish any goal.

REMEMBER

Additional benefits of a college degree include the following:

>> More flexible job opportunities

>> More choices of where to live

>> More familiarity with different cultures

>> Increased likeliness of their children earning degrees

>> Higher standard of living

>> Increased awareness of public issues

>> More active in the democratic process

A recent study showed that one-third of adults who lacked a college degree declined to apply for a job they felt they were qualified for because it required a college degree.

Adjusting to college life

Adapting to college life is one of the major adjustments in a lifetime. The adjustment is socially and culturally — in addition to being academically. Here are some tips for adapting to college and avoiding that meltdown phone call to your parents:

>> **Read more.** Make a stronger commitment to reading more in college than you did in high school (see Chapter 15).

>> **Balance your lifestyle.** Create a balance among study, work, and socializing. When you need more study time, take hours from socializing.

>> **Attend orientations.** Attend all new student orientations. In addition to socializing, you'll learn strategies for adapting to college.

>> **Live your values.** Live a lifestyle that reflects the values you were taught by the significant adults in your life.

>> **Smile.** Be open and friendly toward everyone on campus. Make eye contact with people and give them a smile. Most people will return one.

>> **Attend tech workshops.** You're likely good at technology, but possibly not academic technology. Campuses usually offer regular technology workshops on topics related to academic life.

>> **Attend cultural events.** Enjoy the full experience of college life and attend performances in the arts.

>> **Learn from lectures.** Campus activities include guest lecturers regularly visiting campus. Look for topics that interest you and topics related to your courses. Lectures also provide you experiences to connect to your writing.

>> **Enjoy college sports.** College sports are exciting and major events on campus. Go to different types of events like a volleyball or wrestling match.

>> **Go clubbing.** Join at least one club. The initial recruiting meeting usually has free food.

>> **Attend convocation.** Attend convocation and experience the formality of academic life. It may be your first experience to witness full academic regalia.

>> **Attend an academic awards ceremony.** Attend at least one celebration of academic achievement. Share the excitement of students' academic accomplishments.

>> **Attend graduation.** Attend at least one before your graduation, and you'll have an indelible memory of the most memorable day in your life to date.

» **Showing is knowing**

» **Decoding academic discourse**

» **Focusing on the importance of reading**

Chapter **2**

Sailing into Safe Waters: First-Year Writing Success

First-year college writing, especially the essay, is the first fear of many incoming college students. The fear is justifiable because of college's higher literacy expectations. But the fear is also manageable knowing you were accepted into college, you can learn to write successfully and graduate — and your resources include this book to help you.

The essay is central to your writing success. Your academic writing life began pronouncing sounds of your first letters and will progress through submitting your first college portfolio in your first-year writing course. The five-paragraph essay you wrote in middle and high school expands into the multi-paragraph essay you'll write in first-year college writing.

This chapter explains the evolution of the essay, the essay as a rite of passage, the language of academics and first-year writing, and writing connections that contribute to your writing success. You're on the clock, and you have four years to earn your degree.

Understanding the Essay and College Writing

The essay is to college writing what books are to educated people, what professors are to college teaching, and what wireless is to technology — they're inseparable. The essay has been a major part of students' academic life for more than 15 centuries. With such a storied history, the essay requirement isn't likely to disappear before you graduate. Commit yourself to mastering it; you have on-campus resources to help you. These sections explore the expanded role of the essay in academics and its importance to you as a college student.

Time-honored rite of passage

The rites of passage in your early writing life included the following:

>> Writing words into sentences (see Chapter 8)

>> Writing consecutive sentences on a topic (see Chapter 8)

>> Developing a topic into a paragraph (see Chapter 8)

>> Writing multiple paragraphs on a topic (see Chapter 5)

>> Developing a thesis from a topic with supporting details (see Chapter 6)

>> Writing the five-paragraph essay

The five-paragraph essay that you began in middle school developed into your admission essay, a rite of passage into college. Now you face one additional rite of passage: writing your comp course essays for your first-year portfolio (see Chapter 4) — your rite of passage into your sophomore year.

The expanded five–paragraph essay is integral to your life as a college student and reveals your ability to think and argue an assigned topic. It also shows your verbal aptitude to express ideas clearly concisely and your command of the English language.

Comparing the five-paragraph and college essay

The five–paragraph essay, forms of which are hundreds of years old, serves the needs of emerging writers. It's an excellent tool for learning writing structure with its opening, body, and closing. The opening ends with a thesis that gives direction to the essay. The body contains three middle paragraphs, each explaining a reason that supports the thesis. The closing paragraph summarizes the body.

THE EVOLUTION OF THE ESSAY

The mystique of the essay allegedly developed from an early form of classical rhetoric that began in Greece and Rome about the fifth century. The essay may be the oldest continuous academic requirement taught in schools. It's older than dial-up access to the Internet, the beginning of modern history for many of today's students.

Classical rhetoric is the ancient art of persuasion using grammar and logic.

The study of rhetoric and grammar originated in the 15th century. In the 19th century teachers referred to the five-paragraph essay as the *hamburger essay* because three body paragraphs are sandwiched between an opening and closing paragraph. Two aliases of the essay are *theme* and *composition.*

The *five* serves middle and high school teachers because students learn essay organization. The organization of this type of essay is transferrable to almost every piece of writing because it begins with an opening and ends with a closing.

For the past hundred years, the five-paragraph essay has been the standard in schools because of its accountability and easy assessment for teachers. Developing writers can easily be graded on explaining the importance of a topic with three reasons.

But topics at the middle and high school levels lack analysis and synthesis of college topics. For example, a high school writer may explain three similarities between two contemporary authors, but a college writer may synthesize how those reasons are dissimilar and both authors' contributions to the development of the contemporary novel.

Table 2–1 shows the difference between the two types of essays.

Expanding the five-paragraph format

Think of the college essay as a super app that gives you expansion services to meet your writing needs. If the five-paragraph essay is the hamburger, the college essay is a gourmet buffet because it offers features to satisfy almost every professor's requirements.

TABLE 2-1 **Differentiating between the Five-Paragraph and College Essays**

Criteria	Five-Paragraph Essay	College Essay
Body paragraphs	Three equal-length paragraphs, each explaining a reason	Multiparagraphs with documented supporting evidence
Conclusion	Summary	Synthesis of evidence and wider implication of thesis
Drafts	One	Multiple drafts until portfolio ready
Introduction	All-encompassing opening that adapts to multiple ideas in the essay body	Symbolic representation of an arguable thesis that addresses the assignment prompt
Length	350 to 450 words	550 to 650 words
Revising	Synonymous with editing	Revising at three levels
Structure	Variations of five-paragraph structure	Thematic requirement determines paragraphs
Thesis	Broad thesis that adapts to three reasons	Focused thesis that addresses the prompt question

You as a college student have mastered essay organization (see Chapter 5). Your college requirements include not only complex openings and closings, but also body paragraphs that include analysis (see Chapter 5), synthesis (Chapter 7), and application (see Chapter 5).

At the college level, the five matures with multiparagraph essays developing an arguable thesis, and includes elements such as the following:

» Organization and framework that develops the thesis (see Chapter 5)

» A specific audience and purpose (see Chapter 6)

» Creditable evidence that supports the thesis (see Chapter 7)

» Formal and informal documentation (see Chapter 7)

» Respectful and unbiased language (see Chapter 10)

» A topic that offers value to the academic audience (see Chapter 6)

Showing is knowing

Unlike the true-false test, multiple choice test, and the fill-in-the-blanks test, the college essay offers you an opportunity to show what you know.

The assessment value of the college essay is that it requires showing your knowledge of content, your thinking to explain the topic, and your writing skill to express it clearly — all of which I examine here.

Shows knowledge

Essay writing is built on content knowledge — facts and information fundamental to your ideas. For example, an essay about alternate sources of energy requires knowledge of wind power, solar power, and biofuels. Writing is the process of applying that knowledge to new settings, such as arguing the compatibility of alternate sources of energy with fossil fuels. The major sources of accessing knowledge are reading and listening.

Shows thinking

Writing is frequently described as showing your thinking on paper. Essays show your critical thinking skills such as the following:

>> Prioritizing a topic that addresses the essay prompt (see Chapter 12)

>> Transforming the topic into an arguable thesis (see Chapter 6)

>> Researching credible evidence to support the thesis (see Chapter 7)

>> Analyzing evidence to develop the argument (see Chapter 7)

>> Extending significance of the thesis (see Chapter 5)

>> Comparing and contrasting (see Chapter 5)

>> Showing cause and effect relationships (see Chapter 5)

Shows writing

Your essay also shows your skill to organize your thoughts, develop them, and present them clearly. Writing also demonstrates the following skills:

>> Concise language (see Chapter 14)

>> Respectful and unbiased language (see Chapter 10)

>> Smooth flow of ideas (see Chapter 8)

>> Thesis development (see Chapter 7)

>> Use of writing conventions (see Chapter 11)

>> Knowledge of grammar and usage (see Chapter 11)

>> Tense consistency (see Chapter 6)

>> Parallel structure (see Chapter 11)

Grasping the essay role in college writing

The essay, the heartbeat of the rhythm of college writing, includes the organization of almost all college writing projects. The opening, body, and closing is indigenous to college assignments such as reaction papers, research papers, reports, and reviews of literature (see Chapter 16). The essay structure applies to writing topics in the humanities, in social and behavioral sciences, and across disciplines. However, essay fundamentals don't apply to assignments in the hard sciences such as lab reports and observations or economic assignments such as financial reports.

Essay elements that apply to most types of college writing include audience, purpose (see Chapter 6), tone (see Chapter 6), coherence (see Chapter 8), and style (see Chapter 9). College writing also includes framework such as narration, persuasion, comparison, contrast, analysis (see Chapter 5), and synthesis (see Chapter 7).

Talking the Talk

The culture shock of college is like travelling a foreign country without your translation app. Your new world includes vocabulary uncommon to the non-academic world, and your survival depends on understanding the language.

For example, some unfortunate students learn that the connection between probation and libation is more closely related than rhyme. And don't confuse a TA and RA and ask the TA the time the weekend activities begin.

This section looks at the foreign language of academics, and misunderstandings could have pass/fail implications.

Translating academic-speak

Your knowledge of technology is determined by your understanding of its language, For example, laptop use is restricted without understanding terms such as Bluetooth, operating system, and processor. Your knowledge of the college academic environment requires understanding of academic terminology, called *discourse*. For example, you'll never receive a class schedule without an understanding of your obligations to the bursar.

ADDRESSING COLLEGE PROFESSORS

Address professors as "doctor" or "professor" if they're listed in the syllabus as PhD or EdD. If they haven't earned these terminal degrees, use "professor," "Mr.," or "Ms." Avoid "Mrs." unless they use that prefix in the syllabus.

Don't address professors by their first name unless they tell you to do so in class. If you feel uncomfortable using their first name, revert to "professor."

Misspelling your professor's name on an assignment shows lack of attention to detail. Misidentifying their title represents another language error. If they tell you to identify them as "Dr." or "professor" on an assignment, don't follow their name with the suffix representing their degree.

Categories of academic language include course-related discourse, academic leadership discourse, and student-reference discourse, which I discuss further.

Course-related discourse

Here's a look at discourse related to daily academic life and terminology that you're likely to hear talking with your academic advisor and other students:

>> **Add/drop period:** A brief time period at the beginning of every semester during which students can drop or add a course without penalty

>> **Course load:** The number of courses (total credit hours) taken in a given semester

>> **Declared major:** Primary focus of study for a four-year degree

>> **Discipline:** An academic field of study, such as business management

>> **Electives:** Optional courses that fulfill general education requirement, separate from degree requirements

>> **Lecture:** Type of course delivered primarily verbally

>> **Pass/fail:** A course in which a student doesn't receive a letter grade, but a *pass* or *fail* grade

>> **Pedagogy:** Method and practice of a teaching strategy

>> **Prerequisite:** A course that must be taken before taking a specific course, such as College Composition I, a prerequisite to College Composition II

>> **Registration:** Time frame in which students may enroll in a course

>> **Withdraw:** A student's dropping from a course after the add/drop period

>> **Writing intensive (WI):** Designation of some courses that fulfill general education writing requirements

REMEMBER

Throughout this book, you experience discourse related to writing terminology such as the following: collaborative writing, primary and secondary sources, feedback, rubric, prompt, convention, annotation, and review of literature. I explain these terms within their context.

Academic leadership discourse

The terminology identifies people you may have experiences with:

>> **Academic advisor:** Mentor who shares student's responsibility to sequentially enroll in the courses that result in your degree. Students have an advisor as an undeclared major and an additional advisor as a declared major.

>> **Bursar:** University official responsible for collecting tuition and fees. The first person who validates you're officially enrolled — just as soon as payment clears.

>> **Chancellor:** Similar to the president or highest-ranking administrator of a university.

>> **Dean:** Head of a major field of study within a university, such as the College of Communication and Creative Arts.

>> **Department chair:** Head of a major department or discipline such as Chair of the Writing Arts Department.

>> **Provost:** Most senior academic administrator second in charge to the president.

>> **Registrar:** University official responsible for maintaining students' academic records.

>> **Resident assistant (RA):** Trained peer leader who coordinates activities in a dorm.

>> **Teaching assistant (TA):** Graduate student or equivalent who assists the professor with large classes.

Student-reference discourse

Here's a look at student-reference discourse:

>> **Associate degree:** A two- or three-year degree earned from a community college.

>> **Bachelor's degree:** A university degree representing four years of study.

>> **Dean's list:** List of students who achieve high academic excellence. Dean's list includes students who graduate *magna cum laude* (with great distinction) and *summa cum laude* (with the highest distinction).

>> **Gap year:** A year-long break between high school and college.

>> **Grade point average (GPA):** A student's mathematical computation of how well a student performed.

>> **Independent study:** A nontraditional course of study that allows students to complete an academic project over one semester.

>> **Nonresident:** A student whose legal resident differs from the same state of the university they're attending.

>> **Part-time student:** A student enrolled in fewer than the full-time credit load, usually fewer than 12 credits.

>> **Transcript:** A record of a student's academic progress, which usually includes grades and total credit hours.

Decoding your essay syllabus

The *syllabus*, the document that speaks loudest and most authoritatively about course content, represents what you can't survive without. It's used for planning, organizing, preparing, and verifying information about each course.

It's like the driving manual that tells you what you can do, what you can't do, and the penalty for violating a rule. Professors expect students to decode the syllabus.

REMEMBER

As a legal document, the syllabus identifies the responsibility of the professor as the person who delivers content and your responsibility as a student to learn content.

Here's why the syllabus is important to you:

>> Provides information for contacting your professor, locating the classroom, and visiting your professor during office hours

>> Explains the grading system and grading weight of every assignment and requirement — information that helps you validate the accuracy of your grade

>> Lists assignment dates and important course dates, information needed to include in your course planning and organization

>> Names the texts and materials you'll need for the course

>> Identifies readings and requirements due for every class

Here's a look at the grade–influencing parts of the syllabus:

>> **Contact information:** The professor's name, email, office location, and office hours; the official name and numbers referencing the course; the classroom location and meeting days and times; and prerequisite courses required to enroll in the course (see Figure 2-1 for an example).

Rowan University

College of Communication   Writing Arts Department

Syllabus, Fall 2023
College Writing 101
No Prerequisites required

CW 00101-1   CRN 34951

Meeting days: Tues. / Thurs. 9:30 – 9:45AM   Classroom: Bozen 202
Instructor: Dr. Joseph Giampalmi
GiampalmiJ@Rowan.edu
Office: Carson 101
Office Hours: Tues. / Thurs 10:00 – 11:30

FIGURE 2-1:
A sample of syllabus contact information.

(c) John Wiley & Sons, Inc.

>> **Grading:** Weighted value of every course requirement and criteria that determines A, B, C, and so forth (see Figure 2-2).

>> **Assignments:** Explanations of assignments, weighted values, and due dates.

>> **Attendance:** Attendance policy and penalty for missing class. For example, some universities issue an automatic failure for missing a specific number of classes, and some universities allow unlimited cuts.

REMEMBER

Your primary responsibility as a student is to attend every class. Classes are what you're paying for.

>> **Participation:** Point value associated with participation and the definition of *participation*.

>> **Weekly schedule:** List of activities and requirements for each week of class (see the following sample of a syllabus weekly schedule).

> **Week 4:**
> Essay 2 due by email. Bring to class draft of essay 1.
> Complete reading of Grant's *Originals*.
> Practice sentence variety.

(c) John Wiley & Sons, Inc.

In addition to the attendance policy, the following policies are linked to the syllabus:

>> **Academic honesty:** The examples listed in the plagiarism policy tell you the violations that have occurred at the university. See Chapter 13 for information on plagiarism.

>> **Recycling:** Most universities have policy of using a previously written paper without permission.

>> **Classroom behavior:** Universities have a policy for classroom behavior, if it's needed.

Additional topics in the syllabus include the following:

>> **Accommodations:** Needs of some students to accommodate their learning (see the following example):

> I value your commitment to succeed in the course. If you have circumstances that may affect your performance in this course, please see me during the first week of the course so that we may work together to achieve your success. Documentation for accommodations is available in the Student Success Center, located in the Swartz Center. If you experience a life situation (such as surgery), please see me as soon as possible so that we may talk about your options.

(c) John Wiley & Sons, Inc.

>> **Help availability:** A list of resources available to help performance in the course.

>> **Course description and learning objectives:** An overview of the course and description of what you'll be learning (see Figure 2-3).

FIGURE 2-3:
A syllabus sample of a course description and learning objectives.

> College Writing 101 prepares you for the demands of college thinking and college writing. You are required to complete a portfolio of college-level essays that show continuous improvement from draft to draft. Successful essays include focus, organization, and development that flows from an arguable thesis statement. College writing extends beyond the five-paragraph structure and includes engagement of sources and documentation.
>
> Success in the course requires you to analyze and synthesize information and develop insights from a variety of sources including research, readings, observation, personal experience, discussions, and reflection. The writing and creative process requires constant rethinking and revising content.

(c) John Wiley & Sons, Inc.

Discovering New Partnerships

Walt Disney celebrates children throughout the world with his iconic exhibit "It's a small, small, world." And an earworm that will remain with you for the next few days. With respect to one of the world's most creative people, it's an ever-expanding world for students like you to explore. Some of those areas of exploration include partnerships directly affiliated with your college writing. This section explores partnerships with reading, a partnership that most successful people share, a partnership as strong as an earworm.

Reading and writing connection

Your first-year college writing success and future academic success depends on your reading success. A body of evidence, including landmark studies, shows that reading and writing improve writing. They're skills that improve regularly with practice. Reading and writing also improve academic performance in the present and future.

Your college reading and writing demands will exceed your requirements in high school. The best high school readers, those who regularly read books, usually qualify for honors-level college composition courses, and earn honors-level As and Bs.

Good high school readers, who choose not to enroll in honors courses, usually earn As in Writing 101 courses. Students who don't regularly read books, earn Cs and an occasional Bs in their first-year writing course, and earn B and C grades in their other courses. Readers are rewarded with good grades.

REMEMBER

I regularly share reminders of the importance of reading and the importance of the reading and writing connection. You can improve your grades by increasing your reading minutes.

Reading and lifetime learning

Reading is your major source of absorbing information throughout your career. In the workplace, reading is required for things like understanding data and policies, obtaining information to solve a problem, and evaluating a process or procedure.

Frequently throughout life, you'll become absorbed with projects that require extensive reading such as researching to make a major purchase, preparing for travel, and discovering more about a health-related issue. And frequently your reading is as simple as reading for enjoyment.

When you're assigned a reading selection in college, you're expected to perform activities such as the following:

>> Identify main ideas.

>> Identify the purpose of the writing.

>> Make assessments about the author.

>> Synthesize points of view, their relationship with each other, and the relationship with the main point of the reading.

>> Identify weaknesses in the argument of the reading (see Chapter 7).

>> Identify the structure and framework of the reading (see Chapter 5).

These reading purposes prepare you for other academic projects as well as develop your reading and thinking skills.

REMEMBER

In addition to campuses providing resources to help students with writing, most campuses also provide resources to help with reading.

TIP

If you're motivated by money, studies show readers earn more money than nonreaders.

Writing and career success

A recent study showed that about 75 percent of employers preferred new employees with well-developed writing skills. Students who write well increase their opportunities to land a job. Employees who write well increase their opportunity to receive a promotion. In other words, daily writing to communicate is an essential skill for career leaders.

Writing as a leader in the workplace includes writing for purposes such as the following:

>> Introducing a new product or service

>> Evaluating an employee

>> Explaining the solution to a problem

>> Writing policy

>> Maintaining daily communication with a team

Chapter **3**

Previewing a College Writing 101 Course: Getting Schooled

Your first day on campus you'll quickly figure out that college isn't high school. Your first day in composition class you'll discover that college writing isn't high school writing.

In the first few weeks of your course, you'll the difference between a high school A and a college A. College As are as rare as a full scholarship.

In this chapter, I describe your College Writing 101 course, including the volume of writing you'll be expected to complete. I offer you strategies for balancing family, friendship, and scholarship. I show you a handful of examples of what essay writing is not, and I explain eleven skills you'll learn in the course and use forevermore. Class is ready to begin.

Making First Impressions: First-Year-Writing Classroom

Not only do high school teachers teach about twice as many classroom hours as college professors, they also teach about twice as many students. College professors are allocated more time to prepare for class, evaluate student writing, offer feedback, and suggest revising.

Another difference is that you and your peers are fully committed to earning an education, unlike all high school students. College professors dedicate little to no time managing disinterested students. Your professor and your course are focused on your education.

Consequently, you're held to a higher accountability for the content you write, the audience you address, the insights you offer, the documentation you provide, and the language you use to express yourself.

VARIATIONS OF A COLLEGE WRITING 101 COURSE

College Writing 101 courses, the traditional first-year-writing course, extends one semester or both semesters your freshmen year. The course at different universities includes the following options:

- **Literature study:** Many composition courses include a literature component with writing assignments based on literature. Course readings are literary works. The advantages of such structures is that it provides experiences in classic literature and often fulfills a literature requirement.

- **Theme based:** This approach includes composition and readings focused on a theme such as community service, social justice, music, sports, the environment, and so forth. The advantage of theme-approached courses is that they provide in-depth academic study in an area of predetermined interest.

- **Content affiliated:** A recent trend has been combining composition with a content such as engineering, the arts, business, education, and so forth. The advantage of this approach is that you improve your writing in the language of course content. Chapter 16 offers more information on writing in various content areas.

- **Composition exclusively:** Many colleges with writing or rhetoric departments are offering composition exclusively. This approach studies the processes of writing in depth.

Here, I explain your classroom options — do the work or fail — and show you the requirements of a typical Writing 101 classroom.

TECHNICAL STUFF

Writing is a requirement at almost every institution of higher education. Titles for that first foundation writing course includes College Writing, First-Year Writing, Freshmen Writing, College Composition I (CCI), Composition and Rhetoric, and Writing and Rhetoric. Regardless of the name, it represents a challenging academic experience that predicts your future college success, and this book helps you meet you that challenge.

The professor's way — the only way

You're exercising your new freedoms as a college student with decisions such as to study or not to study, to sleep or not to sleep, to read or not to read, to work out or not to work out, and many more. But when you walk into the classroom, you lack input on what you're required to do and how you're required to do it. Democracy has fallen. Professors rule.

But fear not, the rulers are prepared and focused on offering you the best course money can buy. And why do they have so much confidence in their course? They wrote the course, and they set the expectations for the course. You don't get your say in developing the course because it's not a democratic process.

TECHNICAL STUFF

First-year writing courses differ slightly from other courses. Professors write the delivery of the course, but departments establish consistency and quality control with guidelines such as the number of essays, assignment options, documentation style, types of readings, and choices of skill materials.

Professors write the syllabus (Chapter 2 explains the syllabus) that includes required essays, required readings, supplemental assignments, and final portfolios. Course content and course delivery is their expertise and due dates are as stable as the four presidents on Mount Rushmore. Professors' motto: It's in the syllabus; therefore, it is.

Unlike your high school teachers, professors don't manage classrooms with class votes and class consensus. They learn early in their teaching careers that a change in an assignment date causes a chain reaction in due dates. They also learn that a change in one assignment due date results in an official student evaluation that reads "always changes assignments."

When you're in the classroom, only one vote counts, the one cast by the person in the front of the room controlling the computer. That person also controls the grades. Work hard, play by the rules, and accept responsibility for what's due. Improve your writing, earn your course credit, and progress to the next course.

Just accept it and do it

College may seem like another planet, and you'll eventually like the inhabitants who are committed to offering you a world-class education. But you'll experience an acclimation period adjusting to the assignments.

Your college requirements may include assignments that you may question, such as writing a letter to yourself explaining how you plan to write your assignment. Or you may decide you want to question a professor's feedback on an assignment because you received As on your high school essay and consider yourself an A student.

Save your academic energy and follow the advice of that infamous shoe company, "Just do it." Professors know the *pedagogy* (teaching practices) that support learning. For example, a letter to yourself about planning your essay provides you reflection to think about how you'll approach your essay. Research identifies reflection as a best practice in the teaching of writing.

As a first-year college student, you have little experience with the college and learning process. When an assignment appears irrelevant or unreasonable to you, yield to professors with letters behind their name.

TIP

Develop a connection with at least one professor each semester for the purpose of asking for a letter of recommendation. Composition professors are good candidates because they learn your strengths through your writing. Before asking for a recommendation (in person and in writing), be sure you're performing well in the course and that the professor knows you by name. Ask at least two weeks before you need the recommendation, and be sure you have excellent attendance in the course.

Composition courses require a variation of essay structures designed to meet course objectives. Individual essays (or combinations of essays) usually require the following structures:

>> **Narrative:** Tells a story

>> **Descriptive:** Describes people, places, experiences, and ideas

>> **Expository:** Explains steps in a process

>> **Persuasive:** Convinces the reader to believe in a position or take action

>> **Comparison and contrast:** Identifies similarities and differences

>> **Cause and effect:** Analyzes reasons and consequences

>> **Analytical:** Evaluates, judges, and draws conclusions

Chapter 5 explains these structures in detail.

Looking closer at a typical college comp course

Over the semester, composition course requirements include the following:

» **Writing assignments:** Students are required to write three or four essays and two to three drafts of each essay. Writing assignments generally include options based on a theme in the assignment. Some professors require prewriting submitted with the assignment and thesis approval before writing. Chapter 12 explains prewriting strategies and assignment analysis techniques. Chapter 6 explains thesis writing, and Chapter 7 examines thesis support.

» **Writing process assignments:** Over the semester expect to study numerous strategies related to the processes of writing. They include prewriting (Chapter 12), revising, offering and responding to feedback (both in Chapter 14), openings and closings (Chapter 5), engaging sources (Chapter 7), and sentence and paragraph development (Chapter 8).

» **Readings:** Readings over the course include two to three academic articles for each essay, each ranging between 15 to 30 pages. A nonfiction paperback or two may be required for theme essays or theme courses.

» **Portfolio assignments:** Most universities require a portfolio of essays, including feedback and revisions of each essay. Portfolios typically account for 60 to 65 percent of the final grade. Chapter 4 details information on portfolios.

» **Non-portfolio assignments:** A number of non-portfolio assignments are required over the semester, accounting for the percentage of the grade beyond the portfolio. These assignments include responses to readings, revision assignments, language skills assignments, and documentation assignments.

» **Team requirements:** Comp courses may include two to three team assignments such as creating a technology project, illustrating an essay topic, or teaching an essay skill. The purpose of teams in comp class includes the opportunity to meet and begin the process of working in teams. Collaboration or working in teams is a common strategy throughout college and in the workplace.

Reading and more reading

Your success as a writer depends on your success as a reader. Similar to many academic skills, you can easily improve your reading skills by reading more and reading more challenging materials, especially books. The signature activity of an educated person is reading books.

The major benefits of college students' reading include the following:

>> Improves analytical thinking

>> Builds personal satisfaction and self confidence

>> Improves writing skills

>> Improves concentration

>> Reduces stress

>> Builds vocabulary

>> Provides references for writing and classroom discussion

REMEMBER

A number of studies show that reading improves health. In addition to reducing stress, reading improves brain connectivity, lowers blood pressure and heart rate, fights depression, and contributes to a longer life. Your library offers an unlimited supply of reading materials on an unlimited number of topics. The library and its resources are the heartbeat of your university.

Tips for improving your reading as a college student include the following:

>> Schedule weekly blocks for reading your required materials as well as reading supplementary materials related to course topics.

>> Set a goal for the number of books you'll read throughout the year, around your academic commitments.

>> Establish a distraction-free, technology-free reading zone.

>> Read actively by taking notes and identifying ideas related to course topics.

>> Following each reading section, reflect on what you read and regularly write one-sentence summaries of major ideas.

TIP

Class discussion of assigned reading offers an opportunity to impress your professor with your questions, comments, and observations. Involvement is especially important if participation points are designated as part of your grade. Prepare for class discussion by performing an active reading technique (see Chapter 12). Prepare for discussion classes with a list of questions and observations about the readings and interject them into discussions.

Living a day in the life of a comp class

A typical class day in a comp course follows a combination of activities such as the following:

>> **Writing activity:** Many professors begin class with a ten-minute writing activity such as freewriting on a topic related to an essay, writing a thesis statement, or evaluating an essay opening. Students are then asked to share their writing.

>> **Writing skill mini-lesson:** Every class includes a block of direct instruction with the professor explaining a writing skill such as writing engaging titles, engaging sources, illustrating evidence, revising, and so forth.

WHAT THE FIRST-YEAR-WRITING CLASSROOM ISN'T

Your first-year-writing classroom can easily be argued your most important academic challenge in higher education. The composition classroom grounds you with the skills for writing successful essays and other college writing projects.

Here's a look at what your composition classroom is not:

- **Skills course:** Your course isn't a language skills course with intense grammar, worksheets, and drill. Skills will be taught sporadically as your professor identifies language deficiencies in essay writing, but skills aren't taught every class. Your course materials may include a language handbook that your professor uses to target language issues or references to recommend practice for individual students.

- **Lecture course:** A composition course isn't lecture style with your professor talking about writers and writing. Professors may reference well-known writers and their writing as a comparison to class writing, but professors won't amuse themselves talking about writers and their writing incessantly.

- **Survey course:** College composition isn't a survey of writers and writing, similar to a survey of literature course. Course materials may include an anthology of readings to support essays, but reading texts aren't used as a survey of literature.

- **Personal genre course:** Your course isn't focused on personal writing such as memoir, autobiography, and personal opinion. This genre doesn't meet the objectives of a traditional composition course.

- **Feedback and review course:** First-year writing isn't a workshop course that focuses on students reading their work and other students offering feedback. Feedback and review will be an occasional strategy, but not the focus on the course.

>> **Writing skill practice:** Classes usually include a short block of writing practice responding to a prompt such as developing a piece of evidence, writing an opening, and so forth. Writing is frequently followed by pair or small-group sharing.

>> **Writing feedback activity:** Another typical class activity includes feedback and discussion, such as pairs of students performing feedback and discussion of each other's work, or an essay distributed by the professor.

>> **Reading discussion:** Classes usually include a time block discussing required readings. Preparation for the discussion requires a deep understanding of the readings. These discussions also provide a variety of ideas for essay support.

Identifying the Variety of Writing You'll Do

Writing may not be an activity that you enjoy, but you can learn to write successfully when required academically.

Compared with what you've written in the past, your college assignments will include more genres, more pages, more references, more insight, and more accountability. Those demands are required within a framework of less assignment competition time and a shorter semester to fulfill course requirements. Success requires a positive mindset.

REMEMBER

The term *genre* (plural *genres*) refers to individual categories of writing you'll be required to submit. Types of nonfiction genre include essays, response papers, reports, research papers, memoir, and biography.

In the next few sections, I explain how drafts are coordinated with feedback and the role of drafts as portfolio requirements

Writing drafts, drafts, and more drafts

The writing assignments of college comp will be the most intense requirements of your schooling to date. But the demands aren't insurmountable as evidenced by millions of college students who complete requirements annually.

You may view writing fewer essays in college as easier than high school, but fewer essays mean more drafts of each essay and more development of each essay.

Because most first-year programs require portfolios to show the processes of writing, you'll be required to write two to three draft revisions of each essay. Additionally, some professors require a one-page memo (called a *transmittal memo*) explaining how you plan to revise your essay.

Drafts and feedback

Your improved drafts are built on receiving, evaluating, and applying feedback. Chapter 14 explains how to utilize three major sources of feedback:

> » **Your professor:** Your professor is your major source of feedback because they create the objectives for your papers and they know the process for improving your paper.

> » **Your peers:** Your peers offer you a student perspective on the strengths and weaknesses of your paper, and offering feedback for your peers provides models for improving your writing.

> » **Yourself:** As you continue to evaluate your own papers, you'll continue to develop objectivity toward your writing, but that objectivity takes time and practice.

TECHNICAL STUFF

Writing research supports the importance of students' providing feedback and explains that the person offering feedback benefits more than the person receiving feedback. Feedback and revision is a recurring process during essay development.

Drafts and portfolio requirements

Your drafts show improvements (or lack of) in your writing that will be clear to your professor and should be clear to you. Think of your drafts as evidence that shows what you have done to improve your writing.

REMEMBER

Your revision of drafts with feedback may be required to be submitted with your portfolio. File drafts and feedback for each essay. Organizing them will save you time when you need to prepare your portfolio near the end of the course. Chapter 4 explains portfolio requirements.

Chapter 14 offers you a unique three-level approach to revising. It includes revising on the structural level (opening, middle, and closing), the paragraph and sentence level, and the word level.

Research papers, reports, and more, oh my

Most of your first-year writing will develop from your composition course, but you'll also have papers assigned from other courses, including at least one of the following (Chapter 16 examines them in greater detail):

>> **Research paper:** A college research paper is like an essay on steroids. It's developed from an academic argument — a thesis — and is larger and more developed than an essay.

>> **Reaction paper:** Another common assignment is a *reaction paper,* sometimes called a *read-and-response paper, a critique,* or an *analysis paper*. You write reaction papers in response to specific readings for a course.

>> **Reports:** Reports are another type of assignment commonly required in first-year courses and throughout college. Reports are written to analyze topics common to a field of study. For example, report topics common to a business course include supply chain strategies, management styles, point-of-sale software, and customer service.

The variety of writing genre you'll be assigned in college builds its foundation from the essay.

Writing to discover

You may or may not be familiar with the term *writing to discover* or *writing to learn*. It differs from the primary purpose of writing, which is to communicate. Writing to discover focuses on the purpose of writing to learn new information about a topic. It's a form of brainstorming that you discover in detail in Chapter 12. Your brain will surprise you when it reveals your innate knowledge about a topic.

Writing to discover is a good tool to add to your learning library. It's successful because it generates thinking, and thinking generates additional ideas to write about. As example of writing to discover is creating a to-do list. Each listed item generates additional ideas for your list. Try it.

Checking Out the Skills You'll Learn and Use Forevermore

Educated people are lifetime readers and appreciators of good writing. They are two complementary literacy skills. When you read, you learn writing. When you write, you learn reading — better than a two-for-one snack at the campus bookstore.

Of the two skills, writing is the more neglected one. College is the opportunity to develop your writing skills and refine those skills for career use.

The topics that follow represent some of the skills you'll develop in your composition course and skills that you'll use throughout your career and lifetime.

Writing with a purpose

In high school you learned the importance of writing with a purpose. In college you'll be accountable for writing with a purpose, a purpose that exceeds good grades and a purpose that has relevance to your academic audience.

Chapter 6 features the importance of purpose to your academic writing. You'll discover the value of aligning your purpose with the question asked in the assignment. Highlights you'll read about purpose include the following:

>> Focuses the reader on the purpose that aligns with the assignment

>> Shapes the content of the essay along with audience

>> Determines the language and focus of the thesis statement

The skill of determining purpose applies to almost all career and life projects. Without purpose, a project lacks direction.

Addressing new audiences

Audience and purpose are as integral to a writing project as food and phones are to college students. Similar to purpose, your college writing is required to address needs of the academic audience. Chapter 6 explains the details.

Audience as a career skill means, for example, targeting email to the intended readers, thus eliminating the appearance of spam. Audience means distinguishing information intended for employees from information intended for customers.

Saying more with less

Word economy, saying more with less, is an element of almost all writing styles. Fewer words improve sentence pace and keeps reader interest. Strunk and White's *Elements of Style* advises writers to "omit needless words."

Most word reduction occurs during the revising process. Cut needless paragraphs and sentences. Reduce wordy expressions with power-packed words. Pare repetitious pairs of words such as "baby puppies" to "puppies." Finally, test the need for every word.

As a high school student, you most likely associated revising with editing spelling, grammar, and punctuation. In college you'll discover that editing is editing, and revising is revising.

Famous writers say they spend more time revising than creating their first draft. They've learned that revising is the process that develops writers. You can test this belief by revising a writing assignment that's a year old. You'll see your growth. College revising is as serious as your semester transcript. It shapes your writing future.

Giving credit to earn credit

More than likely, you lack extensive experience with credit in your financial life. And, hopefully, you've learned to give credit in your academic life to sources you use to support your thesis by documenting references.

College essays are built on supporting your thesis with sources, not personal opinion like many high school essays. The lesson is to give credit where credit is due. Chapter 7 shows you strategies for integrating sources into your essays that include researching, summarizing, paraphrasing, quoting, refuting, and avoiding logical fallacies.

Engaging with sources

Incorporating sources is a high school skill; engaging sources (Chapter 7) is a college skill. Engaging sources is like a conversation with your three mythical selves talking about your source. The conversation includes agreement, disagreement, questioning, enhancing, and limiting. Engaging with sources also represents a strategy for incorporating your opinion into your essay.

You may have been introduced to source engagement in high school, but it's expected to appear in your college essay. In the world outside the classroom, engaging with sources is a form of critical analysis.

Valuing evidence and logic

How important is evidence and logic in an essay? Without evidence, readers lack conviction of the value of your thesis. Without logic, they lack understanding your evidence. Without evidence and logic, your argument lacks heart and soul.

The academic audience has high expectations for supporting evidence, which includes facts, studies, statistical data, and expert opinion.

The lifetime lesson of evidence and logic is that without support for what you believe in, you lack believers.

Writing with style

Identifying writing style remains an elusive term to understand as a student, and that misunderstanding in many cases may be attributed to instructors who avoid clarifying their style expectations. Documentation styles are clear: APA, MLA, Chicago, or a number of others specific to a field of study. Formal academic research style is clear: Citations are prioritized; language is formal, and the writer is more important than the reader.

Essay writing style combines clarity, formal language, and documentation, in addition to interesting language that engages, and occasionally entertains, the reader.

College represents your first serious opportunity to develop your writing style — an academic coming-of-age experience. Development of your writing style begins in your comp course where essays permit compositional risks. Chapter 9 explains the fundamentals of developing your writing style.

In the future you'll adapt a style appropriate for the audience you're writing to. If they appreciate a little playfulness in your writing, don't disappoint them.

Thinking and reading critically

Successful college essays require *critical analysis*, the ability to look at an argument from multiple perspectives and distinguish strengths from weaknesses.

Critical thinking looks at an argument with skepticism and asks analytical questions such as:

>> Is the argument reasonable? Why or why not?

>> Under what circumstance is it unreasonable?

>> What assumptions are unreasonable?

>> What biases are revealed?

>> What would a believer and doubter say about the evidence?

Analyze evidence by reading information beyond the facts, by reading how the writer says it. Noncritical readers read for information. Critical readers read for implication. These critical analysis skills aren't only college skills, they're also lifetime skills.

Budgeting your writing time

Your time management skills are as important as your writing skills. If you can't successfully budget your writing time, you won't successfully complete your assignments.

Here's a look at time-saving tips for budgeting your writing time:

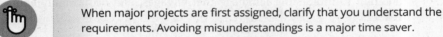

>> **Schedule major assignment due dates at the beginning of the course.** Many students back up an electric calendar with a large full-semester wall calendar attached above their work desk.

When major projects are first assigned, clarify that you understand the requirements. Avoiding misunderstandings is a major time saver.

If major parts of assignments aren't due separately, create your own tentative due dates for completion of major parts.

>> **Meet with your professor to clarify assignment parts.** Ask questions about the assignment. Professors prioritize essay issues that need addressing.

When you meet with your professor to preview your essay, ask questions such as: What part of the assignment has the most point value? What advice do you have for approaching the assignment? Where do students struggle with the assignment? Do you have models of a completed assignment?

>> **Record assignment notes immediately following class introduction of the assignment.** Finalize topic, thesis, and approach soon after. This strategy allows more essay development time.

>> **Use all available sources.** Examples include the writing center, academic success center, and library research specialists. Chapter 17 provides ten resources you can use to create a personal team approach.

>> **Work on writing assignments almost daily.** Completing a writing assignment is like reading a novel. It requires keeping the assignment in your head avoids time to reacclimate.

>> **Schedule a first draft completion date and subsequent dates for revising content.** After scheduling your first draft completion date, schedule days for revising content as Chapter 14 explains.

>> **Schedule a date for final editing (separate from revising).** See Chapter 15 for final editing. Also schedule a date for presentation preparation.

Collaborating with other students

Four is a greater quantity than one, and when four students collaborate on an assignment, they add brain power. Writing is a social activity, and some writing processes include collaborations with your peers such discussions, class brainstorming, and class feedback.

Collaboration includes small-group work such as peer feedback and peer revising. When you're offering feedback, give your best effort. Also, study examples of how other students address essay requirements. Focus on openings, thesis, evidence, development, and so forth. Compliment good examples and suggest improvements for not-so-good examples.

The collaboration you learn in comp class will provide a foundation for collaboration you use throughout college and your career.

Writing resiliency

Writing teaches an invaluable life lesson: Finish what you begin and accept that sometimes you may need to begin again. Always try your best. It's called a growth mindset (See Chapter 5) and belief that you work hard to become educated.

Just as best-selling authors aren't successful with every book they write, you won't be successful with every assignment you write. Learn from your failures similar to creative geniuses such Stephen King, Thomas Edison, Walt Disney, Albert Einstein, Steve Jobs, Abraham Lincoln, Dr. Seuss, and J.K. Rowling.

Remember that becoming an overnight success may take a decade or longer.

THE CHALLENGE OF COLLEGE WRITING

Why are composition courses so difficult? Why do they frustrate almost every student, including those who earn As in high school writing? They're demanding for the following reasons:

- Students are held accountable for the logical development of a thesis and a valued message to the academic audience.

- Writing for the academic audience requires valid evidence that exceeds opinion and is extracted from comprehending complex college reading.

- Professors with fewer students can hold students accountable for higher writing standards.

- The fast pace of the college semester increases the demand to produce higher quality work in less time.

- The essay is a complex genre that requires orchestrating many intricate elements.

- Students lack experience with content revision, the process that professional writers say is more important than composing.

Colleges recognize the challenge of essay writing and provide a team of resources such as the writing center, academic success center, and library research specialists. If you're determined to succeed, your writing support team will help you write successful essays.

Respecting College Genre: What College Writing Isn't

Approach writing, school, and life with the attitude that every effort won't be a home run and that sometimes you'll strike out. Babe Ruth, arguably the best professional baseball player of all time, held the all-time strikeout record (1,330 times) for 30 years.

Successful students, successful writers, and successful people never give up on themselves, and never stop trying. Ever.

If some of your writing strikes out, because you misunderstand it such as any of the following examples of what writing is not, keep trying. You're unsuccessful only when you stop trying. If you've mistaken any of the following examples for an essay, focus on Parts 2 and 3 to get back in the game.

Providing personal commentary

When students begin writing, they write about the subject they know best — themselves, which continues through middle school. In high school, they master the five-paragraph essay. Their high school teachers encourage them to support theses with sources, but opinions require less effort.

College writing requires supporting theses with documented facts, statistical data, research, and expert opinion. High school students who document support and engage with sources are as infrequent as beach days in Alaska.

REMEMBER

Essays based on personal opinion lack preparation, organization, and a research plan to support the thesis.

Chapter 5 explains subtle strategies for incorporating personal experiences in your essay in the form of anecdotes. Chapter 7 explains how to subtly integrate opinion in your essay in the form of source engagement.

Outlining

Outlines don't fulfill requirements for an essay. They're merely part of the process. An *outline* is a prewriting tool that visually displays large amounts of information. The Table of Contents of this book is an outline. It's divided into five major parts of the book, and each part is subdivided into chapters that develop each part. Additionally, each chapter is divided into headings and subheadings. The Table of Contents organizes more than 350 pages of information. But it tells the information rather than shows information.

Summarizing sources

Summaries represent part of the process of completing an essay and a strategy for condensing information from a broader source. Summaries have value as part of the whole, but they aren't the complete a complete essay.

Summaries of sources are easily confused with essays because visually they have paragraph structure and resemble an essay. Professors recognize the deficiency of summaries presented as essays as soon as they read middle paragraphs and identify lack of sources developing and supporting a thesis. Summaries without a purpose are like food destined for a disposal. It hasn't found its purpose in life.

Reacting to sources

Personal reactions to sources are another common misunderstanding of an essay and example of what an essay isn't. Reactions are part of the essay process, but they lack developing a thesis. Professors recognize essays built on reactions to sources when they read the middle paragraphs and neglect to see development of a thesis.

Clarify your understanding of an essay's requirements as explained in Chapters 5, 6, and 7. An essay requires developing a thesis with valid evidence.

Writing only one draft — not

Would you feel confident flying in an airplane that was built once without revision and without testing? Would you feel confident eating an entrée that was created once without testing? Not likely. And neither is your professor confident with one essay draft that you submit without testing or revising.

Research on writing shows that writing is successful when it's completed through recurring processes of writing and revising. The one-draft-and-done approach eliminates regular rethinking and revising. That airplane is much safer and that entrée is much tastier when it's created through processes.

Challenging Yourself: College Writing's Higher Expectations

Higher levels of schooling equate with higher levels of expectations. When you ask mountaineers why they take life-threatening risks and climb mountains, they say, "Because they're there," and they expect to climb it. It's an intrinsic motivation rather than an external one such as climbing for sponsorship.

Intrinsic motivation can drive you to meet the higher expectations of college writing and the goal of earning a college degree. The challenges that follow represent residue obstacles from high school that need to be addressed before fulfilling your dream and reaching your goal.

Performance earns points

A good day's pay for a good day's work — a motto my generation grew up with, believing you earned good payment for good work performance. College grades are earned similarly. If you fulfill the requirements for an A grade, as defined in the syllabus, you earn an A. If you fulfill fewer requirements, you earn a B.

REMEMBER

Notice the verb *earn*. You don't *get* or *receive* a grade, you *earn* a grade. What's earned is valued. If college degrees weren't earned and were distributed like coupons, degrees would lack value. But earning your degree — priceless.

Say goodbye personality points

College doesn't award personality points, sometimes called style points. The college syllabus doesn't include points for "trying hard," "being a good person," "participating in activities," "performing community service," "being named student of the month," or "working in the office." Points are earned for performance. Period.

Courses are islands

Unlike high school, college faculty members across disciplines are usually unknown to each other. They rarely see each other and rarely share information — and many are comfortable with their isolation. Each course they teach is like an island without a system of interisland communication.

Additionally, they have no concern or interest in requirements outside their courses. That's life in higher education. Consequently, your comp course, and other courses you're enrolled in, may share similar major test dates, similar presentation dates, and similar major project dates.

REMEMBER

You have a solution — deal with it and find a way to prepare for it. And unlike high school, you can't ask a professor to change an assignment date because of a conflict with another course. Remember the syllabus calendar is carved in Mount Rushmore, not clay. Because these assignments are scheduled in stone at the beginning of the semester, you know in advance to plan for them.

Planning is how successful college students avoid stress and fulfill their obligations — and perform well with multiple major projects on the same day.

Uncover some life and school balance

Family member, significant other, friend, employee, fitness partner, classmate — the many roles of a college student often collide with the role of scholar. How do you keep everyone happy? You don't. You keep yourself happy by prioritizing what's important to you and learning to say no.

Strategies for balancing life and school include the following:

>> **Pass on perfectionism.** Set your goal as your best effort and best academic performance — not all As and not summa cum laude. Academics is a major part of your life, but not your complete life. Remind yourself of priorities more important than school. Begin with your health and your family's health.

>> **Be where your feet are.** Focus on the present, performing your best effort on your current priority, not the next three. If you need worry and "what if" time, schedule it on your calendar. But separate worry time from your best effort on your current project. You can't worry your way to academic success.

>> **Plan weekly.** Schedule your academic work, including designated time for writing and reading as your highest priority academic time. Schedule exercise, family, friends, and me time. Even schedule a few weekly minutes for career thinking time.

>> **Prioritize study time.** It's not the hours you put into it, but what you put into the hours. Eliminate screen and sound distractions to maximize study time.

>> **Evaluate study strategies.** Are your study techniques as productive? Ask friends their most effective habits for reading, writing, note taking, and test preparation? Check out study materials offered by the student success center.

>> **Celebrate small successes.** Enjoy a well-earned grade, a successful essay, course completions, and semester completions. Each small academic success is a step closer toward the big prize — graduation.

FINDING EMOTIONAL BALANCE

Your life-school balance in college also includes emotional balance. Maintain a healthy range of emotional health well between the extremes of bliss and the blues. Your major tools for managing emotions are exercise and perspective. You have options to manage the stress of school: reduced semester load, an online course, and change of major. Take a deep breath and place yourself in a time-out corner.

When you need help beyond your personal support system, every college offers professional services for managing stress — and it's a phone call away, 24 hours a day. Save the number in your phone for a time when you or a friend needs it.

Sail unchartered waters

College, like life, isn't a smooth sail from orientation to graduation. Life happens. Each time you navigate a storm, you become better prepared for the next one. Encountering academic obstacles is a sign that you're challenging yourself.

Here's a list of academic challenges, not insurmountable, faced by most college students:

>> Fail an essay or test.

>> Drop a course.

>> Fail a course.

>> Face a credit or scheduling issue.

>> Disagree with a professor.

>> Argue with a roommate or friend.

REMEMBER

As an accomplished author, college professor, and person with letters behind his name, I experienced all of the these academic challenges as an undergraduate. Each encounter taught a lesson for the next storm. As Frank Sinatra sings, "That's life."

In addition to navigating these rough seas, plan adventures that exceed your comfort zone. Consider the following:

>> **Play an intramural sport.** Athletic ability isn't a prerequisite; meeting people and having fun is. Most intramurals aren't highly competitive. If athletes were better, they would be playing at a higher level.

>> **Audition for a play.** You never know the identity of some of the people inside you, so discover one of them. It's not Broadway.

>> **Lead a school project.** Or lead a project you create based on your interests. Do you like talking about food, travel, music, or technology? Turn it into a service project.

>> **Attend free lectures.** It's not really free; your tuition includes access to a wealth of knowledge your university brings to campus.

>> **Try a new food.** Get together a group of friends and order take-out food that none of you has tasted.

>> **Go to free food events.** They're common on campuses and serve as bait to attract new members to an organization. You can meet students with similar appetites. Tell others there that you're working on a school project.

>> **Explore a nearby major city.** Many colleges run free shuttles to nearby major cities. Each major city has unique features that attract millions of visitors annually. You can be one in a million.

>> **Sign up for a summer program.** Most colleges offer summer programs for enrichment or academic credit. Programs range from robotic competition to dramatic presentations.

>> **Volunteer to tutor.** Help your peers or young scholars in an area of one of your academic strengths. You'll enjoy the satisfaction of instilling academic confidence.

>> **Sign up for a new technology skill.** Technology departments regularly offer workshops for updating skills.

>> **Advocate for a student cause.** Support what you believe in, and meet people who share your beliefs.

>> **Discover how to cook.** Because eating is a lifetime habit, think of it as a survival skill.

>> **Study a musical instrument.** You don't need experience and your music department may provide the instrument. You could be your own entertainment.

And when your college self-confidence grows, consider the following:

>> Studying abroad

>> Studying a new language

>> Running for student government

>> Starting a side hustle or small business

>> Pitching a business plan

>> Taking a course you'd never think about taking

>> Learning a skills of a trade

>> Volunteering with a friend

>> Applying for an internship your sophomore year

> » **Addressing the details of portfolio organization**
>
> » **Covering all bases with your portfolio cover letter**
>
> » **Practicing a portfolio for grad school or the workplace**

Chapter **4**

Tasting Higher Steaks: Essay Portfolio Requirements

O nce upon a time in college writing, students sat in a room six feet apart (before social distancing) and were assigned an essay topic to write in 40 minutes. They were given no preparation on the topic, and language such as "engaging with sources" was a thing of the future. Every ten minutes proctors would interrupt concentration announcing time remaining. It was the worst of times of writing instruction.

After completing the essay, their professor would grade it on a standard known only to the professor. Some studies at the time showed that better handwriting received better grades. The student's grade determined if they passed their composition course and remained in school — and if their dream continued.

That's how students were graded before the processes of writing were created in the 1980s and before portfolio grading, which became popular about the same time. The course most commonly associated with portfolios is college composition, Writing 101.

One of the earliest uses of portfolios was famous artists who showed samples of their works seeking new commissions. Imagine Leonardo di Vinci applying to the ruler of Milan for a job and showing him sketches of bridges, waterways, public buildings, and armored vehicles — and closing the interview with, "And if you follow me, I'll show you *The Last Supper*, and I'm working on one called the *Mona Lisa*."

This chapter walks you through the what, why, and how of portfolios and explain their importance in your college life and workplace career. I show you sample language of key components of portfolios and explain the advantage it provides students by showing student performance in a course.

Understanding What's It All about: Essay Portfolio Requirements

Kids and collections are as inseparable as college and pizza — or in my case life and pizza. As a kid you may have collected stickers, leaves, cards, and possibly bugs. That experience was practice for what you're collecting today — essays for your writing portfolio.

The theory behind writing portfolios is that over a semester you can apply feedback, make revisions, and improve essays significantly. Your portfolio graders can credit you for your evaluation, analysis, and revision that improves your writing. The following sections explain requirements of portfolios, importance of portfolios, and variations of portfolios.

The terms *drafts* and *revisions* are interchangeable and refer to revised editions of essays based on feedback. Most professors use both terms.

Identifying the ins and outs of portfolios

Portfolios are considered state-of-the-art student-friendly tools for evaluating student writing. They give you the opportunity to argue what you learned in the semester, proving it with your essays as evidence. Most college students prefer this broader method of grading compared with three or four one-time graded tests.

The what of portfolios

A portfolio is a collection of works over a semester. In an anthropology course, for example, students may collect a portfolio of fossils. In a psychology course, they may collect a portfolio of case studies.

Portfolio programs on campus usually begin in composition classes because the processes of writing are conducive to collecting and improving their work over a semester. If portfolios aren't part of your academic life, they'll be before you graduate.

REMEMBER

A writing portfolio is a collection (or selective collection) of writing materials created for college courses. Some portfolios may include preliminary writing such as the following:

>> Notes from background reading (see Chapter 12)

>> Outline and development notes (see Chapter 12)

>> Drafts of thesis statements (see Chapters 6 and 7)

>> Notes of argument development (see Chapter 12)

>> Drafts of openings and closings (see Chapter 5)

In addition to preliminary organizational notes, portfolios usually require feedback by your professor and sometimes peers. The purpose of your portfolio is to demonstrate your writing growth over the course.

The why of portfolios

The value of portfolios is that it shows your growth as a writer over a semester. A portfolio cover letter or reflection piece (refer to the section, "Including cover letters," later in this chapter) argues evidence from your essays that your writing improved.

Here are examples of evidence from your drafts that show writing improvement and corresponding chapters in this book where you can find more information:

>> Improved essay structure, such as a clearly defined and developed opening, body, and closing (see Chapter 5)

>> Clarification of evidence in body paragraphs (refer to Chapter 7)

>> Improved opening engagement (check out Chapter 5)

>> Analysis of the argument (flip to Chapter 5)

>> Synthesis of evidence in the closing (go to Chapter 7)

>> Improved active verbs and specific nouns (head to Chapter 9)

>> Elimination of unnecessary and overused verbs (see Chapter 14)

>> Language that addresses a specific audience (refer to Chapter 6)

Portfolios also offer you an opportunity to improve your essays throughout the course and improve your grade.

Recognizing portfolio types

Portfolios serve a variety of uses across the curriculum. For example, in an art course, students show their best work and in a math course students show their knowledge of processes that complete problems. Writing portfolios can resemble art class and math class.

Here's a look at types of portfolios in a writing course that serve a variety of purposes:

>> **Working portfolios:** The most popular portfolio type in writing courses are working portfolios that include the three or four required essays, in addition to revisions and feedback that developed the essays. Prewriting may also be included with working portfolios.

>> **Showcase portfolios:** Showcase portfolios highlight the best drafts of the best essays. They dress to impress. They're used to show your best writing for job opportunities.

>> **All-inclusive portfolios:** These portfolios show everything you wrote in a course — drafts, prewriting, freewriting, research notes, outline drafts, and so forth. They're used to show production over a course. These are the least popular types of portfolios because of the volume of pages that can easily approach Tolkien's *The Lord of the Rings*.

Eyeing the advantages and challenges of portfolios

Seeing may be believing, but showing is telling when showing evidence of writing improvement. Portfolio evidence is like a team of high-powered attorneys arguing your grade. A good outcome is as predictable as Tom Brady winning another Super Bowl.

Advantages

For students like you who are committed to working at your writing, portfolios offer an opportunity to show what you learned and how you improved.

The advantages of portfolios include the following:

>> Improved writing through the processes of feedback and revision (see Chapter 14)

>> Improved writing through regular feedback from your professor and writing center

>> Improved critical analysis skills (see Chapter 7) through practicing reflection

>> Practice for creating workplace portfolios

>> A sample of writing growth over semester

>> Evaluation of a semester's sampling of writing rather than limited essay samples

Challenges

Portfolios have their challenges primarily centered around the volume of papers required.

The challenges of portfolios include the following:

>> No long-term study has yet validated their effectiveness.

>> Students sometimes make the wrong choice of essays to include.

>> Students are sometimes challenged with the organizational skills required to assemble such a large document.

>> The grading process is intensive for professors because of the 30 to 45 minutes required to read each portfolio.

TECHNICAL STUFF

At the university department level, random selection of student portfolios offers workshop opportunities for professors to evaluate writing and determine need for curricular changes.

The Power of One — Planning Your Portfolio

Compiling your portfolio pieces tests your planning and organizing skills (see Chapter 12). It requires the organizing and coordinating similar to relocating your housing — and you can't call on a party of friends to help you.

Unlike working in teams, you alone are responsible for planning, creating, and organizing your portfolio collection. It's an overwhelming project at a time of the semester when you're most overwhelmed. But it's an invaluable experience for creating future portfolios and making meaning from large quantities of information.

Like advice you'd receive for completing any major project, plan early and organize in small increments. If you haven't organized a writing portfolio in the past, you may find that it requires more moving parts than preparing to enter college—without the help of family and friends.

Checking the list

When you're assigned your portfolio, create a list of tasks that need completing before submitting your portfolio. Your checklist may include items such as the following:

>> Folder for submitting hard copy portfolios

>> Hardware and software for uploading electronic portfolios

>> Essay selection that aligns with portfolio requirements

>> Cover letter that argues essay growth

>> Revised drafts that provides evidence of improvement (see Chapter 14)

>> Table of contents (see Chapter 12) that provides quick-view organization

>> Title page (see Chapter 12) that's aesthetic and functional

>> Authenticity form that validates you are the sole author of all included pieces

>> Essay inclusion form that identifies selected pieces

>> Grading form that expedites receiving feedback and grade

Some items are as simple as filling out a form, and other items represent completing major academic projects, such as the cover letter. Like any major project, completion of the portfolio requires finishing one task at a time, usually beginning with organizational pieces such as the title page and table of contents.

Scheduling dates

Your portfolio project begins with the dating process. Begin planning in the first week of the semester, reducing stress in the last week of the semester. The portfolio due date is usually 7 to 10 days before the end of the semester, which allows time for a committee of professors to grade and return portfolios before grades are due in the registrar's office. Your final portfolio grade usually includes extensive feedback on your portfolio.

Identify completion dates by scheduling backwards from the final project submission date.

Cover letter completion

Plan to complete the cover letter at least a week before the portfolio submission date. You'll have materials — your essays — you need to complete it. Prepare your essays for your cover letter by annotating each essay with the following:

>> Its specific writing strengths

>> Its specific writing weaknesses

>> Its specific writing challenges

>> What the essay contributed to developing you as a writer

REMEMBER

If you're submitting your portfolio electronically, convert each returned graded essay to a pdf file.

Selection of essays

About two weeks before submission date, finalize the essays you'll submit. Guide your selection with the requirement list that includes the types of essays needing submission. Also reference your notes on each essay. Your overall selection guideline is essays that show your strength as a writer.

Revision drafts

Check your guidelines for the number of drafts required for each essay and the definition of a revised draft (see Chapter 14). Organize your drafts at the completion of each essay, and include drafts with the pdf file of each essay.

Completion of forms

About three weeks before submission date, complete forms required with your portfolio. Forms usually include an essay identification form that requires a list of the essay titles you're submitting, an authenticity form that you're the author of works submitted, and a grading form used to return your grade and portfolio feedback. Expect your portfolio ready for you to pick up during the first few weeks of the following semester. The following figure shows an authenticity form that verifies you're the author of portfolio contents.

Portfolio Authenticity Form

I (signature) _____ validate that I am the sole creator of

every document in this portfolio and that I followed APA / MLA / Chicago

guidelines for crediting and documenting sources.

Date_____

(c) John Wiley & Sons, Inc.

Table of contents

About three weeks before submission date, create a table of contents page (see Chapter 12), a file that contains an outline of all materials included in your portfolio. Figure 4-1 shows an example of a table of contents page.

WARNING

You could justify to yourself that the creation of a contents page, the major organizational tool for your portfolio, will only take you ten minutes, and you can create it (and the title page in the next section) the night before your portfolio is due. Wrong. Any academic project you create in ten minutes will be filled with errors. Each page done accurately will take you 30 minutes, and you don't want an extra hour of page formatting when facing the pressure of organizing your portfolio pieces the night (or early morning) the portfolio is due. Save yourself the stress and complete the two pages at least three weeks before the portfolio is due. Each form also serves as a template that can be used for other assignments.

```
                              Contents

                                                              Page

Authenticity statement.................................................................

Essay 1: Title...........................................................................

Essay 1: Drafts........................................................................

Essay 2: Title..........................................................................

Essay 2: Drafts........................................................................

Essay 3: Title..........................................................................

Essay 3: Drafts........................................................................

Essay grading form...................................................................

            [Fill in page numbers, a major organizational feature for your
              portfolio reader to locate documents in your portfolio.]
```

FIGURE 4-1:
A sample table of contents page.

(c) John Wiley & Sons, Inc.

Title page

About three weeks before submission date, you also need to create a title page for your portfolio (check out Figure 4-2).

```
              [One-inch margins on all four sides]

[Position title four double spaces from the top of the page, bold and center.]
                   First-Year Writing Portfolio

[Two double spaces below the title, center your name and contact information.
                 Don't bold contact information.]
                       [Student name]
                       [Course name]
                      [Professor's name]
                         [Due date]
     [Leave blank the remaining three-quarters of the page.]
            [End this page with a hard page break.]
```

FIGURE 4-2:
A sample title page.

(c) John Wiley & Sons, Inc.

Folder purchase

Portfolio submission requirements vary among institutions: Folders, a nonbinder booklet, or a PDF may be required. I discuss submission requirements in the section, "Fill 'Er Up: Portfolio Requirements," later in this chapter.

Frequently a specific two-pocket folder is listed on the syllabus (and available at the bookstore) as a requirement for packaging a portfolio that's submitted as a hard copy. The two-pocket organization usually includes essays and drafts on one side, and cover letter and forms on the other side. Purchase your portfolio folder during the first two weeks of the course.

WARNING

Unless directed, don't insert essays into a plastic sheet that requires extensive grading time to remove them and reinsert them before returning your portfolio. Also, don't use a three-ring binder unless required. Two-sided folders are standard for portfolios at most universities.

Meeting Goals: Department, College, and University

College professors are guided by goals and objectives that flow from the university level, through the college level, and down to the department level. Those goals or learning objectives influence design of the course, essay assignments, and goals of your portfolio.

Here's a look at goals, sometimes expressed as *beliefs,* representative of a department's guidance for portfolio requirements:

>> Writing is a social process.

>> Writing requires recursive feedback and revision (see Chapter 14).

>> Writing requires interaction with text (see Chapter 7).

>> Writing is shaped by audience, purpose, and tone (see Chapter 6).

>> Writers have an ethical responsibility to their audience (see Chapter 17).

Here's an example of language that's representative of a sample reflection for aligning writing improvement with department beliefs:

> My second essay titled "Student Loans Failing Students" exemplifies the belief that writing requires interaction with text. I wrote, "McLaire's 'The student loan bubble' argues that student loans represent a vehicle for many first-generation students to attend college."

> I questioned McLaire and responded to his text with, "McLaire's argument neglects to reveal that while college degrees increase earning power, first-generation graduates earn less money over a lifetime than second and third-generation graduates — a major consideration when financing a college education."

HOW PROFESSORS GRADE PORTFOLIOS

A well-organized portfolio improves efficiency for teams of professors who volunteer to grade portfolios at the end of every semester. Grading portfolios represents one of the most tedious and time-consuming responsibilities of professors who teach writing.

Early in the semester, professors across campus are contacted and asked their interest in scoring first-year portfolios. The number of professors needed is determined by the number of students in first-year writing courses. Grading is usually a two-day process.

Grading sessions begin with an activity called *calibration,* meaning scorers study previously graded portfolios that were scored high, medium, and low. Scorers are then given portfolios to try to match the scoring of the previously scored portfolios. If scorers match the previously scored portfolios, they're qualified to score.

Two professors score each portfolio. When the two agree, the score stands. If the professors disagree on scoring, a third professor also scores. Two professors must agree on the score of each portfolio. Students can be assured their portfolios are accurately and fairly scored.

A common practice during scoring is portfolios scored failing by two professors are validated by another pair of professors. Four professors must agree that a portfolio is a failing grade. Most failing portfolios are the result of missing essays.

Fill 'Er Up: Portfolio Requirements

Attention to detail can make a letter grade difference with your portfolio grade. The portfolio requirements listed here are highly detailed, especially essay specifications. If you need clarification, ask your professor. If you need double clarification because you're a typical conscientious student, ask at the writing center where they don't mind how many times you ask the same question, and they won't tell your professor.

Being clear about essay specifications

Portfolio requirements vary, depending on the writing department's purpose. For example, a department emphasizing fiction and creative writing may require works of writing such as the following:

>> Four pages of poetry

>> Ten pages of short story writing

>> A 15-page summary of a novel

>> Five pages of creative nonfiction

A department that emphasizes research and analytical essays (see Chapter 5) may include choices of three essays from the four you wrote:

>> A cause and effect essay that includes two to three sources

>> A critical analysis essay based on a novel written by an American author

>> An analysis of a major-city problem that includes two to three sources

>> A comparison and contrast essay of two styles of leadership that includes two to three sources

Essays in a Writing 101 course include options. Essay and other portfolio requirements usually contain the following:

>> Four papers totaling 20 double-spaced pages

>> Table of contents (see Chapter 12)

>> Cover letter

>> Student record of contents

>> Revision drafts (see Chapter 14)

>> Form of authenticity

>> Grading form

In addition to the number of essays required, departments have specifications for those essays. The accuracy of those decisions directly influences your grade. Here's an example of specifications for a four-essay requirement:

>> All essays must include formal or informal documentation with APA style and must reference at least two sources.

>> All essays must include at least one revised draft with professor feedback (see Chapter 14).

>> One essay must include persuasive framework (see Chapter 5).

Including cover letters

Your portfolio may include more than 25 pages of documents. Your *cover letter* is an argument that your portfolio represents an improvement in your writing over the time frame of the course. The two or three pages that most influence your grade are the cover letter pages. The cover letter is more important than any one essay because it affects the total grade of all your essays.

TIP

Be sure to address the language that specifies the purpose (see Chapter 6) of your cover letter. Your cover letter assignment question could be asked as:

>> How does your portfolio address course objectives?

>> How did your writing improve over the semester?

The content that answers the question is similar. But one question is answered referencing objectives and the other question is answered referencing writing improvement.

Here are tips for writing your cover letter (see Figure 4-3 for an example):

>> Write primarily in the first person (see Chapter 6), occasionally using the third person.

>> Reference your essays by title.

>> Reference specific language in your essay by quoting yourself. It may be the first time you were ever quoted, but it won't be the last time.

I came to Writing 101 a confident student because I wrote "B" essays in high school. I planned to use my high school strategy to start essays two days before the due date and pull an all-nighter if necessary. After failing my first essay, "Broadband Equity," and receiving professor comments such as: "not college level" and "we need to talk" – something needed to change, and it wasn't going to be my professor. I made an office hours visit.

During the conference, I bought into the writing processes that Professor Colberg so competently taught. I started background reading, prewriting, and analyzing assignments. Most helpful, I visited the writing center to get help with my essays. They taught me the importance of starting early and revising often.

My second essay, "Youth Sports' Grown-Up Problem" earned a "C+" and my third essay "When the World's at War" earned a "B+" and I was complimented for "excellent supporting evidence" and "good synthesis in closing."

I reflected on the differences between "Broadband…" and "Youth Sports…" I learned to write an arguable thesis and in "Youth Sports…" wrote, "The cost of youth sports is more than society can afford." For evidence I chose psychological studies, not like my opinion as evidence "Broadband…." At the writing center they taught me revise by exclusively focusing on verbs and nouns, making them active and specific respectively.

The most significant changes in my writing came from Professor Coeberg who taught me how to give and receive feedback, how to build an argument, and how to write killer openings and closings.

FIGURE 4-3: A sample cover letter.

(c) John Wiley & Sons, Inc.

>> Reference your professor by name, and identify specific ways your professor helped you.

>> Reference specific skills you learned in the course and how examples of those skills are included in your writing.

>> Use the language of writing, such as *reflection, peer feedback, revising, thesis statement, evidence, development,* and so forth. Throw in the high-powered words such as *analysis* and *synthesis.*

Your understanding of writing content begins with using the language of writing, the discourse. Consider this example of language that argues improvement in content:

TIP

My first draft of my second essay titled "Is College for Everyone?" lacked college-level evidence to support my thesis. I wrote, "One of my friends here in college questions his being here because he says he's not an academic person. My professor commented that "one person's experience does not represent strong evidence" supporting the thesis."

I revised my evidence writing, "Wisner and others found that "about 60 percent of students who question the value of college" during their first year, eventually find successful careers in fields such as the trades and technology."

WARNING

In your cover letter reflection, don't identify your revision and writing improvement as correcting spelling, grammar, and punctuation. Referencing corrections tells your portfolio readers that you don't understand revising content, a writing improvement expected of college students.

Showing off your revisions — Multi drafts

The evidence of your writing improvement is found in the feedback–revising–redrafting loop, in other words, the second and sometimes third drafts of your essays. Focus on the revising and feedback processes as you argue your writing improvement.

REMEMBER

Your revision improvements represent your strongest argument that you improved your writing. But your key point is that argument must be your improvement in content.

REMEMBER

Chapter 14 shows the value of revising for legendary writers. They collectively embrace revising as the process that improves their writing. Take that advice and emphasize revising as the major contributor to improving your writing.

Reflecting on improvements — Journals

A body of research shows that quality reflection contributes to quality revision. In other words, if you think about improving your writing, you'll improve your writing. Journals (hard copy booklets or electronic files) offer an opportunity to practice reflection. Critical analysis of your writing — reflection — is a form of feedback and the foundation of revising.

The three-levels of revision in Chapter 14 (global, sentence, and paragraph, and word) also represent three levels of reflection. Here's an example of questions to ask at three levels to generate reflection:

>> **Global:** Are the opening, body, and closing of the essay identifiable? Is the thesis arguable and does it answer the question in the assignment? Does the opening offer a symbolic representation of the thesis?

>> **Paragraph and sentence level:** Are all paragraphs related to the thesis? Do the body paragraphs begin with a topic sentence that introduces a piece of evidence? Is every paragraph connected to the thesis?

>> **Word level:** Are verbs active and nouns specific? Are unnecessary and overused words eliminated? Are redundancies eliminated?

Focusing on organization — Presentation

More than any other college project you submit, your portfolio grade is directly influenced by its presentation and organization. If the reader can't figure out the organization, and can't, for example, locate revisions, your grade is toast.

In addition to the presentation guidelines in Chapter 15, here's a list of questions to ask to before submitting your portfolio:

>> Does the title page look aesthetically pleasing, contain all required contact information, and include correct spelling of key words such as your name, your professor's name, the course name, and the course number?

>> Is the table of contents page aesthetically pleasing, inclusive of all content, and accurate with page numbers?

>> Are essays organized in a logical (or required) sequence such as chronological or from best to least best?

>> Are all required forms included?

>> Are drafts organized with their appropriate essay?

Preparing your e-portfolio

Before you graduate e-portfolios or electronic portfolios will be the standard form. They're more work for you, the student, and less work for professors to grade and administrators to disseminate for program evaluations. For you, they require another level of converting large page files and uploading and more risk of electronic gremlins.

REMEMBER

If your institution doesn't require e-portfolios, or electronic portfolios, more than likely they'll become the standard from at most universities. Colleges are working toward student-friendly procedures for converting files and uploading electronic portfolios, such as cloud storage. Current options include free and paid websites that upload portfolios.

YOUR FUTURE EARNINGS — CAREER PORTFOLIOS

Leonardo di Vinci's imaginary portfolio — refer to this chapter's introduction — is becoming reality for candidates applying for entry-level and career workplace opportunities. They've been common for teacher applicants for a handful of decades.

A *workplace portfolio* showcases your experience and predicts your potential employment capability. It shows your ability to plan and organize as well as a reflection of your work. It creates a professional first appearance and separates you from candidates who don't submit one.

Online portfolios are easily accessible and can be uploaded on professional platforms such as LinkedIn.

Remember: Your portfolio is your professional life, not your hobbies, pets, or memorabilia.

Workplace portfolios are frequently completed as slide presentations and easily updated with new slides. Workplace portfolios usually include the following content:

- Images of diplomas, certificates, awards, scholarships, and transcripts
- Employee evaluations
- Visuals of volunteering
- Infographics
- Visuals of presentations
- Visuals of professional development
- Video clips of answering standard interview questions such as: "Tell me about yourself" and "Why should I hire you?"

Preparing electronic portfolios includes the following:

>> Compiling essays and drafts

>> Including required forms

>> Creating a table of contents page

>> Creating a title page

>> Converting pages into a pdf file

>> Uploading to required site

2

Establishing Essentials: Elements of Composing

Find a writing framework adaptable to the thesis argument and the framework that separates college writing from high school writing, analysis, and synthesis.

Build heavyweight body paragraphs that develop the thesis, explain evidence, support the argument, connect evidence, and synthesize evidence.

Discover a quick-start method of writing by beginning with the middle paragraphs, continuing with the closing, and ending with the beginning.

Create page-turning essays with openings that engage readers with the title and first sentence and offer a symbolic representation of the thesis.

Make a point with inclusive thesis statements that identifies the writing purpose, previews examination of the topic, fulfills reader expectations, and establishes parameters for answering the assignment question.

Lay the groundwork for essays by annotating sources, identifying scholarly publications, quoting, paraphrasing, summarizing, and synthesizing.

Build compelling arguments with five easy-to-follow steps such as writing the thesis, identifying major supporting points, synthesizing data, refuting counterarguments, and forming conclusions.

Chapter 5

Planning Your Essay Success: Organization and Structure

Early in my high school baseball coaching career, I learned that an unstructured practice resulted in an unscheduled meeting with the principal who explained why baseballs and broken glass littered the science lab located near the field. Without an organized and structured practice, high school baseball players may shatter windows and litter floors with broken glass.

Essays also require organization and structure to guide readers through the sequence of evidence that develops the essay's argument. A well-structured essay prevents readers from misunderstanding the focus, just as a well-structured baseball practice prevented me from unscheduled meetings with principal Williams.

The best defense against essays that read like navigating a maze in a cornfield is planning a framework appropriate for the argument, and then organizing information into a smooth flowing opening, middle, and closing. If your essays have the organization of a plate of pasta and receive instructor comments such as "needs structure," "lacks focus," and "needs development," this chapter can prepare your essays for primetime.

This chapter introduces you to organization and structure for your college essays. It also shows you how to write grade-clinching titles, first sentences, openings, and closings.

Getting Organized: Your Mindset

Your development as a student and writer requires a growth mindset and recognition that successful writing results from hard work. College writing never reaches full potential with a fixed mindset, a belief that essays are one and done, and that you either have writing skills or you don't. A fixed mindset writer frequently becomes discouraged trying to achieve perfection composing a single fixed draft.

>> Essay development requires practice, patience, and persistence to address writing issues.

>> Essays flourish with the recurring processes of planning, organizing, drafting, soliciting feedback, and revising.

>> Essay success for some writers may require initiative to capitalize on campus resources to help writers.

>> Writing requires daily practice, regular reading, and recurring revision.

College provides the instruction and resources to improve your writing; you provide the intensity and resolution to achieve your best writing.

Regardless of how skillfully you plan your path through college, the road to your college degree tunnels through your college essay course. You may dislike writing; you may hate writing; but you can't avoid fulfilling your essay course requirements. If you were accepted into college, a committee of admission specialists believed in your potential to perform college work, including essay writing. Work to validate their belief in you.

TECHNICAL STUFF

Colleges recognize students' challenge with writing and provide resources to help you write. No other college skill includes the support system to assist students write. College students have been frustrated with writing since essays were first required at Harvard University in 1636. If you can read this book, have determination and a growth mindset, you can figure out how to write. And you may be a future *For Dummies* author.

DON'T LET A FIXED MINDSET HOLD YOU BACK

During childhood my parents taught me that success required hard work, and they praised me for my effort to achieve academically and athletically. They never told me I was "naturally smart" or "athletically gifted." DaVinci nor DiMaggio I was not. The only comparison with them is that my last name also ends with a vowel.

As an athlete at St. James High School a decade later, the value of working toward goals matured into lifetime habits of commitment, persistence, resilience, and confidence. I believed I could accomplish almost anything — and did: advanced degrees and successful careers in teaching, coaching, and writing. As I earned my doctorate at Temple University, I learned Carol Dweck's theory of mindsets. The Stanford researcher theorized that accomplishments result from determination and hard work — values I learned as a child and teenager.

I regretfully demonstrated a fixed mindset taking trumpet lessons as a teen, thinking I would practice long enough to find out whether I was good enough to play. After six months of lessons and practicing, I quit, incorrectly thinking I wasn't good at music. I neglected to commit to hard work and practice to become a better player — my only life regret. Don't miss a similar lifetime opportunity to achieve a goal because of a fixed mindset. Remember the saying that I first saw posted in Joe Owsley's math classroom at Sun Valley High School: The harder you work, the luckier you get.

Structuring Your Essay's Framework

First-year-college writing programs aren't intentionally designed to add stress to your life and eat up your study-hours budget. But your time management will quickly bankrupt without an understanding of the design and framework of your required essays. The purpose of college essay programs is to provide you with the writing and thinking experiences necessary to succeed in college and careers.

REMEMBER

Your required essays include the following frameworks. These frameworks (sometimes called *genres*) contribute to developing your argument and adding insight to your topic, resulting in earning excellent grades as a college student. Mastery of these frameworks also advances your career skills for completing workplace projects such as the following:

>> Analyze the effectiveness of a staff training program (analytical writing).

>> Justify a staff development strategy (persuasive writing).

>> Evaluate a new advertising program (expository writing).

>> Explain the causes of declining sales (cause and effect writing).

>> Write the history of your company (narrative writing).

These skills can even help you justify to yourself why you need that all–inclusive tropical vacation during spring break.

TIP

Frequently, your assignment dictates your major framework by asking you to explain, argue, evaluate, prioritize, and so forth. Chapter 12 shows you how to analyze essay assignments and determine your essay's major framework.

SUSTAINING GROWTH SPURTS

Responsibilities of a growth-mindset writer include the following:

- **Commitment:** Your professor's success in helping you is dependent on your commitment to help yourself. Commitment to your essay course includes completing readings, submitting assignments before deadlines, taking notes, formulating opinions, participating in class discussions, answering questions, and more importantly questioning answers.

- **Resilience:** Similar to your personal life, your world of essay writing will test your determination to learn from setbacks. Facing adversity builds resilience and helps you accept stumbling blocks common to college academics. Resiliency includes optimistically reacting to your personal and academic disappointments. If you think you may never experience personal rejection or perform poorly on an essay, you're living on a million-viewer YouTube channel.

- **Curiosity:** Inquisitiveness stimulates brain cells and encourages learning. Curiosity generates curiosity, and when your spirit of inquiry triggers an emotion, information becomes easier to recall. Curiosity may have killed one of the cat's lives, but it also ignites writing ideas.

- **Persistence:** The spirit of trying your best and never giving up fuels you through trying times. Your persistence resulted in your academic accomplishments and can drive you to write successfully. Failure is finalized only when you stop trying. Be persistent, master the intricacies of the three major parts of an essay, and work relentlessly.

- **Metacognition:** Developing a growth mindset requires thinking about your thinking — *metacognition.* It requires, for example, analyzing your planning, organizing, revising, and self-questioning such as Did my essay answer the question asked in the assignment? and What can I learn from professor feedback?

Narrative writing — Telling a story

Storytelling dates back thousands of years, the earliest form painted on cave walls recording memorable events. The evolution of storytelling continues on college campuses today — especially on days following a holiday weekend when stories are as common as morning coffee. The written version of the oral tradition of storytelling is narrative writing, common to many types of academic and workplace writing projects. *Narrative writing* recounts the story, usually chronologically, of a sequence of events. Narrative essays tell stories that develop focused themes such as social injustice, redemption, resiliency, and transparency.

Narrative topics common to college essay assignments include telling a story of

>> A life-altering decision

>> A time you overcame adversity

TECHNICAL STUFF

Many professors choose a narrative topic for the first essay assignment because it can be written from a personal experience and lacks research needed for other genres. *Personal narratives* (a narrative written in the first person and ending with a lesson) represent good first writing samples because they demonstrate writing organization, sentence structure, language skills, and thinking levels.

REMEMBER

Although you may be assigned a narrative essay as a standalone portfolio requirement, almost every essay includes some narrative framework.

Here's an example of narrative writing from Steve Wiegand's *American Revolution For Dummies* (John Wiley & Sons, Inc.):

> Before there was a United States of America, there were colonies, and before there were colonies, there were continents unvisited by Europeans, and before they could visit, the Europeans had to come through a whole lot of changes. The changes ran the gamut from new ways of looking at religion to different kinds of governing. These two issues rarely stayed out of each other's way.

The word *before* in the sample indicates a chronology of events, and an element common to narrative writing.

Descriptive writing — Detailing experiences

A Monday conversation between friends usually includes one asking: "How was your weekend? Give me the details." Details represent the description of talking and writing. Similar to narrative writing, descriptive writing is rarely assigned as a standalone college essay and is part of almost every piece of writing. *Descriptive writing* describes people, places, objects, events, and experiences. You've been using description since you first described toys you wanted for gifts and the cake you wanted for your birthday — such as Aunt Helen's chocolate layer cake.

REMEMBER

Successful descriptive writing includes sensory language and many of the other style tools detailed in Chapter 9. Descriptive writing includes observing with your nose and ears, such as smelling rain or listening to the silence of a boring weekend.

Sometimes professors assign in-class descriptive writing prompts such as the following:

>> Describe the sounds and scents you recently observed on campus.

>> Describe the animal that best identifies with how you approach academics.

Effective description creates a memorable impression. Here's an example from my column that reviews Walter Isaacson's *Einstein: His Life and Universe* (Delco News Network):

> During his early years in school, he [Albert Einstein] was described as a slow learner, a challenging student, a non-conformist, and "almost backward." He was slow learning language, and he frequently walked around repeating things to himself. He also struggled with rote learning. But a relative's gift of a compass resulted in a lifetime curiosity for science.

In addition to description that tells about Einstein ("a slow learner" and "non-conformist"), he is also described by his action ("walked around repeating things to himself") and his reaction to receiving a compass ("lifetime curiosity").

Expository writing — Explaining a process

When you think of expository writing, think processes of lifetime accomplishments: learning to read and write, planning your high school course of study, applying for college, rushing a Greek organization (if that interests you), and organizing your social media. *Expository writing* explains a process. It's the language of learning. Other examples of expository writing include completing your resume, securing an internship, and managing your financial life. B-level expository essays explain how a process works; A-level expository essays explain why a process works.

TECHNICAL STUFF

An essay explaining how and when an education system works shows how numerous writing frameworks blend into a successful essay. Expository writing explains how and why it works.

Expository topics common to college essay assignments and frequently required for portfolios include the following:

» Explain why writing is identified as a gateway skill to college and career success.

» Offer a theory to explain breakdowns in the supply chain.

Because of critical analysis required in expository writing, expository essays are frequently assigned as a portfolio requirement.

Here's a look at a sample of expository writing from my *APA Style & Citations For Dummies* (John Wiley & Sons, Inc.):

> Scientists have discovered that people who read novels live longer. Strategies for reading novels and similar fiction include the following:
> * Skim a plot summary to familiarize yourself with setting, plot, characters, and so forth.
> * Read with a pencil and record notes, questions, clarifications, and so forth.
> * Identify how the author's use of literary devices (flashbacks, foreshadowing, symbolism, and repetition) applies to the plot or theme.

These processes or steps in expository writing frequently include a bulleted list to identify each procedure. Each listed item is usually structured parallel. See Chapter 11 for details on parallel structure.

Persuasive — Convincing beliefs

I began my professional career thinking I disliked sales. But looking back, I realize my success resulted from selling. For example, I sold my teaching skills to a high school principal; I sold editors the ideas of my first three books and a dozen magazine articles; I sold educational consulting services to dozens of clients; and I sold department chairs my college teaching skills.

I became more aware of the importance of persuasion in life and writing after reading Daniel Pink's *To Sell is Human: The Surprising Truth About Moving Others* (Riverhead Books). Pink argues that while most people aren't selling in the sense of selling a car, almost everyone is selling in the sense of "if you hire me, I can add value to your company."

You have had similar selling experiences in your life — your college acceptance, a job, and possibly a significant other. Success in life depends on persuading people to take a risk on your skills and work ethic. You regularly persuade your professors that your writing skills fulfill requirements.

The purpose of *persuasive,* or *argumentative, writing* is to convince the reader of a belief or issue and possibly take action. A common belief among college writing faculty is that all writing contains a thread of persuasion, convincing the reader of the value of the thesis. I share that belief and a major purpose of this book is to convince you of the college and career importance of writing five-star essays — not to be confused with five-paragraph essays that I warn you about in Chapter 2.

Writing your way to success can be an entertaining experience. Realistically, I'm not expecting you to tailgate prior to submitting essays, but I'll take satisfaction that writing successful essays results in an occasional fist pound.

Here's a look at persuasive topics common to college essays and frequently required in your portfolio:

>> Argue the role of mental health education on college campuses.

>> Persuade your university board of trustees to reduce tuition.

Persuasive writing is built on logical reasons or evidence supporting a thesis. For example, logical reasons supporting required study of the arts in K–12 schools include the following:

>> The arts drive a passion for learning, and that passion drives reading, writing, and thinking.

>> The arts help express abstract ideas visually.

>> The arts develop the creative right side of the brain.

Here's a sample of persuasive writing from my column (Delco News Network):

Poor modeling by parents and other adults influences children's decisions not to wear helmets. Children wearing helmets needs to be a no tolerance rule for parents: no helmet, no bicycle. But what parents do themselves speaks louder that what they say. The bicycle helmet ranks as important as wearing a helmet when hitting a ball or playing football. Helmet costs range between $20 and $50. Some studies show little difference between the moderately priced and most expensive helmets.

Evidence in the sample arguing for children wearing bicycle helmets includes

>> Children are more likely to wear helmets when parents wear helmets.

>> Bicycle helmets are just as important as helmets for other activities.

>> Helmet costs are reasonable.

Comparison and contrast — Identifying likes and differences

Your college selection process most likely included comparison and contrast, such as qualities that made schools similar and different. You may have selected your college based on national rankings of the top colleges in the country. Or you may have made a business decision and chose the best value for the cost of tuition. *Comparison and contrast* also apply to writing, such as distinguishing similarities and differences between people, places, ideas, and beliefs. (Chapter 9 explains how to integrate comparisons and contrasts, and other figures of speech into your writing style.)

Comparison and contrast topics common to college essays and frequently required in portfolios include the following:

>> Explain differences and similarities before and after the NCAA's NIL (name, image, and likeness) rule.

>> Compare academic environments of two schools you attended.

Here's a look at a comparison and contrast sample from my column that reviews Walter Isaacson's *Steve Jobs: The Exclusive Biography* (Delco News Network):

> Reading Jobs's personal life paralleled my thoughts about another artistic innovator, Ernest Hemingway. I respect their artistic accomplishments, but lack respect for their personal lifestyle. Hemingway was a multi-abuser of women, and Jobs a non-conformist and believer that hallucinatory drugs improved his thinking.

I compare the personal lives of Jobs and Hemingway and contrast their personal lifestyles.

Cause and effect — Justifying reasons and results

Whether everyone needs a cause is debatable; the fact that every cause has an effect isn't debatable — and neither is the value of cause and effect writing. Expect to be assigned at least one cause and effect essay for your portfolio, and at least one such assignment from your other courses.

Cause and effect essays analyze a reason (cause) and its consequences (effect). The essay question can be asked from multiple perspectives:

>> What are the causes and effects of a four-day workweek?

>> What are the causes of a four-day workweek?

>> What are the effects of a four-day workweek?

>> What is the leading cause of a four-day workweek?

>> What is the leading effect of a four-day workweek?

Clarify the focus of the question when you analyze the professor's assignment. Chapter 12 provides detail on assignment analysis. Generally, you'll be asked to analyze the causes and effects of an event, such as: What are the causes and effects of worldwide water shortages?

TIP

Here are tips for writing cause and effect essays:

>> Before beginning background reading (Chapter 12), list spontaneous causes and effects for the topic.

>> Limit your discussion to a maximum of three causes and effects.

>> Designate causes and effects as "most significant," "most interesting," or "frequently overlooked."

Cause and effect writing explains events that lead to specific results. For example, if you lack commitment to writing successful essays (cause), you may not return to college as a sophomore (effect). Similar to other essay frameworks, cause and effect can be assigned as a standalone essay or part of another essay framework. If an assignment asks you for causes, the reader expects effects. When you think of cause and effect writing, think of the relationship. What's the relationship between the cause and the effect?

Cause and effect topics common to college essays and frequently required in your portfolio include the following:

>> Discuss causes of online bullying by adults.

>> Explain the causes and effects of college dropouts.

>> Discuss the effects of poor communication skills in the workplace.

And here's a look at a cause–and–effect sample from my *APA Style & Citations For Dummies* (John Wiley & Sons, Inc.):

Student violations of academic codes fracture the value of individual degrees and frequently result in life-altering consequences such as dismissal from school. Violations of academic codes, though fortunately infrequent, negatively affect all degree holders of a university. When you occasionally see news stories of systematic institutional dishonesty, you question the integrity of every degree holder from that university. Dishonesty is the enemy of teaching and learning.

The sample identifies effects of academic dishonesty: being dismissed from school, devaluing of degrees, and eroding the teaching and learning process.

Analytical — Evaluating and concluding

College athletic coaches frequently warn their athletes of paralysis by analysis — overthinking or overanalyzing on the playing field, which usually results in inaction or the wrong action. What may be a liability for athletic performance, however, frequently results in an asset for classroom performance.

A writing framework that distinguishes nerds from neophytes is analysis. It also distinguishes the As from the Cs. Analytical writing means evaluating, distinguishing, judging, and drawing conclusions.

REMEMBER

Analytical writing uses the part of your brain that earned you acceptance into college. It's sometimes called *critical thinking* because without it, the status of your grade becomes critical. Analysis helps you grow as a writer and thinker and increases your understanding of topics you're writing about. Critical thinking requires analyzing facts and evidence to form a judgment.

Think of analysis as focusing more on how and why than who and what. Analytical writing includes the big picture (How and why does gun violence escalate in major cities?) as well as the smaller views (How and why are the number of illegal guns proliferating?). Analysis also includes explaining the relationship of the smaller picture to the larger picture.

REMEMBER

Almost all writing includes analysis, such as analyzing the advantages of majoring in liberal arts and the disadvantages of majoring in journalism. Success as a college writer depends on the application of critical thinking to every college writing assignment.

Understanding why analysis is important

Analysis is important in college and in the workplace because it interprets and organizes information, and structures it into manageable forms such as essays, reports, research, web pages, and presentations.

Analytical writing is frequently assigned to literary topics such as:

Examine Shakespeare's recurring themes that appear in the novels of Herman Melville and William Faulkner.

REMEMBER

Analytical essays are structured similar to other college essays: opening, middle, and closing. And the thesis is similarly positioned as the last sentence in the opening. The section, "Structuring Your Essay's Framework," earlier in this chapter shows the structure and organization of the essay.

In college, analytical writing shows your ability to think critically (evaluating information) and analytically (break down complex information) — skills that not only earn you a successful grade, but also a successful paycheck. Analytical assignments are frequently required across majors. Here's a sampling:

>> **Science:** Analyze implications of oil spills.

>> **Management:** Analyze the managerial styles at Apple and Amazon.

>> **Political science:** Justify an immigration policy consistent with the beliefs of the Constitution.

>> **Music:** Explain the human body as a musical instrument.

>> **Education:** Justify an equitable system for funding public education.

>> **Literature:** Argue a book that represents the problem of social injustice in the 20th century.

WARNING

Analysis also includes the significance of what isn't said. For example, student surveys identifying the causes of dropping out of college underreport reasons such as "lacked academic commitment," "unprepared for challenges of college academics," and "lacked motivation."

The value of analytical writing includes the following:

>> Develops ability to analyze the big picture, smaller parts, and the relationships of those parts to each other and the big picture

>> Develops thinking for real life situations

>> Develops thinking for the workplace

>> Enhances problem-solving skills

Being successful when writing analytical writing

Tips for successful analytical writing include the following:

>> Analyze the assignment for topics that includes professor interest, audience value, and available supporting evidence. Chapter 12 includes detailed information on assignment analysis.

>> Analyze all evidence and include importance, relevance, strengths, weaknesses, and application.

>> Synthesize the relationship between and among evidence.

>> Present evidence objectively and proportionally without personal opinion.

>> Apply right-brain prewriting strategies described in Chapter 12.

Here's a sample excerpt of analytical writing:

A 40% success rate is easily considered a failure on most scales of measuring success. But in some situations, such as alumni contributions, that percentage is considered an overwhelming success.

But when 40% represents the number of college students who graduate from a four-year institution, that percentage represents an overwhelming failure. The causes of more than 20 million shattered lifetime dreams in recent decades are complex, the responsibilities widespread, and the implications far reaching.

Research by the Loftis and Johnson Foundation shows the following results identified by students as causes of dropping out of college:

* Almost 75% of students identified "work conflict"

* 33% reported "stress" related to balancing school, work, and social life

* 45% reported insufficient academic support because no one in family graduated from college

* 60% said a college degree "lacks value in today's economic environment"

* 20% reported the "inability to focus on classroom lectures" (2020)

Most college students successfully work part-time to help support themselves plus finance their education, and some successful students manage more complex life situations. Managing non-academic life is a pre-requisite to succeeding in college. The 75% of students who attributed "work conflict" as the cause of dropping out lack the organizational skills to succeed academically.

Another cause listed as contributing to students' dropping out was 45% of potentially first-generation graduates identifying "insufficient family academic support." Medis and Balansky found that college programs mentoring such students showed positive results in colleges across the country. These programs require more investigation because of their potential to address other causes of college attrition (2020).

Notable under-reported causes of dropouts were reasons related to self-responsibility such as the following:

* Did not commit adequate hours to classroom assignments

* Did not take advantage of available resources when needed help

* Lacked motivation and purpose to earn a degree

Body Building: Heavyweight Middle Paragraphs

Neatly tucked between the opening and closing, the middle paragraphs of an essay carry the heavyweight lifting of your essay's argument. The body paragraphs perform double duty acting collectively as a body of evidence developing the thesis and acting individually as paragraphs expanding individual pieces of evidence. These sections examine what the middle paragraphs do and how they do it.

Getting a hold of their purpose

The purpose of the middle paragraphs includes developing your thesis, explaining evidence, supporting the argument, and connecting evidence to the thesis. Here's what middle paragraphs think of themselves (refer to Chapter 7 unless otherwise directed):

>> **Develops the thesis:** The middle paragraphs deliver the promise of the thesis. Academicians don't generally use the word "prove," which implies belief beyond doubt. Take a look at Chapter 6.

>> **Explains evidence:** Supporting evidence requires identification, explanation, and relevance.

>> **Supports the argument:** A major responsibility of the middle paragraphs is supporting the argument. A good thesis persuades the reader of the value of the essay's argument. Every academician likes a good argument.

>> **Connects evidence:** Evidence has many responsibilities, none more important than showing its relationship to the thesis.

>> **Synthesizes evidence:** Synthesis shows how the parts are connected to the whole and how they're connected to one other.

Utilizing tools to perform their duties

The middle paragraphs are like iPhone apps. They systematically contain all the information you need in an easy-to-follow format. And like five-star apps, middle paragraphs require iterations of development and revision.

Here's a quick look at the tools they use to perform their duties (refer to Chapter 7 for more on most of the following):

- » **Topic sentence:** The topic sentence identifies the main idea developed in the paragraph. See Chapter 8 for the full story on paragraphs and topic sentences.

- » **Explanation:** The topic sentence is followed by an overview of the topic idea, the promise of content that will be developed.

- » **Illustration:** Illustrations are examples of the main topic idea.

- » **Facts:** Facts about the topic are positioned in the middle of the paragraph, sequenced from general to specific.

- » **Research:** The middle of body paragraphs also includes researched sources that support the topic idea.

- » **Expert opinion:** Quotations, paraphrase, and summaries are also positioned in the middle of the middle paragraphs.

- » **Statistics:** Statistical data are a strong supporter of evidence.

- » **Anecdotes:** Supporting anecdotal references frequently appear as separate paragraphs, following the paragraph they support. Refer to the section, "Including an anecdote," later in this chapter.

- » **Personal observation:** Limit personal experiences used as supporting evidence in middle paragraphs.

- » **Analysis:** Middle paragraphs provide the analysis with relationships. Analysis explains how ideas are similar and different and explains patterns such as agreement, disagreement, and uncertainty.

- » **Significance:** The significance sentences connect the importance of the evidence to the topic. They answer the "so what" question.

- » **Concluding sentence:** The last sentence of the paragraph summarizes the paragraph in one sentence.

- » **Transition sentence:** The transition sentence or sentences, if necessary, bridge paragraphs and enhance flow of paragraph ideas. Chapter 8 provides the details.

TIP

Paragraphs are generally developed in a general to specific format, sometimes call an *inverted pyramid format*. The most specific information is positioned near the end of the paragraph, before the concluding sentence.

BECOMING A MIDDLE BEGINNER

Research supports what writers of all levels have known since hieroglyphics were first carved on cave walls. The hardest part of any project, especially writing projects, is beginning. You may annoyingly stare at a blank screen punctuated with a blinking curser, and your grandparents may have starred at a black sheet of erasable bond paper in a manual typewriter — waiting for the paper to populate.

But you can start as smoothly as "Ladies and gentlemen, start your engines," if you can create your essay out of order: Begin your essay in the middle, progressing to your closing, and following your closing with the beginning. Here's how that works:

- Complete your research, planning, and working thesis statement.

- Create lists, links, and mini outlines for all your supporting information that logically flows from your thesis.

- Sequence your supporting information from weakest to strongest.

- Begin writing your topic sentence that identifies your first piece of evidence.

- Explain your topic sentence with more specific information and provide as example.

- Introduce a source of evidence.

- Follow paragraph developing strategies in Chapter 8.

Keep your engines up to speed and go with the flow of ideas.

Creating First Impressions — Openings

News flash. Your professor, a human being afflicted with a lifetime addiction to reading, determines your essay grade. As much as you've been told about the importance of writing for your audience — like Chapter 6 in this book — your professors are the one member of your audience you need to please. And because professors are sophisticated readers, they value writing that contains a skillfully created opening and closing.

Engaging openings and closings, the intersection of academic and professional writing, offer you the opportunity to impress your professor and stand out among your peers. When you undervalue the importance of an enticing opening and closing, you're leaving points on the page. Here I focus on what you need to know about writing openings, including the first few sentences and the title. The section, "Leaving a Lasting Impression — Closings," later in this chapter discusses closings.

Standing out

Let the gains begin. As a professor who read and graded tens of thousands of essays and research papers, I'm thrilled to see a thoughtful opening that interests me as a consumer of content. My grading experience tells me to anticipate an excellent grade and read the remainder of the essay to justify that grade.

REMEMBER

The purpose of your opening includes the following:

» Engage your reader in the topic and establish the organizational structure of your essay.

» Convince your reader of the importance of your topic and raise reader questions about the topic.

» Clarify your position on the topic question, using language from the assignment sheet.

» Highlight your overall essay plan.

» Demonstrate your command of language.

The opening transports your reader from the symbolic representation of your topic to the specific promise of your thesis — the last sentence in your opening. The structure of the opening progresses from general to specific information, from the abstract hook to the concrete thesis. Your investment in a strong opening yields high returns on your essay grade.

WARNING

Avoid experimenting with a delayed thesis, such as positioning the thesis in the closing, until you regularly write A-graded college essays. (Chapter 6 explains what a thesis is and what it isn't.)

TIP

When you read leisurely, focus on openings and closings that attract your attention. If you want to be nerdy about it, ask Siri to file them. And when you're ready to write your openings and closings, consider re-engineering a favorite one you saved.

While your opening provides background to place your topic within context, college essays usually require a background paragraph following the opening paragraph. Be sure all background content is related to the thesis, not merely to the topic. See Chapter 12 for adding background to the foreground of your essay.

Including an anecdote

A go-to essay opening taught by many professors is the *anecdote*, a brief personal experience story. You can use anecdotes in a wide variety of ways, such as:

» You can connect a different personal experience to each essay you're assigned.

» You can exercise your poetic license by writing an anecdote about an experience that happened to someone else.

» You can write a fictional anecdote that appears believable if you're feeling especially creative.

» You can one as a piece of evidence in the essay body. The more you use them, the better your skills at developing them.

» You can use one as a style tool, similar to those I describe in Chapter 9. Anecdotes are the gift that keep giving.

Here I focus on what to include when writing anecdotes and how you can capture your reader's attention.

Planning to write anecdotes — What to include

Anecdotes are scenes, not narratives with a beginning, middle, and ending. They range between five and six sentences within essays between 600 to 650 words. They aren't the recount of an experience from beginning to end.

Strategies for writing anecdotes include the following:

» Name relevant people, places, and events.

» Identify relevant time references.

» Consider a twist or surprise ending.

» Add brief dialogue when appropriate.

» Brainstorm your anecdote similar to how you brainstorm your essay.

» Reference conclusions from your anecdote that apply to your essay's thesis.

TIP

Anecdotes are successful only when the experience connects with the essay topic. For example, an anecdote that tells a story about never quitting in athletics can be applied to an essay about never quitting in a challenging course.

Grabbing your reader's attention

Similar to opening an essay, begin an anecdote with an attention-attracting first sentence. Language for beginning your anecdote and setting the scene includes the following:

>> When I visited Alaska, I experienced the highlight of my travel experience — walking on glacier.

>> I will never forget the desperation on animal's faces when I volunteered at the center for abused animals.

>> Some of my most memorable lessons I learned in middle school occurred outside the classroom on camping trips.

>> I hide emotions well, but holding tears failed me when I recognized the name on the post.

Consider this opening anecdote:

> I boarded the helicopter from the heliport in Juneau, Alaska — aware that one crashed in recent weeks — anticipating the experience of flying above an ice field, landing on the Mendenhall Glacier, and walking across frozen tundra, thousands of years old. I walked to the edge of crevasses, looking down hundreds of feet at the flow of blue glacier water. I witnessed the excitement of one of nature's unique performances. But on the helicopter flight back to Juneau, nature offered one additional surprise that changed my comfort level with nature's majesty.

Using additional openings strategies

Here's a look at other opening strategies:

>> **Series of questions:** Many professors consider a one question opening a cliché strategy common to high school writing. But a series of questions raises the curiosity level and raises even more questions. Here's a sample from my column reviewing *Choke* by Sian Beilock (Delco News Network):

> What's the cause of high-performing students underperforming on a high-stakes standardized test such as the SAT and GRE (Graduate Record Examination)? What's the cause of a professional athlete underperforming on a game-winning play or a pressure putt? Do underperforming students and athletes share common characteristics for their "choke"?

>> **What if? picture this:** Another opening is the hypothetical "What if?" which raises questions and curiosities. Here's a sample on a topic that interests you:

What if colleges accepted more responsibility for ensuring graduation for the students they accept? What if their accountability included partial refunds of tuition and student loans for students who drop out? What if colleges fulfilled the promises to students and their parents made during freshmen orientation?

REMEMBER

In addition to the previous opening strategies, openings also include the importance of the topic, the approach to the assignment, your position on the topic, and the thesis (Chapter 6).

Steering clear of these types of openings

Here's a look at openings as unappealing as a broken popsicle:

>> Previewing your intentions for the essay, such as what you plan to cover

>> A dictionary or encyclopedia definition of the topic

>> Restating the topic

>> Presenting an overview of the topic

>> An all-encompassing phrase such as: "Since the dawn of time . . ."

>> Quotations that suddenly appear in text without context or follow up

When I read these openings as a professor, I thought no effort, no thought, and no good.

Focusing on the first sentences

Are you surprised to hear that some professors will stereotype you as a student? Your professor's assessment of your grade begins the first day of class with behaviors such as:

>> Arriving early and introducing yourself

>> Sitting in the front row and assuming an academic position

>> Actively participating in class discussions and taking notes

>> Saying thank you on the way out of class

Your professor will also stereotype you by a strong opening of your essay, especially the first sentence.

TECHNICAL STUFF

Unlike professional writers, inexperienced writers rarely prioritize first sentences and openings. Professional writers quickly learn that their most important sentence is the first because editors frequently buy or reject a piece of writing based on the reader connection of the first sentence. A lackluster title, first sentence, and opening won't cost you money as a first-year student, but it can cost you a scoring opportunity.

Here's a look at a couple of first-sentence strategies that will engage your reader, impress your professor, and score the grade (you can easily develop these first-sentence strategies into opening strategies):

>> **Surprise information:** Readers enjoy a surprise. When the first-sentence surprise raises curiosity and questions, you have the ingredients for an engaging opening. Here's a sample:

Sleep researchers studying mice observed that the brain's synapses, message connectors, surprisingly decrease about 20% after a few hours' sleep. But they also discovered that the reduction makes you smarter.

The second sentence (*But they also . . .*) shows a sentence that transitions into the thesis. Chapter 6 details more information about thesis statements.

>> **Expert quotations:** Opening an essay with a quotation by an expert interests the most sophisticated readers, including your professor. Here's an example:

"Progress is made by trial and failure, the failures are generally a hundred times more numerous than the successes; yet they are usually left unchronicled," said renowned chemist William Ramsey (1852–1916). Ramsey was referencing science, but his advice applies beyond science and into everyday life, including writing.

The second sentence (*Ramsey was referencing . . .*) also shows a sentence that transitions into the thesis.

>> **Essential content connection:** What is the most emotional part of your essay? For example, if your essay's about the college dropout rate, play the emotional card by opening with a sentence describing what a college degree means to you and your family. Here's a sample:

I dreamed of my college graduation since my first day of school, but I didn't dream of its financial and emotional toll on my family.

When your first sentence connects with your readers, you're set up to deliver your second sentence and the remainder of your opening. Midway through your opening, your professor formulates a projection of your grade. Capitalize on the opportunity to impress your professor with a high-interest opening, and remember that good openings generate good grades.

Writing a title to highlight your essay

Titles, the high rollers and one-percenters of essay real estate, command penthouse location on the printed page. They additionally call attention to themselves with skyscraper letters and center stage seating. Titles' absence, like your absence from class, is judged unfavorably by serious readers like your professor. Titles highlight your essays are like beach days in Alaska.

The goal of your title is to tease and entice your reader. The mere inclusion of a title tells your professor you're more than a casual college student who writes essays on autopilot. A successful title identifies the essay topic, references the thesis, suggests the approach, and addresses the major question of the assignment.

The following sections discuss how you can begin writing a title, how you can draft a memorable title, and what types of titles to avoid.

Starting with a working title

After reading background material on your topic and creating your thesis, formulate your *working title*, a title that provides flexible boundaries for developing your thesis, but is subject to change.

I encourage my students to paste their working titles and thesis at the top of every draft page as a reminder of their intended focus. If your argument drifts from your working title and thesis, you have two options: Refocus your argument or revise your title and thesis. The latter is usually the better option.

Begin creating your working title by searching key nouns and verbs from the assignment sheet, thesis statement, and background reading. For example, an assignment that requires you to analyze the college retention rate might include the following key words: "college dropout causes," "college dropouts and economics," college dropouts and work," and "college dropouts and family support."

Possible titles from the previous key words (dependent on the thesis statement) include the following:

>> Diving into College Dropout Rates: Statistics That Surprise

>> Solving the Dropout Problem: More Mentoring

>> Answering the Dropout Question: Is It More Than Financial?

>> Acceptance Rates and Retention Rates: An Unfaithful Relationship

>> Hidden Costs of Degreeless Dropouts

Many academic titles include a subtitle following a colon, which reduces the topic focus. Take a look at this title and subtitle:

College Students and Sports Gambling: Entertainment or Epidemic?

The title example identifies the content (college sports gambling) and references the thesis (Is college sports gambling harmful to college students?). It also answers the assignment question (Does sports gambling negatively affect college students?). The subtitle (Entertainment or Epidemic?) focuses the topic as benign or harmful. The title also includes a catchy repetition of the "e" sound and parallel rhythm of both words containing four syllables. (Refer to the next section for other title strategies.)

REMEMBER

Make sure you punctuate and format your titles and title page correctly, too. For more information, flip to Chapter 11.

Drafting a memorable title — The how-to

A good title suggests that your essay offers reader value for their time invested. Here's a look at techniques for creating memorable essay titles:

>> **Repetition:** Repeat sounds that attract reader attention, such as:

- Academic Essentials for Sustainable Success

- Exploring the Essay: From Title to Termination

>> **Rhymes and opposites:** Strategically position rhymes and opposites, such as:

- Low Return Value of High-Tuition Universities

- How College Students Get Hooked on Books

>> **Play on words:** Words with double meanings playfully appeal to readers' sense of humor, such as:

- Businesses That Make Dollars and Sense

- Careers That Air with Caution

>> **Poignant question:** Ask a question that the essay answers or sheds new light on, such as:

- Is the Spirit of Shakespeare Alive in Contemporary Fiction?
- Are Colleges Admissions the Primary Cause of the High Dropout Rate?

Steering clear of these heading no-no's

Essay titles aren't news story headlines, which preview a story much less focused than an essay. Avoid broad language in your titles, which is common to news stories, such as the following:

>> **The big reveal:** Secrets of . . .

>> **Unlimited advice: 100** Tips for . . .

>> **All encompassing:** Complete Guide to . . .

ESSAY GRADING: INSIDE INFORMATION

Grading essays and offering feedback represent the most time-consuming activity of a professor's responsibilities. Many professors are trained to evaluate essays applying an evidence-based time-management strategy called *holistic scoring,* an overall impression that corresponds to a pre-determined validated essay score. Many institutions train holistic scorers with a 1–6 scoring scale or rubric, meaning if an essay is scored a 6 (equivalent to an A), that "6" essay corresponds to other "6" essays professors studied during training.

The scoring process includes professors' formulating an overall upper-half (6, 5, 4) or lower-half grade as they read the beginning of your essay. Engaging titles, first sentences, and openings are infrequent in college essays can easily elicit a preliminary 6 or 5 (A or B) from most professors. A creative title stands out like the North Star; your professor is inclined to think A or B after reading the first few words. A strong closing can solidify a top grade by leaving your professor a lasting impression of the essay. Professor's also like A essays because they reduce grading time. A essays don't require the justification of lower grades.

Another advantage for you is that additional research shows after professors form a belief, such as an essay deserves an A, they're reluctant to contradict that belief. And professors don't like to be wrong. Effective openings and closings are well worth the investment of your time.

Furthermore, avoid these essay title tragedies:

» Prefacing titles with constructions such as

- An Analysis of . . .

- An Overview of . . .

- The Rise and Fall of . . .

- The Life and Death of . . .

- All About . . .

» Using generic titles such as "Essay #2" or "Assignment 3"

» Abbreviating in the title

» Underlining, italicizing, or enclosing the title in quotation marks

» Ending the title with an exclamation point

Leaving a Lasting Impression — Closings

Mariano Rivera, New York Yankee Hall of Fame pitcher, is recognized as baseball's all-time closer. When the game was on the line in the last inning, he thrived on closing out the win. Your essay also needs a winning closer — you — someone who can dramatically end the essay with your professor thinking: This is a hall of fame essay.

A successful essay ending requires a closer's mindset such as planning, practicing, and perfecting a closing strategy. You can't think: "I finished the essay, included supporting evidence, and summary endings were successful for me in high school."

That effortless approach tells your professors you don't know how to end your college essay and don't care to learn. The closing, like a memorable dessert, is the last message you leave the reader.

REMEMBER

The purpose of your closing is to convince your professor your evidence supports an argument that meets assignment requirements. Your goal is also to leave your reader with a sense of closure, like the satisfaction of earning an A in a challenging course.

The following sections break down how to write an effective closing in five easy steps and what types of closings to avoid.

Creating a closing in five steps

Begin your closing by studying your opening, thesis, and supporting evidence — three stars of a five-star essay. Here's a five-step plan that closes your essays with the drama of a standing ovation at the closing a Broadway show:

1. Transition to the closing.

Use a transitional strategy to clarify that the middle has ended and the closing is beginning. For example:

With the college dropout rate increasing as a result of less commitment to study time and more hours committed to sports betting, retaining students need new strategies. And those strategies are showing promise in a handful of Midwest schools.

2. Reference your main points of evidence.

Briefly explain your evidence sheds new light on your argument. Here's an example of what that looks like:

Successful strategies to improve the college retention rate include assigning student tutors to all incoming students, mandating advisor meetings for students projecting a C or lower GPA at the mid-semester mark, and mandating a ten-hour time-management workshop for students with a projected GPA lower than B.

3. Synthesize your argument.

Explain the interdependence of the evidence. What does each piece of evidence mean in relation to each other? For example, if you're arguing to improve the college dropout rate, synthesize evidence that suggests more mentoring for at-risk freshmen with evidence that shows at-risk freshmen who met with a writing tutor in person ten or more weeks a semester improved grades more than freshmen who met with tutors online.

4. Explain the broader application of the new evidence.

In this last section of the closing (usually a new paragraph), return the reader to the real-world application of your argument. Identify new questions the topic raises. For example, the college dropout topic raises questions such as: Who benefits from a 40 percent dropout rate? Why aren't colleges accepting more responsibility for improving the retention rate? Follow the questions with the application of the topic to the everyday lives of readers, language such as:

Broken college dreams are not the story of one college dropout, but twenty million dropouts, a formidable number that if improved would have the following effect on society: a stronger economy, fewer people needing financial assistance, fewer college loan defaults, more family role models of degree earners, and a more literate society for making decisions to perpetuate the democratic process.

Also consider how the essay topic applies to class topics, popular books, and current events.

5. End with a closer sentence.

Close with a bang that causes your professor to look at the name of the student who caused it. A common closing strategy among professional writers is closing with a reference to their opening. Here are examples of opening-and-closer relationships from my column:

- **Opening:** Most articles written about grammar interest me; most articles written about dating disinterest me. But when I see titles such as "Bad Grammar a Dating Deal Breaker," I not only see a topic of interest, but also an opportunity to discuss specific grammar with my college students.
  Closer sentence: Using deal-sealing language not only gets the date, but also gets the grade.

- **Opening:** Similar to the transformation needed to reduce dependence on fossil fuels, higher education needs to reduce its dependence on fiscal foolishness.
  Closer sentence: And one of those high-cost educated graduates may discover a low-cost source of energy.

Avoiding crash endings — Closing don'ts

Steer clear of language that tells your professor your closing skills are in the age of dial-ups:

>> Don't introduce new evidence.

>> Don't apologize or undermine your credibility.

>> Don't write an ending that sounds like you can't think of anything.

>> Don't include language that tells the reader you're closing.

>> Don't patronize the professor and beg for a good grade.

>> Don't play the emotional card with a medical history.

>> Don't include quotations that you think speaks for themselves — they don't.

Chapter **6**

Determining Your Reasons for Writing: Audience and Purpose

Audience and purpose prepare you for LAC (life after college) when you may be writing to audiences such your supervisor and corporate leaders and writing for purposes such as admittance to grad school.

Audience identifies the readers you're writing to; purpose identifies your message to those readers. Audience and purpose also shape development, organization, tone, and style of your writing. Your audience determines your purpose, and your purpose determines your focus and thesis.

This chapter details the audiences and purposes you'll be required to address in your college writing and the tone appropriate for your message. I also develop strategies for writing the thesis statement, the most important sentence of your college writing projects.

Audience and purpose are sometimes described as the air and water of college writing, the life of a piece of writing. But some instructors think they're much more important than that.

Identifying Who: Audience

You communicate with many different people in your everyday life: parents, peers, roommates, siblings, acquaintances, significant others, professors, and so forth. Each person you address requires decisions such as what content to include and exclude, how much and how little to explain, and what tone and language you use to say it. An example of an inappropriate tone is emailing your professor a greeting such as: "Hey, Dude."

Here's another example: Describing a spring break experience requires different content for difference audiences. Your account to parents and younger siblings may stretch the truth to include descriptions of books you read and papers you completed. Your account to your college friends may exclude your academic enrichment because they not only don't care, they also don't believe you.

REMEMBER

Just like audience determines your content, language, and tone telling your spring break experiences, *audience* also dictates similar decisions with your writing assignments. Writing research shows that audience awareness improves thinking, writing, voice, and writing style.

The following sections focus on the recipient of your message and clarify the point of what you're saying.

Figuring out who your audience is

Before addressing your audience, formulate assumptions about who your audience is by answering the following questions:

>> What's their background and what's their experience with the topic?

>> What motivates and interests them and what are their expectations?

>> What's their attitude toward the topic? Is it agreeable, disagreeable, or hostile?

>> What's their political, cultural, and other beliefs on the topic?

>> What questions do they have about the topic?

>> What common interests do they share with the author?

>> What kinds of sources do they value?

>> What parts of the topic do they lack interest in?

>> What part of the topic will be most difficult to explain to them?

Assumptions based on answers to those questions determine your content, purpose, word choice, tone, and examples. For example, my assumptions about you as my audience include no need to convince you of the value of a college education. You already made that decision by enrolling in a college writing course and reading this book. And because you accept the need to improve your writing, I can write in a friendly conversational tone and you'll accept my attempt at occasional humor. I hope.

Writers make assumptions about their readers, and I make assumptions about you. You can read about those assumptions in the book's Introduction.

You, as a writer, make assumptions about the academic audience to which you're writing. Those assumptions include qualities readers value about writing such as the following:

>> Topics that stimulate new thinking or new approaches to old thinking

>> College-level evidence that supports a thesis

>> Arguments built on logical reasoning and ethical responsibility

>> Tone appropriate for the message

Visualize or look at a photo of a person who is representative of the audience to which you're writing. Your audience needs nurturing. Table 6-1 provides some thoughtful food to nurture their interest.

TABLE 6-1 **Feed and Nurture Your Audience**

Food for Nurturing	How to Feed
Establish an emotional connection.	Show humility and respect with tone, language (see Chapter 10), and examples.
Maintain interest.	Use appealing anecdotes (see Chapter 5) and tools of style. Utilize active verbs and specific nouns (see Chapter 9).
Establish an interesting pace.	Choose appropriate lengths of explanations and quotations. Eliminate personal digressions (refer to Chapter 9).
Establish an appealing rhythm.	Apply style tools to create linguistical music (see Chapter 9).
Fertilize with words.	Choose audience-appropriate language, formality, and explanation terminology.
Practice ethical responsibility	Present ideas acceptable within the mainstream of the academic community.

First-year college writing assignments frequently identify the audience and purpose, which then shapes content, language, and tone (see Chapter 6).

Recognizing what the college audience expects and doesn't expect of you

Your college audience demands (notice the tone of that verb) more than you've achieved in the past and more than even you expect to accomplish. Chapter 1 mentions the expectations of the academic audience are nonnegotiable. Those expectations define college — the academic way or the highway.

Here's what the college audience (your professors) expects from you:

>> Read, write, research, and think to satisfy curiosities.

>> Prepare for class, take notes, and engage in class discussions.

>> Participate in campus activities that will further develop your academic interests.

>> Maintain a healthy lifestyle that allows you to physically fulfill your academic obligations.

>> Take advantage of campus resources when you need help.

>> Perform with a work ethic that results in your best effort with everything you do, occasionally exceeding the expectations of yourself and your academic audience.

And here's a list of what the academic audience doesn't expect from you:

>> **Acting contentious, annoyed, and generally unhappy about assignments:** If you find that you're generally unhappy or depressed, take advantage of your school's confidential resources to help you. They can help you address the causes of your unhappiness and resume your academic productivity.

>> **Missing deadlines:** The first indication that college demands are overwhelming is missing assignments. Research shows a high correlation between missing your first college essay assignment and failing out of college your first year. The connection is that strong.

>> **Missing class:** The classroom is the cathedral of the learning experience. Attend class religiously. In my decades of teaching college, students with perfect attendance rarely earn less than an A. If life happens and you need to miss a class, email your professor before missing class. Don't insult your professor and ask if you'll be missing "anything important." Every second of class is important and expensive.

>> **Submitting poorly presented work:** You show pride in your work with near-perfect presentation (see Chapter 15). Allocate presentation time in your assignment planning.

Hard-working college students frequently exceed the expectations of their audience. Overachieve by referencing the following content connections in your writing and class responses:

>> Outside readings, especially books

>> Past class lectures and discussions

>> Current events

>> Ideas from other courses

>> Personal experiences such as work, travel, volunteerism, and entrepreneurialism

Differentiating among audiences

You need to address a specific audience when you speak and write. When you speak and write to everyone, you speak and write to no one. And if you enjoy a good audience, your assignments offer three specific ones to write to. Here's a description:

>> **Primary:** Your *primary* audience is the academic community — the readers that expect you to perform at the college level and beyond.

>> **Secondary:** Your college writing addresses two *secondary* audiences:

- An audience identified in the assignment such as a board of trustee member

- Fringe readers who have interest in the topic

  For example, an assignment written to the academic audience on the topic of social injustice also appeals to the criminal justice community, the political community, and the general public.

>> **Your professor:** Time for a reality check: Who designed and taught the assignment? Who grades your paper? Determines if it's focused? Knows the requirements better than you do? And has the experience of possibly having graded thousands or tens of thousands of similar assignments? The grader-in-chief, your professor, a member of the academic audience who needs to be pleased first. Please your professor by seamlessly referencing appropriate books, events, discussions, interests, and so forth that you heard mentioned in class. Your professor is the one member of your audience who directly controls your future supply of food, clothing, shelter, and quality of life.

MY REFLECTION ON YOU, THE AUDIENCE OF THIS BOOK

As I write to you as my audience, I'm thinking of you as students in my first-year-writing course (College Composition I: Sports Concentration) in room 201 Whitney Hall on the campus of Rowan University. You're academically invested, committed to improving your essay skills, and willing to work to earn an A or B. Any grade lower is a disappointment, and a B is only okay.

When you write your college essays, think of your professors as representative of the academic community, the reader who shares excitement of your topic and is anxious to hear your unique approach and slant — and who cheers for you to write an essay that both of you are proud of.

Don't think of your professor dressed in academic regalia who overpowers you with degrees that you can't spell or abbreviate. Think of your professor as your writing coach who entered the teaching profession to help students like you. Your professors can't be successful teaching essays unless you're successful writing essays. They believe in themselves and their skill to coach you to write your best essays ever. They believe in you.

And as the author of this book, I believe in you and your ability to write exceptional essays, succeed in first-year writing, graduate from college, and make your mark in the universe.

TIP

Studies show that people who carry written goal cards have a 90 percent chance of achieving their goal. I encourage my students to do the following: Carry with you a copy of your anticipated college graduation date. Under the date write "college graduation date" and your name. Carry it, photograph it, post it where you study, and think about it. And on that date, share it with the people who love you and thank them for supporting you on your degree journey.

Matching tense and tone to your audience

Just as you a college student like consistency and stability in your life, your writing audience likes consistency with verb tenses and writing tones that you choose to communicate your message. I delve deeper into tense and tone here.

Tense: When something happens

Verb *tense* indicates the time action takes place: present, past, and future. Tense inconsistency, primarily interchanging the present and past tense, challenges writers (and readers) at all levels. Verb tense establishes time relationships among your ideas, and corrections are most effective in the revision process when tense can be revised within large chunks of information. Table 6-2 looks at simple tenses in college writing.

TABLE 6-2   **Feeling Tense**

Tense Name	Tense Function	Example
Present	Identifies current action.	I frequently think *(present)* about life after college.
Past	Identifies action completed.	I gave *(past)* little thought to life after college.
Future	Identifies action that will occur.	I will think *(future)* more about life after college.

RECOGNIZING ILLOGICAL TENSE SHIFTS AND AVOIDING THEM

An illogical tense shift is like is telling a story about an experience last weekend (past tense) and suddenly shifting the story as if it were happening today (in the present tense). Illogical shifts in tense confuse your audience and cause grade attrition. Here's a look at illogical tense shifts and its revision:

> **Illogical tense shift:** After my essay is returned *(present)*, I looked *(past)* at my professor's comments. My past essays are earning *(present)* sour-tasting grades. I used *(past)* to think I want *(present)* to major in English.

Before this writer can think about majoring in English, they need to standardize tenses.

Here's a look at revising the illogical tense shift:

> **Revised tense consistency:** After my essay is returned *(present)*, I will analyze *(future)* my professor's comments. My past essays earned *(past)* good grades.

WARNING

Unfortunately, tense shift errors stand out to your professor like an Easter ornament on a Christmas tree. Tense inconsistencies are errors of sound more than errors of sight — like the sound of your grade hitting rock bottom.

HOW SHIFT HAPPENS

Illogical shifts in tense occur when you begin, for example, an anecdote in the past, get emotionally involved in the story, and shift to telling the story in the present. Here's what shift sounds like:

> When I recalled *(past)* the lessons I learned *(past)* growing up in the small seaside resort town of Cape May, New Jersey, I remember *(present)* walking into Swain's Hardware and Russell asks *(present)* me what I'm building. I'm explaining *(present)* how I am building *(present)* my Lionel railroad empire and I am looking *(present)* for copper wire to light my houses. He walks *(present)* me to the back section of the store . . .

BEING MORE CONSISTENT WITH TENSE

Here are general guidelines for tense consistency that can help you navigate college writing. This first group of guidelines applies to nonliterary works, text you're not referencing from literature such as books, poems, plays, and studies:

» **Use the present tense to identify actions that remain consistent in present time.** A Senate Committee is considering *(present)* reducing $10,000 of student debt for serving *(present)* a year of national service.

» **Use the past tense to identify actions that occurred exclusively in the past.** Government-backed student loans were first offered *(past)* in 1958 for students studying in fields such as science or education.

» **Avoid tense changes if the time frame for actions are similar.** When I begin *(present)* a writing presentation in the classroom, I ask *(present)* students to identify the biggest single obstacle that prevents *(present)* them from becoming a better college writer.

» **Generally use the present tense to reference ideas as the first-person narrator.** I expect *(present)* my students to make the same commitment to their writing that they make *(present)* to athletics.

» **Combine the present and past to identify actions considered timeless and actions that occurred in the past.** Writing is *(present)* arguably the highest intellectual activity performed *(past)* by humans. First-year college writing resulted *(past)* in 40 million students dropping out of college.

SIMPLIFYING THE PRESENT TENSE

As a general guideline for your college writing such as essays, reports, and reaction papers, writing that doesn't analyze literary works, use the present tense as follows (refer to Chapter 7):

- **Writing the thesis:** This paper argues *(present)* that specialized mentoring offers a strategy for improving the college retention rate (refer to the section, "Making Your Point: Thesis Statement," in this chapter.

- **Referencing a source without a formal citation:** Mu's *Endless College* (Parker Publishing) offers *(present)* untraditional college tradition strategies.

- **Attributing sources:** Poeland's research on poverty supports *(present)* the belief that poverty correlates with employment.

- **Connecting evidence to the thesis:** Morgan's research shows *(present)* that college retention can be improved.

- **Making general statements and conclusions:** The effects of dropping out of college have *(present)* extensive financial implications.

- **Introducing and analyzing evidence:** A body of evidence by Gibson and others shows *(present)* the connection between admissions and college dropouts.

And here are tense guidelines for referencing literary works:

>> **Use the present tense to reference or cite an author or source whose research was completed in the past.** Brogan and Miles' landmark study in 1964 examines *(present)* compatibility of civilians and military students in higher education.

>> **Use the present tense, sometimes called the *historical present* to identify fictional events that occurred in literature.** Dawidoff's *The Catcher Was A Spy* explains *(present)* how major league baseball player Moe Berg is selected *(present)* to spy on Hitler in WWII.

>> **Use the past tense to identify author actions completed exclusively in the past.** Shakespeare drew *(past)* his extensive vocabulary from his experiences in the trades.

>> **Use the past tense to reference an event that happened before the literary story began.** In the opening of Isaacson's *DaVinci,* the author explained how DaVinci wrote *(past)* a job application letter and mentioned *(past)* as an afterthought that he was *(past)* an artist.

Tone: How you view the topic

Here I talk tone and triangles, not love triangles, not the Bermuda triangle, and not isosceles triangles, but rhetorical triangles such as audience, purpose, and tone. The rhetorical triangle represents the interior working elements of your message. Each part plays its role: Whom are you communicating to? What are you communicating? How are you communicating? Lack of triangle integration results in a message such as: Professor, the dude tutoring doesn't know squat about college essay stuff.

Tone and *voice* (terms frequently interchanged) express the writer's attitude toward the topic and audience. Think of tone as the conversation about the writing that writers and readers hear in their head. Tone is frequently expressed subconsciously, such as speaking aloud something you didn't intend to say. Be sure that the tone of your words say exactly what you want to say. Tone is frequently expressed with emotion. Be sure that you have control of your emotions and that your emotions don't control you.

Think of tone as that expression on your unsophisticated teenager face that you were frequently told to wipe off. Note tone differences in language variations asking for potatoes on the dinner table:

Child, get those potatoes down here.

Who's got the spuds?

Will someone get me those blasted potatoes?

Please pass the potatoes.

Academic writing generally requires a serious and formal tone — which results in some boring and bland textbooks. Academic stylebooks such as APA, MLA, and Chicago/Turabian endorse a tone described as formal, serious, and professional. But essay topics such as sports and college life frequently lack seriousness and are conducive to tones of satire and humor. Essays about college life frequently express tones of laughter and tears. Yes, there is crying in college.

Although tone may vary with some academic writing requirements, the general tone of your academic language necessitates inclusiveness, optimism, helpfulness, friendliness, simplicity, respect, and objectivity.

Because tone is better heard than seen, analyze tone by reading your work aloud.

If you're a regular *For Dummies* reader, you notice the absence of a formal academic tone and a somewhat edgy irreverent tone toward content. Notice the headings in this book: Scoring Personality Points: Stars of Style; Heart of speech:

Verbs; Scrutinizing Your Paper for Sneaky Errors; and Ordering A La Carte: Optional Assignment Sections. *For Dummies* likes its authors to show a little irreverent text, which some people don't need any practice to achieve.

Justifying Why: Purpose

An essay without a purpose is like a life without a plan — both need immediate interventions. *Purpose* is the reason you write, and writers write for a variety of purposes. Writing purposes at the college level generally exceed earning an A grade. Of course, you want a good grade, but you also want to educate yourself and reach for higher goals.

TECHNICAL STUFF

Research on motivation shows that people who reach high levels of success are motivated internally rather than externally. For example, students achieve a higher level of success when they're motivated by improving their writing and thinking rather than improving their GPA. Additional internal motivation includes earning the first degree in your family, preparing yourself for a career in education, and writing your best essay.

Here I help you determine the purpose of the message you want to say to them.

Figuring out your writing purpose

Purpose is the major influence for determining the framework (see Chapter 5) for your assignment. Many professors reduce purposes to three: inform, persuade, explain, which include the foundation for other purposes such as compare, trace, evaluate, prioritize, and synthesize. Seldom are college writers asked to write for the primary purpose of entertaining. But appropriate humor complements your writing style. For more on writing style, flip to Chapter 9.

REMEMBER

To determine your writing purpose, answer the following questions:

>> Does the purpose offer value to your professor and the academic audience?

>> Does the purpose address the assignment's major question?

>> Does the purpose read like a college paper, rather than a high school paper?

>> Can the purpose be fulfilled by you as the writer and are sources available to defend it?

College students are frequently required to address multiple purposes, such as describe and explain; persuade and inform; and illustrate and evaluate. Identify your writing purpose from the assignment sheet. (See Chapter 12 for analyzing assignments.) Look for professor language such as:

>> Explain and compare the causes of . . .

>> Analyze and prioritize the importance of . . .

>> Describe and evaluate leadership styles of . . .

>> Explain and justify a plan for . . .

Considering person

Person, (first, second, and third) sometimes referred to as the *point of view* of the writer or speaker, influences the purpose of the writing. Table 6-3 explains how the three and how they're used in writing.

TABLE 6-3   **Getting Personal**

Person	Pronouns	Purpose / Example
First	I, we, me, us, . . .	Express personal experience, personal reaction to sources and experiences, and assertiveness.
		For example: I dislike cold weather.
Second	You, your,. . .	Offer advice or explanation.
		For example: If you believe in yourself, you can accomplish almost anything.
Third	He, she, it; noun and pronoun references	Establish content objectivity. For example: Writing is a gateway skill to college and career success.

REMEMBER

The third person is almost exclusively used in academic writing because of its objectivity. An essay frequently switches from the third person to the first person to use an anecdote. The second person has its limited uses for the essay.

WARNING

Many first-year-writing professors ban students from writing in the first person because it encourages personal perspective and lacks the objectivity needed for essays. The first person adds value to college writing when used judiciously. Very few essays are written exclusively in the first person, with the exception of personal narratives used as writing samples at the beginning of the semester. Before you write any essay, verify first person use with your professor. Writing an essay exclusively in the second person is as rare as a Golden Retriever with an attitude problem.

MY REFLECTION ON PURPOSE OF THIS BOOK

Publishing a book, especially a *For Dummies* book, represents a satisfying academic experience. Educators are motivated to publish books by many writing purposes; however, earning big amounts of money and making the bestseller list not being two of them.

During the early writing of this book, immediately following the publication of *APA Style & Citations For Dummies*, I told my wife Carole that this is the book I always wanted to write in my lifetime. I also shared that dream with my agent Margot Hutchison at Waterside Productions and editors Vicki Adang, Lindsay Lefevere, and Chad Sievers at John Wiley & Sons Inc.

Every educational experience in my life — earning advanced degrees, teaching in high school and college, consulting in K-12 schools, presenting hundreds of writing workshops, and publishing nearly a million words — has contributed to the content of this book.

My internal motivation for the book includes providing simplified strategies for college students to write successful assignments that contribute to improved academic performance and successful careers.

My purpose also includes contributing to more first-year college students writing successful essays, advancing to their sophomore year, and eventually earning their degrees. The nearly 40 percent attrition rate of college students is a national tragedy, and my purpose for this book is to contribute toward the solution of that problem.

TECHNICAL STUFF

Note the varied use of person in this book. The third person explains information. The second person speaks to you directly about information, and the first person occasionally offers personal reflection.

Making Your Point: Thesis Statement

Just like slogans communicate the promise of the company, a *thesis statement* communicates the promise of your piece of writing. If your thesis is successful, your readers, especially your reader–in–chief, will buy into your argument. Your thesis is your port connection hub. Every paragraph going into your essay funnels through the thesis statement.

TECHNICAL STUFF

A thesis statement is sometimes called a *claim statement* because it asserts claims, the argument of the paper. Although the term *thesis* is common to essays, all college writing assignments include a thesis, claim, or purpose statement that reveals the direction and extent of the piece of writing.

The following sections explain thesis statements — what they are and aren't and how write them.

Understanding what a thesis is

Your thesis is the focus statement of your essay that advertises the specific argument of your essay. A good thesis is a grade-clincher; a bad thesis is a grade-buster. Your thesis shows your professor your position on the assigned topic that answers the assigned question.

Eyeing what's important about your thesis

Here's the importance of the thesis and what it does for your essay:

>> Identifies the purpose of the writing.

>> Tells the reader how you'll examine and sequence the importance of the topic.

>> Fulfills readers' expectation for development, emphasis, and scope of the topic.

>> Establishes parameters for answering the assignment question.

REMEMBER

The thesis establishes the importance of all information in the essay and shows how that information connects to the topic. When you begin your assignment, establish a working thesis that is subject to change.

Finding out more about your topic

Before creating your thesis, address the following questions about your topic:

>> Does the thesis have value for the academic audience?

>> Does the topic have professor appeal?

>> Can I locate at least three college-level pieces of evidence to support it?

>> Is the topic too broad, too narrow, or too complex?

>> Does the thesis include an argument that reasonable people can disagree with?

Here's a look at thesis statements that are too broad, too narrow, and too complex, followed by a good example:

Too broad: Homelessness is overwhelming our society.

Too narrow: Homelessness can be reduced by providing more low-cost housing.

Too complex: Homelessness is overwhelming major cities and addressing the issue requires improving mental health services, providing more low- cost housing, and offering job search training.

Good: Society can reduce homelessness by improving and expanding mental health programs and addressing the problem in educational systems and the workplace.

TIP

A good thesis includes debatable issues and extenuating circumstances. Debatable issues and extenuating circumstances in the previous example include: What is the cost or improving and expanding mental health programs? Can upgraded mental health programs succeed? What problem will be caused by adding responsibilities to educational systems and workplaces? How will added responsibilities affect education and work production? A weak thesis is as useless as cup holders on a laptop.

Recognizing what a thesis isn't

A thesis isn't a thesis when it's the following:

>> **A question:** A thesis doesn't answer a question, it argues a debatable issue.

>> **A list:** A thesis doesn't contain a list of items about a topic. It argues a focused issue on a topic.

>> **An announcement:** A thesis doesn't announce a topic such as: Online learning is a good way to learn.

>> **Includes vague language:** A thesis doesn't contain vague language such as: This paper will talk about. A thesis doesn't "talk about" a topic; it argues a position.

REMEMBER

Also, a thesis doesn't include an unarguable topic. You may not be a person that likes disagreement, but you'll be regularly asked to argue academically. A thesis topic requires addressing disagreement. For example, you can't logically argue against the need to discover cures for diseases that afflict people worldwide. But you can argue for prioritizing funding for the sequence of how diseases should be researched.

Here are examples of bad thesis statements:

>> Everyone should read Shakespeare for his literary value.

>> The *Great Gatsby* is the greatest novel of all time.

>> College students should take the courses they're most interested in.

>> The trades are a good career for people who don't want to go to college.

WARNING

In your first-year writing, generally avoid arguing a value. Not that higher education lacks values, but value papers are difficult to write, and — unless your course includes values content — your professor's expectations and your writing skills offer you a better chance of success if you avoid abstract topics, such as arguing religious values.

TIP

Because your writing purpose includes writing a successful essay, you may be more successful writing the side of the issue that more resources are available rather than the side you strongly believe.

TIP

To avoid planning your paper around a fatal thesis, ask your professor to review your thesis. You can either ask to have it reviewed by email or ask during office hours. If your professor can't review it, ask at your writing center.

Writing a successful thesis: The how-to

These tips can help you write a successful thesis:

>> **Identify the assigned task.** Look for key words that identify what you are being asked to address, words such as *analyze, evaluate,* and so forth. Chapter 12 identifies and explains these key words. Frame your thesis around the task you're assigned to complete. For example, if you're asked to analyze online learning, your thesis should include language such as this example:

Online learning offers learning opportunities for populations of students who lack the availability of face-to-face learning. But all programs are not created equal and students should search for programs that have a track record of success.

>> **Utilize background information in the assignment.** Professors usually provide background facts, statistics, and terms to justify the importance of completing the assignment. Use this information for identifying search terms and generating ideas and approaches to the assignment.

>> **Search background reading.** Search assigned sources and additional background reading for trends and patterns on the topic. Look for points of contention and disagreement.

>> **Reverse the assignment question.** Convert the question into an assertion or claim. For example, if the assignment asks you to analyze the causes of college dropouts, reverse the request into a statement such as this example:

The causes of dropping out of college include the lack of preparation to complete successful college writing assignments, the lack of college-level reading skills, and the lack of assertiveness to utilize available resources.

>> **Anticipate and identify counterarguments.** Academia respects logical disagreement. Many topics will include qualified people who share a contrary opinion. For example, educational experts will argue a major cause of college dropouts is the admission of unqualified applicants. If you can't identify disagreement, look for common ground of contrary evidence — for example the belief that colleges should accept a number of marginal applicants because some of them capitalize on the opportunity and make significant contributions to society.

REMEMBER

Follow your thesis with a sentence or two that provides background on the importance of the topic.

Determining how: Writing forms

Golf, tennis, swimming, and pickle ball are frequently identified as carry-over sports, meaning activities you learn in the active years of your life and carry over in the not-so-active years of your life as forms of exercise.

Essays are similarly a carry-over skill. The essentials you learn building an essay carry over to other forms of writing. Here's a list of essay skills that represent the foundation of other college writing assignments:

>> An opening, body, and closing

>> A focus or thesis statement

>> Support of major ideas

>> Appropriate audience, purpose, tone, and style

>> Respectful language

>> Respectful grammar, usage, punctuation, and spelling

>> Application of the processes of writing, especially planning and revising

In addition to similar essentials, college writing includes a variety of writing forms or formats for different messages. Here's a look at forms (in addition to essays) that may be required during college writing (see Chapter 16):

>> **Research papers:** Research papers are a form of writing you're experienced with. But you're inexperienced writing research papers to the college audience with college expectations. For more information on college research papers, check out *Research Papers for Dummies* by Geraldine Woods and my previous book, *APA Style & Citations For Dummies* (both by John Wiley & Sons, Inc.).

>> **Reaction papers:** Reaction or response papers encourage you to respond to assigned readings and critically analyze them. They're frequently assigned in various courses across the curriculum.

>> **Reviews of literature:** A review of literature is like a research paper on steroids. They're usually required in courses specific to your field of study and require you to analyze literature on a given topic.

>> **Reports:** Reports are like cell phones, they come in a variety of sizes, strength, and content, but they all talk and take selfies. A report is a focused package of information with many moving parts. Reports are discipline specific and required in many fields of study. One of your early experiences with reports was your kindergarten report card.

>> **Email:** First distinguish between email for your personal audience and email for your professional audience. Professional email as a form of writing begins with a subject line that focuses your purpose. Paragraphs are short and concise with one topic per paragraph. And more than any other form of writing, email reveals your language skills.

Chapter 7

Showing Evidence: Thesis Support

A defendant in a court room can't be judged guilty without compelling evidence; an essay in the classroom can't be judged successful without compelling evidence.

The strength of your college essays, and the major difference between college and high school essays, is the evidence that supports your argument. And as good attorneys will tell you, evidence and its presentation makes or breaks the case — and your essay. When you're gathering evidence, think of defending yourself against a charge you're falsely accused of. You need stronger evidence than: "I didn't do it."

Here I explain the DNA of evidence that develops your argument, including how to search it, prepare it, present it, and cite it. I also show you the kind of evidence professors like and don't like and five easy-to-follow steps for building compelling evidence that supports a *thesis statement* — the focus sentence of the essay (see Chapter 6).

Search and Rescue: Sourcing Your Argument

Most kids grow up playing hide-and-seek. The object of the game is finding a person who is hiding from you. And if you're the person hiding, you accept the challenge of finding a hiding place that no one can find — and some kids are so proficient at hiding that they get lost for days.

As a college student you're playing a similar game — your essay evidence is hiding and you need to find it. Also similar to your childhood game, evidence has its favorite hiding places. Let the games begin.

Discovering a couple of search strategies

You have been searching computers since your first playdate, but you may be frozen when considering where to start to look for sources. Don't worry. Check out these two options:

>> **Schedule a session with the person who can help you the most with your writing research — your college reference librarian.** Visit in person. You can get point-and-click directions, and then email your sources to yourself. You can also get help with searching parameters such as full-length scholarly PDF articles that include a reference.

>> **Ask that librarian about card catalogues if you prefer the slower and less efficient method.** Begin your search by creating key search terms from your assignment sheet, working thesis statement (see Chapter 6), background reading (refer to Chapter 12), required readings (check out the next section), and class discussions.

TIP

Create word combinations that identify your topic. For example, if your topic are sports betting among college students, search *sports betting, fantasy sports, college gambling,* and so forth. Follow the key word topic with qualifiers such as: and . . . *academics, causes, abuses, dropping out,* and so forth. Connect qualifying terms with *and* or *not.*

Tapping into required sources

After a few weeks in college, you quickly discover the meaning of what's required. It means readings listed on the syllabus and on assignment sheets. It also means professor's classroom sound bites about essays such as: "You may think about including . . . ," "It may be a good idea to . . . ," "Don't forget to . . . ," and "I strongly suggest you . . ." I strongly suggest you include in your essays what your professors strongly suggest.

REMEMBER

The requirement that's indisputable for your essay is required readings, which are frequently included to address specific department and university goals. Required readings

>> Provide essay-related topics for classroom discussion.

>> Identify content to be included in the essay argument.

>> Illustrate examples of scholarly articles from academic sources.

>> Discourage plagiarism because professors are familiar with source content.

>> Provide a starting point for first-year students unfamiliar with college-level sources.

SEARCHING TIPS TO FIND ESSAY SOURCES

In addition to integrating required readings (sources) into your essay, you're frequently required to include a few additional sources. Here are searching tips for finding those sources:

- Find basic search parameters such as publication dates, scholarly sources, available PDFs, and so forth.

- Use the library staff. They have expertise in searching databases, as well as assignment knowledge similar to what you're working on. It's also a service covered by your tuition.

- Read abstracts, prefaces, and introductions to determine if the article will be helpful, but these synopses generally aren't accepted as sources. Introductory sections such as abstracts offer background on the topic and paths to additional sources.

- Discover other Boolean search terms. For example, "AND" between search terms produces results that contain both terms connected by "AND." Other Boolean terms include OR and NOT.

- Use DOIs (digital object identifiers) when available in place of URLs (uniform resource locators).

- Search bibliographies, works cited, and references for links to additional sources.

What are you expected to do with the sources? Without sources, essays are merely opinioned–supported, similar to many unsuccessful high school essays. The purpose of the required reading is to show your writing skill by integrating source ideas into your thesis development.

When professors grade your essay, they specifically look for your references to required readings. Without them, you can't write an essay that will earn a passing grade.

Begin searching with Wikipedia for general topic information and background sources. Although some professors may accept Wikipedia as a reference source, many don't. And if it's accepted, you can impress your professor with much better sources.

Using extended sources

Professors appreciate students who take academic initiative and exceed assignment expectations. One way to impress your professor is referencing one or two sources beyond your essay's requirements. Such sources include the following:

>> **Artifacts:** Consider objects of cultural or historical significance (stone tools, pottery, clothing) as support for historical and cultural topics.

>> **Artwork:** Consider original artwork as support for art and cultural topics.

>> **Audio recordings:** Audio recordings, such as the original radio broadcast of the Hindenburg disaster, support a number of topics.

>> **Blog posts:** Current blog posts add relevance to many current topics.

>> **Court cases:** Famous court cases (*Marbury v. Madison, Brown v. Board of Education, Miranda v. Arizona*) add credible evidence to essays.

>> **Current books:** Impress your professor with your knowledge of nonfiction books and support your topic with credible evidence.

>> **Diaries:** Original diaries support many literary and historical topics.

>> **Documentaries:** Reference documentaries as trustworthy sources for many topics.

>> **Documents:** Analyze an historical document as a source of primary evidence.

>> **Maps:** Reference historical maps to validate locations of appropriate topics.

>> **Museum pieces:** Refer to museum pieces as another primary source of evidence for cultural topics.

» **Other professors:** Many professors are honored to be interviewed on their specialty as evidence for your topic.

» **Photographs:** Original photographs offer evidence for many topics.

» **Speeches:** Recordings of historical speeches offer evidence for a number of topics.

» **TED Talks:** Many experts offer creditable evidence with their TED Talks.

» **Tweets:** Relevant tweets represent a source of evidence for many current topics.

Laying Groundwork: Noting Sources

You've probably learned that navigating the adult world requires building successful relationships. Source and reader relationships are built on similar trust. Your academic audience, including your professor, trusts you as an academician-in-training who scrutinizes your sources and ensures they meet the expectations of your academic audience. Your readers' trust in the quality of your sources is as important as the trust in your adult relationships.

These sections examine what makes a source acceptable and how to identify sources to use (and not use) in your essay.

Figuring out whether sources are acceptable to use

A strong argument begins with persuasive evidence that meets criteria for currency, relevance, credibility, accuracy, specificity, and fairness. Here are questions to ask to determine if your sources contain the trust your readers expect:

» **Is it current?** Verify that the date of your sources correlates with the timeliness of the topic. For example, sources on the topic of technlogy and mass media may become outdated within a year. Sources on the topic of environmentalism may be current within three years.

» **Is it relevant?** Your audience expects sources relevant to your topic and relevant to the development of your thesis.

» **Is it creditable?** Creditable sources are written by credentialed authors who are experts in their field. Such sources are published in respected professional journals.

>> **Is it accurate?** Standards of source accuracy include current and reliable information documented with appropriate formatting style and with error-free writing.

>> **Is it specific?** The academic audience expects sources with focused support rather than general applications to the topic.

>> **Is it unbiased?** Trustworthy sources are written in a style that includes respectful and unbiased language. See Chapter 10.

Finding sources for your essay

Your research could be easier if your sources came prepackaged, cited, referenced in your text, and copied in your bibliography, but that's just as unrealistic as expecting a million dollars as a graduation gift. Sources need vetting for credibility. Acceptable academic sources are written by credentialed experts who title their work. The minimum length of their work commonly ranges between 12 to 15 pages and is printed in a scholarly publication. They're generally reviewed by other experts and contain citations and an extensive list of references. The work is written in formal language with a serious tone, using academic terms. The pages of academic sources lack a glossy finish and don't include advertisement. The following sections give you an idea of some sources to use (and not to use).

Sources that are acceptable to use

The strength of your essay is determined by the scholarly value of your sources. Essays usually require between four to six sources, including one or two sources from required readings. Here's a sample of top scholarly publications and websites:

>> Journal of *Advances in Physics*

>> *African Journals Online*

>> *American Literary History*

>> *Business Ethics Quarterly*

>> *Cell*

>> Google Scholar

>> IEEE Xplore

>> JSTOR

>> *Journal of Finance*

>> *Journal of Music Theory*

- » Library of Congress
- » *Nature*
- » *Science*
- » *Science Direct*
- » *Web of Science*
- » WorldWideScience

And here's what professors generally accept as academic sources for essays:

- » Academic (nonfiction) books and chapters from those books
- » Academic journal articles and academic websites
- » Conference papers
- » Articles from EBSCO, JSTOR, and Project Muse
- » Almost all scholarly sources from your library
- » Some articles from websites with URL extensions such as .edu, .org, .gov, and .net

Sources to avoid at all costs

And here's what professors generally don't accept as academic sources for essays:

- » Abstracts
- » Articles from .com sites
- » The Bible, The Quran, and religious documents
- » Book reviews
- » Dictionaries, encyclopedias, and Wikipedia
- » Essay sharing websites
- » Famous quotation sites
- » Google books
- » Introductions
- » Movies and television shows
- » Nonacademic YouTube and podcasts
- » Popular magazines and newspapers

>> Unrelated fiction

>> Your professor

Using the sources wisely

No single source should overpower your essay. Each source plays its role developing your essay, with no source dominating.

If you're using electronic sources, evaluate them with these questions:

>> Who created it?

>> What affiliations are listed?

>> Is advertisement included?

>> Does it contain language errors?

>> What contacts are listed?

>> What's the URL extension?

>> Does it ask for money?

>> When was it updated?

DIFFERENTIATING PRIMARY AND SECONDARY SOURCES

Research sources are classified at primary and secondary, and both are used in college research. Here are the differences:

- **Primary:** Data collected directly from the source such as novels, art collections, diaries, government documents, and original letters, maps, videos, speeches, and photos

- **Secondary:** Data based on analysis and interpretation of primary sources

Research papers and similar level topics are usually supported by a majority of primary sources. College essays are supported by a majority of secondary sources and an occasional primary source.

If you have any question or uncertainty, visit your professor during office hours and ask to review your sources and evidence.

Recognizing the Different Ways You Can Use Sources

Sources don't speak for themselves. They need content, formatting, and language that makes them relevant as evidence. Their speaking preferences are quoting, paraphrasing, summarizing, and synthesizing, all which I discuss in these sections.

Quoting

More than any other type of evidence, quotations don't speak for themselves. Here's an example: "All work and no play make Joe a dull boy." That quotation has no relevance to the topic of the book, chapter, or heading. And it also lacks an introduction and a follow-up discussion. The quotation appears as a popup in the text. You don't like popups on your devices and professors don't like popup quotations in your essays.

TIP

In order to use quotations, you need an introduction that integrates them into your writing. They also need a brief follow-up discussion of their relevance to your writing. Here's an example of a successful use of a quotation:

> Education solves many societal problems and improves lives. Segran's "Solutions" in *Tomorrow's Educator* argues, "As little as thirty minutes of daily book reading contributes to improving problems such as poverty and unemployment." Segran's advice adds meaning to the importance of improving literacy in schools today. It improves lives.

TECHNICAL
STUFF

The previous example includes an informal citation, commonly accepted in college essay writing and similar short papers. See the section, "Informal Source References," later in this chapter.

The introduction to the quotation (*Education solves. . .*) prepares the reader for the context of the quotation. The verb *argues* as a signal phrase (see "Signal phrases referencing sources" later in this chapter) identifies Segran's endorsement of the quotation. And the last two sentences represent the writer's follow-up discussion.

A more flexible use of quotations in your writing, especially your essays, is partial quotations. Choose a string of words from the quotation that drives home a point. Here's an example:

> Reading is a game-changing skill in the battle to improve education. Segran's "Solutions" emphasizes that reading books only "thirty minutes. . . five times a week" improves students' skills.

The two partial quotes (*thirty minutes. . . five times a week*) separated with ellipsis emphasize the reading time.

Paraphrasing

When you think paraphrase, think highlights of a source in your own words. *Paraphrase* references a broader use of information than a quotation and more specific use of information than a summary (which I discuss in the next section).

REMEMBER

Your plagiarism-protection phrase for paraphrasing is "in your own words." Paraphrase with words you'd use to describe what you read to a friend.

Here's an example of paraphrased evidence to support college programs for non-traditional students:

> **Original:** Lockland argues the need for advisory programs to support nontraditional students, a forgotten student population with the highest dropout rate. She recommends programs helping them schedule courses for the upcoming semester, navigate financial aid, and master technologies relevant to their course work.

> **Paraphrase:** Lockland's research on the college retention rates of nontraditional college students recommends advisory programs for financial aid, registration, and technology.

Summarizing

Summaries provide an overview of longer text, such as referencing a few paragraphs for essays and full-length articles for major research papers. Summaries are especially effective for a Review of Literature, which may include summaries of a dozen or more full-length sources.

Here's a summary of the original Lockland reference in the previous section:

> Lockland researched the high college dropout rate of nontraditional students. She found evidence that retention rates could be improved among this forgotten population of students. Her recommendations include advisory programs to help these students in the following areas:

- Assisting with course registration for the upcoming semester
- Navigating the maze of financial aid forms and documents
- Enhancing technology for course instruction

Synthesizing

Synthesis, an analysis of relationships of multiple sources, distinguishes college writing from high school writing. You may be inexperienced with the word, but synthesis is what makes college essays college level.

The good news is that much of your academic success to date can be attributed to your success of looking at all sources of information and arriving at a new conclusion. For example, your college search may have resulted in the decision that the flexibility you need to attend college is only available through online programs. Your conclusion was the synthesis of your collective college-search sources of information. Here I delve deeper into the why and how of incorporating synthesis into your essay.

Why synthesis is important in college writing

Discovering how to synthesize your essay sources — find meaning between and among them — is the college skill that separates the dreamers from the dream makers, the A from the B–C students.

The purpose of synthesizing sources includes the following:

>> Develop new insights and new conclusions.

>> Identify differences, similarities, and outliers.

>> Draw broader conclusions at the intersection of source agreement and disagreement.

>> Integrate information from multiple sources.

>> Link your ideas with those of multiple sources.

TIP

Distinguish between synthesis and summary in your essay. A synthesis is like a salad — some tastes are distinct, some blend well, and occasionally you bite into a raw onion. A summary is like eating a sampling of lettuce, carrots, tomatoes, and so forth.

How you can use synthesis in college writing

Synthesis, a critical thinking strategy, creates meaning from multiple sources, showing relationships of the sources to themselves and the sources to the thesis. Synthesis is your most intellectual strategy for preparing sources as evidence. Here are a few pointers for synthesizing sources:

>> Plan paragraphs by source topics.

>> Begin analysis by distinguishing reasons for agreement and disagreement, such as "Baylor and Chew argue that inexperience with college-level reading contributes to poor writing performance."

>> Explore additional patterns and outliers, such as "Only Kim identified 'inability to socialize' as a major contributor to not completing assignments."

>> Justify your own reaction to your new information, such as "Colleges offer orientation programs to expedite student socialization; perhaps schools need to identify nonparticipants and extend personal invitations to encourage participation."

>> Formulate new insights and connect to the thesis, such as "The research of Kim and others suggest a possible solution to retaining freshmen may be implementing individual personalized approaches to encourage participation in orientation experiences."

>> Recognize the absence of information, such as identifying the causes of college dropouts and not including underage alcohol abuse.

Use language patterns to begin synthesis statements. Follow statements with transitional statements (refer to Chapter 8). Table 7-1 looks at some language patterns for starting synthesis sentences.

TABLE 7-1   Language Patterns Common to Synthesis

Agreement	Disagreement	Blends
Similar to . . .	On the contrary . . .	Somewhat similar to . . .,
Author A agrees with Author B in that . . .	Author A disagrees with Author B in that . . .	Somewhat dissimilar to . . .,
Also . . .	But . . .	Somewhat surprising, . . .
According to Authors A and B, . . .	Contrary to Authors A and B, . . .	Somewhat ambivalent . . .

SIGNAL PHRASES REFERENCING SOURCES

Signal phrases (or words), a set of indispensable verbs, help determine the writer's relationship with the source. Here's an example:

> McCarthy (2022), a renowned public health official, questions (signal word) the findings of the committee.

Additional signal phrases include the following: *argues, contradicts, challenges, explains, endorses, refutes, doubts, adds, recognizes, debates,* and *highlights*.

You can also use synthesis to create a thesis from background reading and use synthesis to support an existing thesis. Here's an example synthesis paragraph:

> The Covid pandemic shed new light on employees' desire to work remotely with Adams (2021) reporting that 1 person in 100 worked remotely before the pandemic and 1 in 7 works remotely after the pandemic. Adams and Chadson attributed the remote work trend to the pandemic revealing the value of working in a non-office environment and identifying a home office as "the perfect work environment right here in my home." Brooks disagrees with Adams and Chadson finding that "the game-changing difference" was the absence of travel and its complications. "The elimination of travel and wardrobe costs was equivalent to a 10% raise," she reported. Brooks also suggested a phenomena identified as "work burnout" as a contributor to the remote trend. I agree with Brooks "work burnout" theory because of the increasing workplace stress that began in the '90s and continued to the pandemic when employees finally saw relief.

Extracting What You Need from Sources

As any foodie knows, the quality of the food you eat is the direct result of quality of the ingredients in the recipe. Similarly, the quality control of your essay reflects the quality of the notes you take from your sources. The following sections identify the three categories for taking notes and getting the essential information from your sources.

Selecting sources

In addition to your usual two or three required reading sources for your essay assignments, search another two or three sources using key search terms from your assignment and working thesis. See the section, "Discovering a couple of search strategies" earlier in this chapter. If your assignment doesn't provide required readings, search four to six sources.

The purpose of your preliminary reading of sources includes refining your thesis and reading for evidence and counterevidence that develops your thesis.

REMEMBER

Work with a manageable number of sources, four or five. If two sources are supplied in your assignment, select another two or three.

TIP

Use skimming strategies to identify your best couple of sources, in addition to your required reading sources. To do so, skim your source with the purpose of identifying evidence and counterevidence that develops your argument. Read the introduction, topic sentences of each paragraph, and conclusion. From that information evaluate whether the source contains evidence supporting the thesis and additional topics and subtopics related to the thesis and assignment.

Organizing sources

You have successfully organized your academic materials since you positioned your first book on your eye-level bookshelf. Since that time, the iPhone was invented and the world of electronic organization. Here's a suggested approach for organizing information from your sources. It works with paper organization or pixel organization.

TIP

Start by organization your notes, such as a separate print out, a notecard, or page in a word-processing document. For each source include the formatted documentation style required such as APA or MLA. If applicable, include the URL and DOI (digital object identifier). Also create an abbreviation identifying each source, such as "Br" indicating the first two letters of the author's last name.

In each source file, complete the following background data:

>> A one-to-five-star rating identifying how well the source provides information for your essay

>> A one-sentence summary

>> A brief paraphrase

>> A brief summary

>> A list of factual information about the topic

To identify source ideas related to your thesis, complete the following:

>> Topics related to the thesis

>> A significant quotation

>> A memorable sentence

>> Supporting evidence

>> Ideas that refute the thesis

>> Ideas appropriate for your opening and closing

>> A list of who and what is affected by the topic

>> Ideas you agree and disagree with

>> Ideas you question

>> Ideas that surprise you

>> Ideas that are controversial

>> Ideas that remind you of class topics, current events, books, and so forth

Synthesizing sources

After you gather information from each source, create a synthesis page by listing topics and identifying sources they originated from. Topics to synthesize include summaries, paraphrases, quotations, memorable sentences, counterevidence, thesis-related topics, and so forth.

After you finish organizing all the source information, record a brief insight on the information. Look for patterns, agreements, disagreements, questions, controversies, and so forth. See Figure 7-1 for an example.

Here's a list of tips for taking notes from sources:

>> Record all notes in your own words — the first step for internalizing them and preparing them for inclusion in your essay.

>> Create a personal system for abbreviations in your notetaking, such as Sum = summary, Par = paraphrase, Ev = evidence, Re = refutation, and quotation marks = quoted text. Also consider a five-star rating system for sources and content.

>> After a session of notetaking, return to your notes in a few days and clarify notes as necessary.

FIGURE 7-1: A sample page of synthesizing sources.

© John Wiley & Sons, Inc.

In addition to these tips, consider using these items to take notes:

>> Traditional 3 x 5 notetaking cards

>> *Mind mapping,* a diagram of brainstormed topics with lines and circles identifying relationships between ideas

>> A Venn diagram, overlapping circles of three topics with overlapping content in overlapping circle sectors

>> Sticky notes

>> Audio recordings of notes followed by speech-to-text software

Vetting Your Sources in Greater Detail

Quality evidence produces a quality argument. In this section I explain the details of quality sources, the foundation of good evidence. I also describe the importance of counter–evidence.

Putting together the evidence

The sweet spot of your evidence paragraphs is the analysis of sources (see Chapter 5) and the connection between your evidence and thesis. Follow these three steps for building evidence from sources (I include examples):

1. **Create the topic sentence of the paragraph, followed by a sentence introducing the evidence.**

   - **Topic sentence:** Research shows students identify finances as the primary reason they drop out of college, while colleges report a large amount of financial aid remains unused.

   - **Evidence sentence:** Jai's "Dropouts in Desperation" (2021) analyzes the complexity of dropout statistics and questions finances as the major cause of dropouts.

2. **Illustrate the evidence with examples.**

   For example, Jai's statistical analysis shows that dropouts who list "financial" as the major cause are also likely to have a GPA under "C." In other words, poor academic performance may contribute to the dropout rate.

3. **Connect the evidence to the thesis.**

   While college retention strategies focus on increasing financial aid, Jai's research shows that academic remediation remains insufficient to alleviate the problem.

TIP

After professors read your evidence, they look for you to connect the evidence to the thesis.

TECHNICAL STUFF

When you're looking for reasons to support an argument, you can categorize potential evidence into four topics, beginning with an expression you frequently hear: "Follow the money trail." The categories are economic, political, cultural, and legal. Then find the sources to support your argument.

Refuting evidence as easy as 1, 2, 3

If you're assigned an argumentative essay, a rebuttal is required. A *rebuttal, a counterargument identifying the weakness of the argument and refuting the thesis,* is usually optional for other essay genres, unless specified by your professor. Regardless of the inclusion of a rebuttal, your reader requires information that ethically represents your evidence. Here's a three-step approach to refuting evidence for the following thesis: Salaried employees are less productive working four ten-hour days than five eight-hour days.

1. **Identify the opposition's argument, such as the following:**

   Opponents of the 4-day work week argue that the last two hours of the work day are non-productive because employees are mentally fatigued.

2. **State your position, such as the following:**

   Proponents of the 4-day work week argue that 3-day "weekends" will energize employees for the longer work day and that the last two hours eliminate common afterhours work from home such as checking email.

3. **Find common ground, such as the following:**

   Opponents recognize some value in the mental-fatigue argument and suggest a ten-hour organized day that includes brain-smart strategies such as scheduling the most complex work activities in the first half of the workday.

Building Your Compelling Argument in Five Easy-to-Follow Steps

College students generally aren't argumentative people. But they do have the assertiveness to defend their beliefs. The time has arrived to put on your game face and argue your thesis. Your *argument* is your essay, and here are five easy-to-follow steps to win your argument.

Step 1: Write your thesis statement

A successful argument begins with a successful thesis that's focused, interesting, and debatable — and addresses the assignment question. A strong *thesis* results from analyzing your assignment (Chapter 12), reading for background on the topic, and researching for topic approaches.

Step 2: Identify major supporting points

Identify three or four pieces of evidence that appeal to your audience. Remember to choose from facts, statistics, experts' assertions, and study results. Focus on evidence of logic and avoid arguments based on ethics and emotions. Smoothly transition from idea to idea.

Step 3: Synthesize data from multiple sources

Synthesis is the step that makes your argument compelling. It's like evidence on steroids and represents the strength of your evidence individually and as a body of information. See "Synthesizing," earlier in this chapter.

Step 4: Refute counterarguments

A compelling argument includes revealing the weaknesses of opposing ideas. It also identifies common ground between the evidence and counterpoints. Represent the opposition professionally, fairly, and logically. (See the section, "Getting Real: Avoiding Logical Fallacies" later in this chapter.)

Step 5: Form conclusions

Avoid a summary conclusion. Offer new insights and new questions raised as a result of your argument. Refer to Chapter 5. What are the implications of your argument outside classroom walls? What does your topic mean beyond a college assignment?

Giving Due Credit: Citing Sources

Everyone and everything deserve their due, especially the information sources taken from scholars and referenced in research papers and essays. Due respect for sources referenced in text includes recognition with unique sentence formatting. Here's one style of what an in-text formal citation format looks like:

> Sonnesta (2021) explains the benefits of pet-friendly campuses saying that pets on campus reduce stress among student pet owners.

The citation that identifies the source is the name of the author (Sonnesta), followed by the date in parenthesis (2021). This formal style is required in college research papers and similar research documents. The next couple of sections explain the difference between formal references and informal references.

REMEMBER

Universities, departments, and professors require specific documentation formats for recognizing scholarly work that is referenced in writing.

Formal source references

The academic community values consistency and formality. (Attend graduation and you'll see an example.) Documentation styles such as APA (American Psychological Association) and MLA (Modern Language Association) provide that consistency by standardizing citing sources, listing references, and standardizing document pages from the title page to reference page.

TECHNICAL STUFF

Other documentation styles common to undergraduate research include Chicago Manual of Style, Turabian, Harvard, and the MHRA (Modern Humanities Research Association). Styles are consistent to academic disciplines, but frequently styles will be consistent within a department or discipline.

Citations, references, and page formatting for college research papers and research reports require formal documentation, commonly APA or MLA. The style you're assigned requires mastery of all its power and glory, including illogical spacing, bolding, italicizing, and indentations.

Informal source references

Many first-year writing departments also adapt an informal citation and reference style. Departments explain it in a two-page handout, approximately 600 pages fewer than some formal publication manuals. Informal documentation styles are created to maintain the smooth writing style of essays and similar short papers that require minimal use of research sources. The informal style also avoids reader detours of formal documentation.

The general requirement for informal source references include information required to retrieve the document. Here's an example of an informal in-text reference:

> Bagwell's "Causes of Supply Chain Shortages" in 'Management Review' January 2021 contradicts traditional causes of food shortages.

Essays and short papers usually require a formal reference page listing sources cited informally, and occasionally references require annotation.

Finalizing Recognition: References

Sources like to get together for a final farewell on their own page. APA calls the page "References" and MLA calls the page "Works Cited." Professors expect you to use labels associated with specific documentation styles.

Here's an example of an MLA Works Cited entry looks like for a journal article:

> Works Cited
>
> Renduci, Alex. "College Success: Capitalizing on Opportunity." *College*
>
> *Attrition,* Vol. 12, no. 2, 2022, pp. 56-68.

Meanwhile, here is an example of an APA Annotated Reference entry for a journal article (annotated) with a DOI:

References

Swarez, J. G., & Lewis, M. S. (2022). Reading strategies for reading ready

students. *Reading Readiness Journal*, *9*(12), 84-102.

https://doi.org//10.0000099-444

The authors examine reading strategies for successful high school readers who show comprehension deficiencies reading complex text such as numerical charts and bulleted lists. Remediation strategies included isolated close reading activities with a mentor to validate discussion. The authors reference studies that show success with this technique.

Professors sometimes require an annotated bibliography (or annotated works cited) that includes a three to four sentence summary of the source. The preceding reference contains an annotation. *Note:* Annotations appear in an Annotated Bibliography, not a Reference page.

For more information on citing and documenting sources, see my book *APA Style & Citations For Dummies*. For more information on research paper writing, see Geraldine Woods' *Research Papers For Dummies* (John Wiley & Sons, Inc.).

Getting Real: Avoiding Logical Fallacies

Successful essays require a logical flow of ideas from sentence to sentence, paragraph to paragraph, and from opening to closing. The interruption of logical flow is like discovering sand in a snack. It gets your attention.

Here's an example of an interruption in the flow of logic. You're justifying logical reasons to purchase a new million-dollar database for your college library and your opposition thinks it's too expensive. You argue saying that your competitor school has the database and more of their students graduate with honors. Your reference to "more honors graduates" connection lacks logic; using the database is unlikely to result in more honors students graduating. You fed your audience sand.

Here's a list of logical fallacies, illogical thinking common to college essays:

>> **Generalization fallacy:** One incident applies to numerous incidents. For example, if one student writes an "A" essay after eating chocolate ice cream, you illogically argue that every essay writer who eats chocolate ice cream will write an "A" essay. Writing essays isn't as easy as eating chocolate ice cream — even with *College Writing For Dummies*.

>> **Either/or fallacy:** This presents two choices rather than all options. For example, we either buy the database or fewer students will graduate with honors. Problem solving requires much more thought than an either/or solution. The either/or fallacy also resembles the I-can't-think-of-anything-else, so-it-must-be fallacy.

>> **Bandwagon effect:** This refers to thinking that it must be good because everyone is doing it — logic that won't get you the million-dollar database. Independent thinkers avoid bandwagons.

>> **Slippery slope:** This fallacy uses the thinking that a series of similar events will follow. For example, spending one million dollars for this database results in spending one million-and-a-half-dollars for the next database.

>> **Evidence absence:** This fallacy follows the thinking that there is no good reason not to buy it; therefore, we should buy it.

>> **Ignoring counterpoints:** This fallacy refutes evidence with an unrelated argument, for example, "You get what you pay for."

>> **Anecdotal evidence fallacy:** This believes that one occurrence will result in numerous occurrences. For example, an English major used the database and was accepted into a prestigious law school; therefore, if more students use it, they will be accepted into similar law schools.

>> **Cause and effect fallacy:** This shows illogical cause-and-effect relationships, such as believing your cause (buying the database) results in your designated outcome (higher entry-level salaries). Starting salaries are influenced by much more complex data than a database.

3

Writing with Style, Language, and Grammar

Refresh your knowledge of parts of speech and basic grammar terminology that will help build sentence structure and variety.

Improve your sentence variety skills with sentences that branch and various sentence patterns.

Recognize the importance of two parts of speech that improve writing style — verbs that show action and nouns that identify specific images to the writer and reader.

Discover danceable rhythms that can mature your writing style, such as sentence rhythms, punctuation rhythms, word rhythms, and syllable rhythms.

Top off your style with figures of speech that compare and contrast, repeat memorable patterns, and surprise readers.

Respect your reader with language that respects people with disabilities, racial and ethnic references, age, gender, sexuality, and socioeconomic references.

Grow your grammar skills by avoiding common college errors and reviewing sneaky errors.

» Avoiding incompletes and sentence malfunctions

» Branching out in all directions

» Transitioning to additional relationships

Chapter **8**

Establishing Structure: Sentences and Paragraphs

Picture this early elementary school memory. You formed your first letter, probably an A, your favorite letter. You followed letter writing with your first words, your name. You were so proud that you couldn't wait to use all 26 letters. Nothing could stop you. Sentences were followed with paragraphs and essays — and today you're writing college papers.

And now you're returning to studying sentences and paragraphs, but you're now a college student analyzing how words make meaning and variety improves writing. In this chapter I show you engine parts of sentences and paragraphs. Their power and precision. Their abruptness and their coherence. I also show you sentence patterns with as much variety as a college course guide.

TIP

You can begin by testing your sentence and paragraph knowledge at the college level with a few questions:

» What's the differences between an independent clause, dependent clause, and Santa Claus?

>> When is a fragment a fragment and when is a fragment a sentence?

>> How do you achieve sentence variety?

>> How many directions can a sentence branch?

>> Will college professors accept sentences that begin with "and" and "but"?

If you missed any questions, you'll find the answers as you go through this chapter. Grammar up!

Variety Packs: Sentence Organization

In the beginning, before the heavens and earth and grammar books, cave people created sentences as a survival tool. Caveperson may have said: "I need a sharp spear." The first complete thought was spoken; and the simple sentence was born. Think of the simple sentence as basic sentence structure, your reliable transportation through paragraphs and essays.

Sentence structure continued to expand into a variety of structures, purposes, and formations. And cavepeople showed a sense of humor by creating fragments and run-ons.

The following sections break down sentences into their parts and explain the language of sentence organization. I give you a quick review of parts of speech, sentence structure, and sentence purposes.

Identifying parts of speech

The language of sentences requires understanding principles of a few grammatical terms. Here is a quick look at the eight parts of speech followed by their definition and some examples:

>> **Noun:** Names people, places, events, and ideas: Ben Franklin, Great Barrier Reef, Fourth of July, romanticism

>> **Pronoun:** Takes the place of nouns: I, you, he, she, him, her, it, they, them

>> **Verb:** Words that show action (or state of being): sprint, decide, write (am, is, are, was, were, be, been)

>> **Adjective:** Words that describe nouns: Stately, educated, tall

>> **Adverb:** Words that describe verbs, adjectives, and other adverbs: quickly, unceremoniously, rigidly

>> **Preposition:** Words that introduce phrases and show relationships with other sentence elements: in, to, after, before, at

>> **Conjunction:** Words that connect: and, but, nor, for, since, while, yet

>> **Interjection:** Words that show surprise: Wow!

Recognizing important grammar terms

The simplicity of the definitions in the previous section serves the purpose of understanding content of the chapter. Here's more Grammar 101. You can refer to these terms as you read this chapter:

>> **Prepositional phrase:** Three or four words including a preposition and a noun or pronoun as the object: *in the fitness center, from the library, after class,* and *near the end.* Common prepositions include *of, from, for, over, in, at,* and *after.*

>> **Independent clause:** A subject and verb, a complete sentence: The orange sun dipped below the horizon.

>> **Dependent clause:** An incomplete thought with a subject and verb that depends on an independent clause to complete its meaning: *When the sunset,* the college town came to life.

>> **Linking verb:** Inactive verbs such as *am, is, are, was, were, be,* and *been* that link the subject with the object complement: Cardez *is* president of his class.

>> **Subject complement:** Noun or pronoun that follow a linking verb and refer back to the subject: Tuesday is a *holiday.*

>> **Subject:** The person or object that performs the action of the verb: The *president* congratulated the graduates.

>> **Verb:** The action completed by the subject: The president *congratulated* the graduates.

>> **Object:** The receiver of the action: The president congratulated the *graduates.*

>> **Verbal phrase:** Phrase beginning with "ing" verb form: *Having fulfilled my purpose,* I left for home.

>> **Noun clause:** Clause acting as a noun: She *said that her requirements were completed.*

>> **Appositive:** A group of words acting as a noun, clarifying the previous noun: Writing for Managers, *a course for management majors,* is offered as a hybrid.

Focusing on sentence structures

Sentences may not be mightier than the sword, but they're powerful enough to earn your degree. The power of sentences is in their simultaneous simplicity and complexity. Here's a look into the four basic sentence structures.

TIP

For essay writing and similar short papers, aim for a general sentence length between 21 and 25 words, the approximately length of a complex sentence. For traditional research papers, write slightly longer sentences.

Simple sentences

Simple sentences are complete thoughts with at least one subject and one verb. Here's an example:

A *winter storm* (subject) *stopped* (verb) traffic on Interstate 95.

TIP

When a writing idea eludes you and loses translation between your brain and your fingers, write it in the simple structure of an simple sentence. Identify the topic you're talking about (the subject) and follow it with an action verb (take a look at Chapter 9 for action verbs). Here's an example:

I enjoy reading Walter Isaacson's biographies.

Compound sentences

Compound sentences contain two or more independent clauses, connected with a conjunction or comma. For example:

Traffic was stopped on Interstate 95, and cars detoured to Route 301.

The two independent thoughts (similar to simple sentences) are connected with the conjunction *and.* When two independent clauses in a compound sentence have a strong relationship, they're joined with a semicolon. Here's an example:

Carlos and Maria travelled to Philadelphia (independent clause); *Maria suddenly returned to Pittsburgh* (independent clause).

Complex sentences

Complex sentences contain one independent clause and at least one dependent clause. Take a look at the example:

When Interstate 95 began to freeze, motorists detoured south on Route 301.

The dependent clause (*When Interstate 95 began to freeze*) is a partial thought that can't stand alone and depends on the independent thought (*motorists detoured south on Route 301*).

REMEMBER

Compound sentences are one of your most useful sentence tools. They offer you the power to express a complete thought with a partial thought, breaking the monotony of strings of simple sentences and compound sentences. Complex sentences are a college essay writer's best friend, but remember that a simple sentence is your safety net sentence for an unclear thought.

REMEMBER

The comma that follows the introductory dependent clause (following *freeze* in the previous example) is one of the major comma omission errors by college writers. Other subordinate conjunctions that introduce opening dependent clauses include: *since, because, although, even though, until*, and *while*. See Chapter 11 for punctuation tips.

Compound-complex sentences

Compound–complex sentences consist of two or more independent clauses and a dependent clause. Here's an example:

> The snowstorm stopped traffic on Interstate 95, and ice blocked the detour on Route 301 south when we questioned if we would ever get to sunny Florida.

Let me break that down: The two independent clauses (*The snow storm stopped traffic on Interstate 95*) and (*ice blocked the detour on Route 301 south*) are followed by the dependent clause (*when we questioned if we would ever get to sunny Florida*). This sentence structure requires inches of line real estate. Use it sparingly.

Addressing sentence purpose

In addition to varied structures, sentences also include the flexibility of varied purposes.

The four basic sentence structures (simple, compound, complex, and compound-complex) serve four writing purposes (which the following sections discuss further):

>> **Declarative:** Provide information.

>> **Interrogative:** Ask questions.

>> **Imperative:** Issue requests.

>> **Exclamatory:** Express emotion.

Declarative sentences

Declarative sentences make a statement, provide information, and declare facts: *I enjoy Florida's sandy beaches with warm water and summer winds.* It's a fact that I enjoy Florida beaches, and also a fact that declarative sentences provide the most useful purpose for your college writing, offering information. For example:

> Without a college degree, you don't know the lifetime opportunities you are missing.

Interrogative sentences

Interrogative sentences ask questions and are followed by a question mark. Interrogative sentences are a good tool for sentence variety. They're also a natural transition because the answer to the question transitions to the next topic. Use an interrogative sentence once in an essay. Two are usually one too many. Here's an example:

> What's the major cause of financial insecurity?

Imperative sentences

Imperative sentences offer advice, give directions, and issue orders or directions. They end with a period or exclamation point. Use them sparingly — both imperative sentences and exclamation points. And you don't want to make a habit of telling people what to do, either. Here's an example of an imperative sentence:

> Please respect diverse opinions in the classroom.

A common use of imperative sentences is explaining a process. A *For Dummies* book is chock-full of imperative sentences that explain how to improve your writing. Flip to Chapter 5 for more on expository writing.

Exclamatory sentences

Exclamatory sentences show emotion, any kind of emotion: *What the #@$%!* Place exclamatory sentences at the bottom of your writing toolbox. Use exclamatory sentences as infrequently as long holiday weekends. Here's an example:

> Tonya earned her first A essay!

REMEMBER

Exclamation points and exclamatory sentences are severely overused in college essays. One exclamatory sentence and explanation point is effective; two are overuse. And never use repeating points!!!

Inspecting sentence formations

Sentence formations and emphasizing techniques are easy-to-use tools for adding interest to your writing and engagement from your audience. Sentences formations include branching out and adding more detail. They branch right for security, left for variety, and middle for slowing the pace. The following all represent the structural elements of sentence writing, the tools to express ideas interestingly, and clearly — and with sentence variety. These elements are especially common to college essay writing and similar short writing projects.

REMEMBER

When sentence structure fails, paragraphs fail. When paragraphs fail, writing projects fail. When writing projects fail, . . .

Branching to the right

Right branching sentences begin with a simple sentence. The subject–verb–object pattern is usually followed by descriptive information about the object of the sentence. Here's an example:

> Reading (*subject*) prepares (*verb*) students (*object*) (right branching) for a lifetime of learning, satisfying curiosities, and experiencing ideas to share with others.

Here's an X-ray view of the structure: The heart of the sentence is the subject-verb-object (*Reading-prepares-students*), words that identify the independent idea of the sentence. The less important dependent ideas follow the object *students* and describe the circumstances of how reading prepares students. Here is another example of a right branching sentence:

> The professor explained her position on reading assignments required for essays.

The subject–verb–object pattern (*professor-explained-position*) is followed by the right–branching elements that explain the conditions of the professor's position.

REMEMBER

Right branching sentences frequently include one of the following:

>> Series of items

>> Bulleted list

>> Explanation following a colon or dash

Here's an example of a right-branching sentence following a colon:

> The professor clarified again: no popular sources in essays.

And here's a right-branching sentence with a bulleted list:

Nancy brought to college the following:

- home theater hardware
- snow survival equipment
- a laser printer
- a half dozen novels.

Right-branching sentences, the standard building block of first-year college writing, also represent the standard speech pattern and the reason for the advice to write like people talk. After mastering right-branching sentences, be aware of the danger of overusing them and boring your readers. Right-branching sentences are a major tool of successful college writing, but not the only tool in the toolbox.

Branching to the left

Left branching sentences position the less important dependent ideas before the subject and verb, delaying the independent idea of the subject-verb-object pattern. But a pattern of left-branching sentences in your essays will frustrate your reader (your professor) into thinking: "Please get to the point." Use left branching dependent clauses judiciously. Excessive use of left-branching sentences should remain locked in the toolbox.

Left-branching sentences are common to historical documents and proclamations. Here's an historical example of a left-branching sentence:

When in the course of human events, it becomes necessary for one people to dissolve the political bands which have connected them with another, and to assume among the powers of the earth, the separate and equal station to which the Laws of Nature and Nature's God entitle them, a decent respect to the opinions of mankind requires that they should declare the causes which impel them to the separation.

Notice the half dozen left branches before the sentence gets to the point, the independent clause: *They should declare the causes.* You're not writing history in college, you're writing to make history with historical essays and other writing projects.

Branching in the middle

Middle branching sentences suffer from an identity crisis by hiding the main sentence thought between the subject and verb. But they do offer readers a breath of fresh words in the middle of an independent thought. A middle-branching sentence looks like this:

The professor, after explaining the purpose of required readings in essays, asked for questions.

The independent clause (subject–verb) in the example is *The professor asked for questions.* The middle branching element of the sentence (*after explaining the purpose of required readings in essays*) provides the conditions that the professor did the asking.

Here's an example of a middle-branching sentence with excessive middle branches:

The professor, after explaining the purpose of required readings, previewing the next essay assignment, and collecting book projects, asked for questions.

The point about burying the point in middle branching is clear.

Emphasizing your point

Sentence ideas without emphasis are like one ice cream flavor — nothing stands out. Some sentence ideas require more emphasis than others. Here's a list of strategies for emphasizing your high-priority ideas to your readers and examples:

>> **Sentence position:** Position ideas for emphasis at the beginning or end of the sentence:

- **Beginning emphasis:** *One million dollars,* that's how much some people can earn with a YouTube channel.

- **Ending emphasis:** Some YouTube channels earn as much as *one million dollars.*

>> **Punctuation:** Emphasize ideas following a comma, colon, semicolon, or dash. Take a look at these examples:

- Bernadette's reward was her ultimate dream — *a bachelor's degree.*

- Every student in the classroom experienced the same thought: *too much lecturing.*

>> **Key words:** Use key words to emphasize the importance of ideas:

- The opening of an essay is read *first* by the reader, but it's written *last* by the writer.

>> **Transitional phrases:** Use transitional phrases (*such as, for example, in addition to,* and *also*) to prioritize ideas:

- Carlene earned academic honors for the year, *in addition to* being named musician of the year.

>> **Conjunctions:** Use conjunctions such as *and, but, except,* and *however* to prioritize ideas:

- Josh was first to arrive for the academic bowl, *but* he was also the first contestant to be eliminated.

>> **Intensifiers:** Use words such as *most important, especially, foremost, above all,* and *consequently* to highlight an idea:

- Your essays are written for the academic audience, but *the most important* member of that audience is your professor.

Using intentional fragments

One or two intentional fragments add pop to your essay writing, but don't use them without first talking with your professor and having a history of successful use. But keep intentional fragments in your writing toolbox.

Short fragments focus on a point of emphasis. For example:

The hospitality majors served the best food on campus. *Free*.

Intentional fragments get to the point quickly. They're like Carolina Reaper peppers. They either enhance the flavor of your writing, or they blow up your grade. Unintentional fragments are the first sign of language skills issues and the need to visit the writing center. Same with the unintentional use of run-ons (refer to the section, "Avoiding (Unintended) Incompletes: Fragments and Run-ons," later in this chapter for more information).

SENTENCE FORMALITY: ESSAY VERSUS RESEARCH PAPER

Sentence structure tools are as plentiful as snowfall in Alaska, and every tool has a home in an essay except one, run-ons. With your professor's guidance, use intentional fragments, use "ands" and "buts," but don't use run-ons. Save those for the professionals. Your essays and similar papers are a playground for most sentence structures.

But research papers are a different set of rules. No run-ons, no fragments, and very few "ands" and "buts." And little to no use of playful style tools in Chapter 9. The style and sentence structure of research writing is as formal as a classroom lecture.

Starting sentences with "and" and "but": Yes or no?

As a college professor, I get questions. Sometimes untimely. And, yes, some questions are bad, such as: What essay that was due yesterday?

TECHNICAL STUFF

High school teachers, overburdened, underpaid, and underappreciated, sometimes create rules for instructional purposes, such as no fragments, and no "ands" and "buts." But college essay encourages your experimentation with new language patterns.

ADDING VARIETY TO YOUR SENTENCE PATTERNS

The sentence patterns and the examples that follow are common to college writing:

- **Prepositional phrase-subject-verb:** During rush hour, a winter storm stopped traffic.

- **Dependent clause-subject-verb-prepositional phrase:** When the storm subsided, traffic resumed on Interstate 95.

- **Independent clause-dependent clause:** She wrote a successful essay because she had her paper reviewed by the writing center.

- **Subject-linking verb-complement-appositive:** Another optional back section of a research paper is a glossary, or list of terms used in the research project.

- **Subject-verb-noun clause-prepositional phrase-dependent clause:** Many professors prefer that you embed figures and tables within the text where they have more relevancy.

- **Verbal phrase-subject-linking verb-complement:** Having read the directions for the installation, I felt confident.

- **Verbal phrase-subject-verb-compound object:** Depending on the course or topic, professors usually require an abstract or executive summary.

- **Subject-verb-object-prepositional phrase-prepositional phrase-appositive-dependent clause:** We investigated the causes of online bullying through social media, a phenomenon that has been increasing in recent years that resulted in a number of deaths in past years.

- **Prepositional phrase-subject (understood)-compound verb:** From your answers, delete unnecessary and overused words and revise your list of key words.

- **Subject-prepositional phrase-verb-verbal-prepositional phrase:** The language of sentences requires understanding principles of a few grammar terms.

Look at the sentence in the first paragraph of this section: *As a college professor, I do get questions.* It's followed by the intentional fragment: *Sometimes untimely.* You as a student can identify with the fragment and with some students who ask untimely questions, such as when a test is beginning. The meaning is clear. Agree?

REMEMBER

Don't ask questions that are answered on the syllabus (check out Chapter 2). You're telling your professor you didn't read the syllabus.

Two questions I'm happy to be asked, usually early in the semester, are: Can we use fragments? and Can we begin a sentence with "and?" The questions tell me the student understands fragments and that they had a high school teacher who put "and" on the Covid "unable to perform" list. I encourage the use of "and" and "but" as a form of sentence variety. The questions also tell me they need a lesson in "can" and "may," but at another time.

Avoiding (Unintended) Incompletes: Fragments and Run-ons

Unintentional fragments, and their close friend, run-ons, are the red flags of sentence structure. Their incorrect use attracts your professor's attention like a cell phone ringing in class.

WARNING

At the first identification of an unintentional fragment or run-on sentence, run to the writing center for help. Trained tutors can help you with these language errors that I examine more here — if you provide determination and practice.

Cutting a thought short: Fragments

Unintentional fragments are incomplete thoughts lacking a subject and verb. The problem with unintended fragments is that your professor can't distinguish between an unintended fragment that shows lack of sentence structure knowledge and an intended fragment that shows skillful use of a style tool. During my decades of college teaching, I haven't seen more than a handful of college writers successfully use fragments.

Here is an example:

> After binging on Netflix and watching a few YouTube episodes on the large screen in the recreation room where they have surround sound and snacks.

This fragment represents an incomplete thought, dependent clauses that lack a subject and verb. Here's how to revise it into a complete sentence:

After binging on Netflix and watching a few YouTube episodes on the large screen in the recreation room where they have surround sound and snacks, Patricia began working on her essay.

Erroring with punctuation: Run-ons

Run-on sentences are two or more independent thoughts (sentences or independent clauses) that run consecutively without a mark of punctuation. A variation of a run-on is a *comma splice* (two independent clauses joined incorrectly by a comma without a conjunction). Here's an example of a run-on:

> Writing can easily be argued the most demanding intellectual activity performed by humans think of what we create with twenty-six letters interpreted with small lines, curves, and dots.

In the example, two separate sentences (independent clauses) run together without punctuation. They are

> Writing can easily be argued the most demanding intellectual activity performed by humans.

> Think of what we create with twenty-six letters interpreted with small lines, curves, and dots.

REMEMBER

Run-ons can be repaired by separating them into two sentences, as done in the previous example, or separated with a semicolon like this:

> Writing can easily be argued the most demanding intellectual activity performed by humans; think of what we create with twenty-six letters interpreted with small lines, curves, and dots.

Or you can separate run-ons with a coordinating conjunction and a comma like this:

> Writing can easily be argued the most demanding intellectual activity performed by humans, and think of what we create with twenty-six letters interpreted with small lines, curves, and dots.

Indenturing Sentences: Paragraph Structure

Sentences that experience a good childhood, grow up to be strong healthy paragraphs. Problem sentences that don't work hard and hang out with the wrong crowd of words are destined to a life of intentional fragments and runs-ons. Not a bright future.

Topic sentences represent the alphas of paragraphs and control the pattern of paragraph development. The following sections show you how to write and incorporate paragraphs into body sections of your college writing and how to vary sentence lengths in paragraphs.

Focusing on topic sentences

A good topic sentence acts like the safety patrol of developing sentences, ensuring all sentences contribute to paragraph development. Topic sentences identify the focus of the paragraph, the one piece of evidence that steps up center stage to perform for the thesis. Topic sentences guide paragraph development similar to how theses guide direction of the essay.

TIP

Reading your topic sentences sequentially offers an overview of evidence supporting your essay.

Topic sentences aren't just another sentence in your writing assignment. They're the second most important sentences in your college writing — next to your thesis statement. The next two sections explain how to create and position topic sentences.

Putting together a topic sentence

Create your topic sentence by answering these questions:

>> What's the major piece of evidence you're introducing into the paragraph?

>> What's the purpose of the evidence?

>> How's the evidence connected to the thesis?

>> Does the sentence predict the development of the paragraph?

Here are a couple examples of topic sentences:

> Rodson argues that the iPhone in 2007 started a revolution of technological advances that continues today.

This topic sentence introduces a piece of evidence that the iPhone started a technological revolution in 2007 that continues today. Here's another topic sentence:

> Literary critics argue Ernest Hemingway is America's best writer because of his unique style emphasizing active verbs and specific nouns.

The topic sentence introduces one piece of evidence, critics arguing Hemingway America's best writer because of his unique style.

Here's an example of a bad topic sentence:

> The iPhone influenced communication.

The bad example lacks specificity identifying *influenced communication.*

Positioning your topic sentences

Topic sentences for essays and similar short papers are ideally positioned as the first sentence in the paragraph, but they may be preceded by a transitional sentence. Here's an example of the transitional sentence:

> Another piece of evidence supporting today's technological revolution is the recent invention of the iPhone.

The transitional word *another* alerts the reader that what follows is another strategy.

Follow the topic sentence with an explanatory or overview sentence that includes "such as" or "for example." Until you become a sophisticated college writer, or a writing major, avoid positioning your topic sentence in a location other than the top of the paragraph.

Developing paragraphs

Paragraphs are the organizational units of essays and most other pieces of college writing. Those unit ideas serve as the builders of evidence in the body paragraphs. Writing effective body paragraphs is an essential skill for writing essays that earn a B or A.

REMEMBER

The opening and closing paragraphs differ from the body paragraphs and are detailed in Chapter 5.

The following sections explain how paragraphs are structured and how they vary in length.

Structuring paragraphs

An essay paragraph usually includes the following structure and sequence:

>> **Topic sentence:** The topic sentence, detailed in the previous section, introduces the paragraph topic, similar to a mini-thesis.

>> **Follow-up sentences:** The topic sentence is followed with a sentence(s) that emphasizes the importance of the topic.

>> **Supporting evidence:** Paragraph supporting evidence includes references to studies, experts' observation, statistical data, survey results, and anecdotes.

>> **Analysis and synthesis:** Analysis and synthesis (see Chapter 7) interpret the evidence by showing its relationship to other pieces of evidence and topics related to the thesis.

>> **Conclusion:** The paragraph ends with the importance of the evidence and its connection to the thesis.

REMEMBER

Every paragraph sentence adds insight to the development of the topic sentence. If a sentence doesn't add to the topic sentence, it doesn't belong in the paragraph.

Here's an example of a body paragraph developing a piece of evidence:

> Lonetta's study showed that job-interview preparation lasting twenty or more hours resulted in increased job offers. Bleven explains that "the interview is the decision-maker in the job search process" and requires "intense preparation." College students' preparation for a job interview requires preparation similar to a research project, and searching to answer questions such as: What are the strengths of the company? What are the liabilities and how can they be turned into opportunities? In addition to searching key words from the company web site, the industry requires searching to determine the company's position among similar competitors in the industry. Students should synthesize research by looking for similarities and differences among competitors and identifying recent trends and the importance of those trends. "You can never overprepare for an interview," said career consultant Abigail Arietta from Job Solutions, and "it determines whether or not you get the job."

Varying paragraph lengths

Paragraph length subtly signals the importance of the content to the reader, importance that ranges from judging paragraphs as "only transitional" short paragraphs to "overly complicated" for extended paragraphs.

Varied paragraph length, similar to sentence length, also creates writing interest. And like all writing tools, length has its strengths, limits, and perspective.

Here's an analysis of the roles of paragraph length in essay and other college writing:

>> **Long paragraphs:** The high-priority paragraphs for essays, long paragraphs carry the evidence load of your essay. For essay-length papers (approximately 650 to 700 words) paragraph length shouldn't exceed three-quarters of a

page. Long paragraphs develop evidence with research references, illustrations, examples, expert testimony, and so forth. Long evidence-building paragraphs require readers' use of high brain wattage. Avoid successive long paragraphs because of the visual appearance signifying challenging content.

>> **Medium paragraphs:** Approximately five to six sentences, medium paragraphs capably function as extensions of evidence paragraphs and a placeholder for shorter pieces of evidence. Medium paragraphs are also adaptable to openings and closings where they frequently function in pairs.

>> **Short paragraphs:** They consist of one or two sentences are like a quick snack — a short burst of intellectual satisfaction. Short paragraphs in an essay provide a change in rhythm and a quick transition. Don't use more than two short paragraphs in an essay. Avoid short paragraphs in other academic papers.

>> **Extended paragraphs:** A page or longer, extended paragraphs are the evidence-building paragraphs of extended research projects and are common to formal research such as a reviews of literature, thesis, or certificate-granting project. These monster paragraphs are unwelcomed in essays.

Flowing Smoothly: Coherence

Cohesion is like gravity that pulls paragraphs towards the thesis and also bridges sentences and paragraphs, preventing them from gravitating to outer space — a condition your professor describes as "off topic." Cohesion enhances comprehension. The lack of it is frequently detected with language instinct, that inner voice that says, "This sentence doesn't fit."

The following sections discuss the two techniques that build coherence: transitional strategies and transitional words.

Being consistent: Transitional strategies

Transitional strategies frequently function behind the scenes. They provide consistency, and consistency provides coherence. Transitional strategies for building coherence include consistency using the following:

>> **Person:** Use first, second, and third person consistently in a piece of writing. Unexpected person shifts are like sudden gear changes for the reader. Chapter 6 provides details for person uses.

» **Pronoun references:** Pronoun reference consistency also provides a smooth, cohesive flow of information. Ensure pronouns agree with verbs and antecedents in person, number, gender, and case. See Chapter 11 for details.

» **Number:** Consistency in number also establishes coherence. Ensure that singular and plural uses are consistent (refer to Chapter 11).

» **Tone:** A consistent tone also contributes to coherence. Chapter 6 warns about sudden changes in attitude that disrupt coherence.

» **Tense:** Similar to tone, verb tense needs consistency to maintain coherence, and shifts need to follow logical reasons (see Chapter 6).

» **Noun references:** Throughout a piece of writing, noun references need consistency to maintain coherence. For example, if you reference *automobile* in the beginning of a piece of writing, remain consistent with *automobile* throughout the writing and not change to *auto, car,* or *vehicle.* In this book the three essay parts are consistently labeled *opening, middle,* and *closing.* They don't shift to "introduction," "body," and "conclusion." Consistence builds coherence.

Eyeing relationships: Transitional words

When you think of transitions, think of relationships — relationships between ideas, relationships such as similar, dissimilar, exceptional, emphatic, sequential, high priority, and low priority. Use transitional words to connect ideas and show relationships among sentences and paragraphs. Use transitions at the beginning, in the middle, and at the end of sentences and paragraphs. Table 8-1 lists some transitional words.

TABLE 8-1 **Transitional Words**

Relationship	Examples
Additional	In addition to, furthermore, besides, along with
Consequence	Therefore, consequentially, subsequently
Dissimilar	Unlike, in contrast to, on the contrary, nevertheless, despite, conversely, on the contrary
Emphatic	Primarily, in addition to, such as, for example, however
Sequential	First, next, finally, in conclusion
Similar	Likewise, also, similarly, along with

To see the importance of transitional words, try reading without them. Transitional words power the sentence train to run smoothly.

Chapter **9**

Scoring Personality Points: Stars of Style

Think of the style or brand of your university. Is it country club or community center? Is it intercollegiate or intramural? Is it boardroom or meeting room? Is it motor scooter or motorhome?

Your writing contains a similar style. Is your part of speech emphasis active or inactive? Is your word choice fast food or fine dining? Is your sentence structure heavy traffic or county road? Is your writing rhythm symphony hall or battle of the bands?

Language represents not only a visual experience, but also a musical experience that accompanies the meaning of words. Your writing style includes the sounds of words and the rhythms of sentences as you express your message.

Chapter 8 explains the structural patterns of sentences. This chapter focuses on the rhythm and beats of those patterns as well as other tools for creating style. Your content selection attracts readers; your style selection keeps readers interested. Time to start dancing to the words.

TECHNICAL STUFF

Your professor may use the term *syntax* as analysis of word arrangements, sentence structure, grammar, and figurative language.

Knowing Who's Doing What: Active Verbs and Specific Nouns

Ernest Hemingway's alleged advice to beginning writers was to write with more nouns and verbs than adjectives and adverbs. His advice applies to almost all writers, including you. For college students, specific nouns and action verbs are a point producer. Verbs are where the action is, and nouns are who's doing it. They're the foundation of your writing style, especially when verbs are action-packed and nouns are pixel-perfect.

Science today has advanced Hemingway's advice with fMRI brain-scanning machines showing that specific nouns and active verbs activate the brain, while vague nouns and inactive verbs don't.

Here's an example: Picture the noun *pet* and what you see in your head. Now picture *Golden Retriever*. See the difference? Picture the verb *went*, and picture the verb *jogged*. See the difference? *Golden Retriever* photographs a fluffy, furry friend and *jogged* shows a human in the process of slowly trotting. Your writing style begins with your selection of active verbs and specific nouns.

The Nobel Prize winner's advice identifies a successful writer-reader connection. Writers choose words that represent a picture in their mind. When readers read that word and develop the same picture, writing and reading connects. That connection begins with good verbs and nouns. The following sections explain how to strengthen your verbs and nouns and clarify your ideas to your readers.

TIP

Hemingway, arguably America's best novelist, is considered master of the simple sentence, the subject-action-verb-object sentence pattern. His novels include *A Farewell to Arms*, *The Sun Also Rises*, and *For Whom the Bell Tolls*. His *The Old Man and the Sea* is popular with many students. Pick up a copy or two of these books and enjoy Hemingway's stories with style techniques worthy of duplicating in your writing.

Heart of speech: Verbs

If you like action, adopt verbs as your favorite part of speech. Your writing style thrives on action verbs, the heart of your style system. Like a heart, verbs need regular exercise and disease protection from inactivity. Choose verbs that show action when they're screenshot in your mind, verbs such as *sprint*, *process*, *analyze*, *initiate*, *volunteer*, and *coordinate*.

These sections explain tips for converting inactive verbs to active verbs and tips for converting verbs that tell action into verbs that show action.

Understanding active and passive voice

Verbs are identified with one of two voices, active or passive. When verbs are active voice, the subject performs the action. Here's an example:

The professor *dismissed* class.

The subject (*professor*) performed the action (*dismissed*).

When verbs are passive voice, the subject receives the action. Here's a passive voice example, the kind of sentence you usually want to revise:

Class *was dismissed* by the professor.

In this example the subject (*class*) receives the action of being *dismissed*.

The passive voice is formed with the verb "to be" (*was*) in the example. The doer of the action (*professor*) is positioned at the end of the sentence. If you unintentionally write with a pattern of passive voice verbs, convert them to the active voice.

To do so isn't difficult. Here's an example:

Passive voice: My computer *was infected* by a virus.

Active voice: A virus *infected* my computer.

In this passive example, the doer of the action (*virus*) is positioned at the end of the sentence. Revise to the active voice by positioning *virus* as the subject.

TIP

Use the active voice for almost all your verb needs, but here are two occasions when the passive is acceptable:

>> **The receiver of the action is more important than the doer of the action.**

Lincoln *was shot* by Booth.

Lincoln was the tragedy of the story, not Booth, the assassin. Because Lincoln is more important than Booth, position Lincoln as the subject.

> **» You choose not to identify the doer of the action.**
>
> The project *was mismanaged*.
>
> The performer of the mismanagement is intentionally unidentified, a common practice in business writing.

Table 9-1 lists some active verbs commonly used in essays and other forms of academic writing.

TABLE 9-1   ## Common Academic Verbs

argue	support	synthesize	analyze
categorize	evaluate	implement	trace
predict	conclude	focus	survey
integrate	investigate	survey	coordinate
align	recommend	attribute	determine
highlight	insert	contradict	confine
classify	identify	allocate	prioritize

Limiting linking verbs

Linking verbs are inactive verbs that connect a noun or adjective to the subject and can frequently be revised to active verbs. Linking verbs, sometimes called *being verbs*, represent static existence and lack movement. They include *am, is, are, was, were, be,* and *been*. A few other verbs are frequently included in this group because they act like linking verbs: *seems, appears, feels,* and *looks*.

TECHNICAL STUFF

Linking verbs are called being verbs because they represent conjugated or categorized forms of the *to be* verb. *Conjugate* verbs means identifying verb forms in the first, second, and third person singular and plural. The following conjugates the verb *to be*.

Person	Singular	Plural
First	I am	We are
Second	You are	You are
Third	He, she, it is	They are

Revise almost all linking verbs to active verbs. Here's what revising looks like.

Linking verb: I *am* the person who spilled the coffee.

Active verb: I *spilled* the coffee.

Linking: The speaker *is* very interesting.

Active: The speaker *tells* stories about travel throughout the Southwest.

In each example the linking verb is converted to the action performed by the subject. A form of the action verb is frequently found later in the sentence.

Forms of "to be" also function as helping verbs to the main verbs, as in these examples:

I *am looking* for my phone charger.

Writing classes *were scheduled* to meet in the writing lab.

REMEMBER

When linking verbs function as helpers, they aren't considered inactive verbs because they help the action of the main verb.

Using active verbs rather than inactive verbs

Verbs that generate specific actions in your mind as a writer communicate these same actions to your reader. Here are examples of inactive verbs revised to active verbs:

Inactive verb: Ophelia *has* a city apartment.

Active verb: Ophelia *resides* in a city apartment.

Inactive verb: I *went* to Harrisburg to pick up my certificate.

Active verb: I *drove* to Harrisburg to pick up my certificate.

In the examples, the inactive verbs (*has* and *went*) lack the specificity of the active verbs (*resides* and *drove*).

TIP

When you choose your verbs (and nouns — refer to the section, "Never nameless: Nouns," later in this chapter) use the screenshot test. Can you see in your mind the details in the actions of your verb? For example, when you screenshot the verb *sprint,* did you see facial expressions, streams of sweat, and arms pumping? Similarly, when you picture the verb *earn* (as in the sentence: You *earned* an A.), do you picture hours of intense study?

Utilizing show verbs over tell verbs

Strong verbs show action rather than tell action. Verbs that tell follow the sentence pattern of subject–linking verb–complement (see Chapter 8 for grammar terms).

Here are examples to differentiate *show* from *tell*:

Tell verb: *Moby-Dick is* an interesting story of Ahab chasing the whale.

Show verb: *Moby-Dick accounts* the story of Ahab avenging Moby-Dick for biting off his leg.

The verb *is* tells the reader that *Moby-Dick* is an interesting story. The verb *accounts* shows the reader that Ahab avenges Moby Dick for biting off his leg. Here's another example:

Tell verb: Tuesday *is* trash collection day.

Show verb: The city *collects* trash Tuesday.

The verb *is* tells the reader that Tuesday is trash day. The verb *collects* shows the reader trash is collected Tuesday.

Finding hidden verbs

Frequently active verbs are hidden in three- or four-word phrases. When you identify three or four words to express the verb idea, look for one word that expresses the action. Table 9-2 lists some examples.

TABLE 9-2 ### Locating Hidden Verbs

Wordy Verb Expression	Action Verb
come to agree on	agree
offer a comment	comment
reach a conclusion	conclude
make a contribution	contribute
offer a suggestion	suggest
cause a reduction	reduce
have a requirement	require

Avoiding adverb corruption

Adverbs, the enemy of verbs, corrupt active verbs and compromise verb integrity by weakening the verb action. For example, if *look* is the verb, and needs a qualifier such as *quickly*, revise *look quickly* to the more specific verb *glance*. Table 9-3 examines verb and "ly" adverb combinations adaptable to a stronger verb.

Converting Adverb + Verb to Active Verb

Verb + Adverb	Action Verb
drove quickly	sped
made sure	checked
ran quickly	sprinted
read quickly	skimmed
talked loudly	shouted
thought quietly	meditated
wrote quickly	scribbled

Never nameless: Nouns

How important is a noun or name? Imagine your campus buildings without names, your town's streets without names, and students in your classes without names. Nouns name people, places, objects, and ideas: nameless nevermore.

Similar to verbs, nouns aren't created equal. Nouns such as *thing, gadget, stuff, factor,* and *ways* need more education before they qualify for college writing. Hemingway recommends nouns that generate specific images. For example, the noun *e-bike* elicits a more specific image than a noun such as *vehicle* or *transportation*. Table 9-4 looks at a continuum of nouns from general to specific.

Using specific nouns and action verbs

The most important tip that this book offers you to improve your writing is emphasizing specific nouns and active verbs. Here's a sample paragraph showing you their effectiveness:

> We exited the 4-Train along with the Bronx faithful at Yankee Stadium Exit. We were distinguishable by our red Phillies caps and wheeled luggage. A polite young Yankee fan in a blue cap offered to carry our luggage down three flights of subway

stairs. He then directed us toward a bowling alley that checked backpacks and luggage. We walked past a storefront awning that displayed the years of 26 World Championships, 25 more than the Phillies.

TABLE 9-4

General to Specific Nouns

General	Less General	Specific
animal	amphibian	frog
art	painting	White Umbrella
book	nonfiction	*Einstein*
foot covering	shoe	boot
leader	administrator	principal
tool	wrench	rachet
vehicle	hybrid	Prius

Table 9-5 shows the specific nouns and active verbs that appear in the sample paragraph. They represent the kinds of verbs and nouns to focus on in your writing.

TABLE 9-5

Identifying Specific Nouns and Action Verbs

Nouns	Verbs
4-Train	exited
Bronx faithful	offered
Yankee Stadium Exit	directed
Yankee fan	checked
awning	passed
26 World Series Championships	displayed
bowling alley	walked

REMEMBER

When you choose a noun, ask yourself if a more specific form of the noun is available.

A WORK IN PROGRESS — YOU AND YOUR WRITING STYLE

You entered college with the basics of building your writing style and with tools such as grammar, mechanics, sentence structure, sentence variation, and figurative language. College is ground zero for continuing to develop your style. Fortunately, the emergence of style tools into your writing has little influence on your essay grade — assuming you continue mastery of fundamental elements of style that I explain in Chapters 5–8.

The essay and your first-year writing course offer you the opportunity to develop a more complex writing style, beginning with expanding the five-paragraph structure as described in Chapter 2. College topics and analysis require college-level writing tools such as writing frameworks (Chapter 5), varied sentence structures (Chapter 8), varied paragraph structures (Chapter 8), source and documentation integration (Chapter 7), and higher expectations of the academic audience (Chapter 6).

The style tools in this chapter offer you an opportunity to safely experiment with style in your essay writing and similar writing projects — especially the tool of rhythm. Rhythm aligns the sound of sentence patterns with the sound of spoken language patterns. It helps you emphasize and dramatize ideas. "Feeling Risky: Styling with Figures of Speech," later in this chapter, provides additional tools for increasing audience interest.

As an academician you're a work in progress; as a writer your style is also a work in progress.

Pacing Makers: Varying Patterns

We live in a world surrounded by sound — people talking, nature singing, music playing, technology beeping, and transportation screeching. Each sound contains its rhythm and its systematic pattern. In the world of reading, your ears demand high expectations from words that speak to you from the page. They demand a rhythm that duplicates spoken language.

The rhythm of writing includes sound variations of sentences, punctuation, and words, which the following sections examine. It also includes variations of stressed and unstressed syllables, the music of language. When the rhythm of sound lacks variety, it's as annoying as back–up beeps of trucks in reverse.

Recognizing sentence rhythms

This is a simple sentence. The rhythm of that simple sentence is as unappealing as the rhythm of a cell phone alarm. Novice writers create simple sentences, such as the reader primer sentence: *See Spot run*. Experienced writers orchestrate complex messages with combinations of structures and rhythms, like a 72-piece orchestra.

Rhythm controls reading pace. Shorter sentences and end punctuation slow pace; longer sentences and serial commas speed pace. Pairs of commas and dashes invite reader reflection. Bullets, headings, and graphic organizers warn readers to slow down smell the sound.

Length and rhythm

Short sentences combined with long sentences establish a rhythm that sets up short sentences for impact. Long-, long-, and short-sentence patterns build drama. Rhythm variations are a writer's major tool to emphasize ideas.

Here's an example of sentence with a variety of rhythms from award-winning poet and playwright Oscar Wilde:

"Life is never fair, and perhaps it is a good thing for most of us that it is not."

The rhythm of the opening four-word independent clause (*Life is . . .*) is short and snappy with three one-syllable words and one two-syllable word. The short opening clause prepares readers for the 15-word longer clause (*and perhaps . . . not*) that explains *life is never fair* and extends the rhythm with single-syllable words. The longer clause (*and perhaps . . . not*) includes short words, visualizing the simplicity of the message.

This example shows the rhythm of a short sentence between longer sentences:

The art of writing, a complex learning activity, extends back almost five thousand years. *Reading is similarly old*. Reading, another brain add on, requires the complex integration of manipulating twenty-six letters with multiple-meaning combinations expressing multiple meaning.

The sandwiched short sentence emphasizes that reading is as old as writing.

Variety and rhythm

Sentence structure and length create a variety of rhythmical patterns. Your style goal as a college writer includes awareness of sentence structures that add variety to writing, duplicate human speech rhythms, and emphasize ideas.

Here's an example from Herman Melville's *Moby-Dick* that includes sentence variety and rhythm. Take a listen:

> Call me Ishmael. Some years ago — never mind how long precisely — having little or no money in my purse, and nothing particular to interest me on shore, I thought I would sail about a little and see the watery part of the world. It is a way I have of driving off the spleen and regulating the circulation. Whenever I find myself growing grim about the mouth; whenever it is a damp, drizzly November in my soul; whenever I find myself involuntarily pausing before coffin warehouses, and bringing up the rear of every funeral I meet; and especially whenever my hypos get such an upper hand of me, that it requires a strong moral principle to prevent me from deliberately stepping into the street, and methodically knocking people's hats off — then, I account it high time to get to sea as soon as I can. This is my substitute for pistol and ball.

The paragraph begins with the 3-word, *m*-sounding repetitious *Call me Ishmael*. The short sentence is followed by the left-branching (see Chapter 8 for branching sentences): *Some years ago . . .* that includes a dash rhythm-breaker (*never mind how long precisely*). This long 40-word sentence is sandwiched between the 3-word opening and a 15-word right-branching: *It is a way. . .*

The following 87-word, left-branching sentence (*Whenever I find myself . . .*) includes repetition of *whenever*. A short 8-word sentence follows: *This is my substitute . . .*

Melville creates variety and rhythm by integrating sentence structure and length — splashed with dashes and repetition. Store Melville's techniques in your toolbox. This sample, obviously, is from a novel and not an essay, but its structure represents professional use of variety and rhythm.

Identifying punctuation rhythms

The origin of punctuation was aligned with the rhythm of music, duplicating beats that tell musical audiences and readers of literature when to pause, stop, reflect, emphasize, and connect. The rhythm of music and writing is guided by the sounds of silence used to focuses reader attention on emphasized and deemphasized information.

Punctuation patterns that guide sentence rhythm include the following:

>> **End punctuation:** Periods, question marks, and exclamation points stop readers for an uninterrupted moment of reflection on the previous sentence. End punctuation produces rhythms of stop-and-reflect (declarative sentence),

stop-and-question (interrogative sentence), and stop-and-perform (imperative sentence).

>> **Introductory comma:** A comma following an opening dependent clause produces a stop and switch in rhythm from the less important dependent clause to the more important independent clause. The introductory comma has the effect of a temporary loss in communication because it breaks flow and introduces an unknown independent thought.

>> **Dash:** A dash interrupts rhythm and introduces explanatory material.

>> **Double dashes:** Double dashes are serious interruptions dressed in formal attire. They're equivalent to fingers pointing to the head saying, "Listen to me. This is important."

>> **Comma combination:** Comma combos lack the confidence of dashes, but ask for a minor break in rhythm to add a quick or nonessential thought.

>> **Semicolon:** Semicolons are the heavy machinery of punctuation. They're warnings of serious rhythm interruptions that require intense concentration. Minor interrupters such as commas are within the jurisdiction of semicolons.

>> **Colon:** Colons grow up dreaming to be semicolons, but lower SAT scores sentence them to less-complex responsibilities such as introducing a series of items or a bulleted list.

You can find examples of these punctuations throughout this book.

Hearing rhythm variety

Punctuation determines how readers hear your words and rhythm. Read these sentences aloud and listen to the rhythms. Which punctuation rhythm identifies the professor's highest impression of the essay?

>> **The professor read the essay. It was a work of art.**

The combination period and capital letter produce the longest stop (of these four examples) and reader reflection time to think about the essay. The period provides reflection for the professor to evaluate and determine the essay was a work of art.

>> **The professor read the essay, a work of art.**

The comma produces a shorter pause than the period and less reflective time to evaluate a work of art.

>> **The professor read the essay — a work of art.**

The dash offers a strong argument for the professor's highest impression of the essay.

>> **The professor read the essay: a work of art.**

Like the second example, the colon offers a shorter pause than the period and less reflective time.

This next example builds rhythm toward a dash and dramatic ending. Listen to the rhythm of skillful punctuation in the statement from Internet entrepreneur Gurbaksh Chahal:

"If you genuinely want something, don't wait for it — teach yourself to be impatient."

The sentence begins with the longer dependent clause (*If you genuinely . . .*) that builds drama toward the comma's short rhythm break. The independent clause stresses the point *don't wait for it.* The dash creates a longer pause than the comma before delivering the sarcastic *teach yourself to be impatient.*

Noticing short- sentence rhythm

American poet Robert Frost shows the rhythm of a short sentence with small, high-impact words:

"In three words I can sum up everything I've learned about life: it goes on."

The sentence rhythm begins with a prepositional phrase consisting of three one-syllable words. The introductory prepositional phrase builds drama with a short reflective silence that precedes the main clause (*I can sum up . . .*), and centers on the multi-syllable *everything.* The colon provides another reflective silence prior to the understatement — *it goes on.* Life goes on regardless of its trials and tribulations.

Here's an example of a seven-word, rhythm-building sentence with a twist from Franklin Delano Roosevelt:

"If you're going through hell, keep going."

The introductory dependent clause (*If you're going through hell,*) establishes a fast-paced rhythm that ends with a comma. The reflection pause is followed by the unexpected advice — *keep going.*

REMEMBER

The influence of rhythm in writing style is underestimated, underutilized, and often misunderstood. Remember that your first step toward rhythm development is awareness in your reading.

Noting word rhythms

Novice writers use words to create meaning. Professional writers manipulate words to create music that complements meaning. Write your essays with your eyes on what you say and an ear on how it sounds. Awareness of sound is the "scholar in training" part of your college education. It's reaching for higher expectations of writing. It's like shooting for the moon, and if unsuccessful, hurtling toward the stars.

REMEMBER

Awareness of rhythm applies primarily for essays, occasionally for reaction papers and report writing. It's generally avoided in research writing.

The sections that follow complement your writing style with rhythm of syllables, while avoiding repetitious syllables.

Styling with syllables

Words are designed with patterns of stressed and unstressed syllables. The human ear distinguishes between syllable sounds in words such as *design* and *descent*. For example, the ear hears *design* as the unstressed *de* syllable and the stressed *sign* syllable. The ear hears *descent* as the stressed syllable *de* and unstressed *scent*. A general rule is that every word has only one stressed syllable, one upbeat sound that influences rhythm.

The following words show examples of stressed syllables:

>> **Disassemble:** First syllable *dis* is stressed.

>> **Accommodate:** Second syllable *com* is stressed.

>> **Identical:** Second syllable *den* is stressed.

>> **Allegation:** Third syllable *gat* is stressed.

How do you develop an appreciation of word and sentence sounds? Duplicate your strategy for appreciating music. Listen and identify what's pleasing. Read, listen, write, and revise. Study how writers adapt rhythm to complement their message. Read and re-engineer, adapting it to your content.

TECHNICAL STUFF

The building blocks of words, letters, also contribute to sounds of words. Letters that support pleasant sounding words include *l*, *m*, *n*, *s*, and *b*, which appear in words such as *mellow, melancholy, syntax, serendipity, imbue, eloquence, cataclysmic*, and *propensity*. Harsh-sounding letters include *c*, *k*, *t*, and *g*, appear in words such as *cacophony, raspy, atonal, draconian, flak, aghast*, and *guttural*.

Steering clear of unpleasing rhythm

Successful essay rhythms avoid patterns of similar sounds. They're called lullabies, designed to help babies sleep. If your writing sounds like the monotone rhythm of a boring professor's lecture, your writing rhythm needs resuscitation. If you haven't yet developed an ear for humdrum college lectures, and similar-sounding syllables exceeds your decibel level, file these techniques in the bottom of your toolbox. It's available when you hear a need for it.

Listen to the repetitive rhythm in the following example:

Sadly we face the threat of rain all day.

The rhythm is a combination of five patterns of an unstressed syllables followed by stressed syllables. For example, in *Sadly*, the *sad* syllable is stressed, and the *ly* syllable is *unstressed*. The pattern follows with *we face*, *the threat*, *of rain*, and *all day*.

The pattern creates memorable poetry, but boring prose. Read poetry for an awareness of rhyme and rhythm, but recognize that prose, such as essays, dislikes repeated rhythmical patterns. Prose likes variety.

TECHNICAL STUFF

The combination of an unstressed and stressed syllabus is called an *iamb*. Five iambs in a line is called *iambic pentameter*, a form of poetry written by William Shakespeare.

Identifying single-syllable rhythm

You've heard about the power of one, one person. One syllable contains a similar power. Here's a look at the power of a simple sentence (see Chapter 8) with a pattern of one-syllable words from William Cullen Bryant:

"Truth, crushed to earth, shall rise again."

Five compact, one-syllable words communicate the simplistic, yet powerful, message that truth prevails, including suppressed truth. Sentence rhythm is created by the optimistic reflective pause *crushed to earth*.

A similarly constructed sentence from Thomas Edison communicates a similar powerful message of optimism:

"I failed my way to success."

Edison uses the tool of irony and contrast (see "Feeling Risky: Styling with Figures of Speech," later in this chapter) to show his message. Edison's advice for success is written with five simple words familiar to a third grader.

WRITING STYLE DEFINES YOUR VOICE

Style and voice are as closely related as people and personality. Your writing style defines your writing voice and your writing personality. Similar to your personality, your voice is a developmental process that results from your writing and literacy experiences.

Most academic writers begin developing their writing voice as college students. If you developed your voice in high school, send a note of appreciation to the high school teacher who helped you discover it.

Your writing style develops with awareness of your writing personality. Here are questions to begin:

- Is your purpose (see Chapter 5) inclusive of all people?
- Does your sentence structure, variety, and rhythm align with your purpose?
- Do you develop your purpose with specific nouns, action verbs, and concise sentences?
- Do you create writing interest with figurative language?
- Do you write with awareness of the sound of language?
- Do you read with awareness of style?

As you read, identify tools of style. Experiment with figures of speech. If you're an over-achiever, study past essays for opportunities to insert style-building tools.

Making the Right Word Choices

At the end of a flight, airlines remind you that you have many choices of air travel for your transportation needs. Then they thank you for choosing their airline. In reality, you don't have many choices because selected airlines own the travel routes that match your travel preferences.

Word choice for essays is similar. You lack an unlimited supply of words. You're limited by the words of your content, audience, and purpose. Similar to what you heard frequently from the significant adults in your life — make good choices, word choices.

You begin learning language with short one-syllable words: *dog, cat, hat, see, run, chair,* and *toy.* As your reading and speaking vocabularies grow, writing complexity grows. One-syllable words develop into polysyllabic words. But the foundation of clear writing remains grounded in short familiar words. When word production slows, return to the simple words that started you on your writing journey.

The sections that follow explain the role of word variety in your writing — words that shortcut to the brain, carry concentrated meaning, and have withstood the test of time.

Implementing sensory words

You live in a world with overstimulation of sight and sound. How often are you distracted by your cellphone? The other three senses (touch, taste, and smell) are underutilized and undervalued by college readers and writers.

TECHNICAL STUFF

Sensory words help readers shortcut ideas to the brain for easy recall. Research shows sensory words are processed in a part of the brain that positions them for easy recall. Sensory words activate the brain similar to specific nouns and active verbs, and science supports it.

Sensory words connect directly to the brain's storage drive of experiences — like tasting flavors of your favorite childhood ice cream store.

Here are sentences with sensory words:

>> Experienced writers avoid *musty* words that contaminate their style.

>> Writers quickly learn that *disheveled* sentences lack rhythm and reason.

>> Successful writers *adorn* their style with specific nouns and active verbs.

The examples include switched-sense words, words that usually describe one sense used to describe another sense. For example, *musty* usually describes smell, whereas *disheveled* and *adorn* don't usually describe sentence structure.

Enjoy the following words in Table 9-6 that fast track to the senses. They may evoke memories:

Practice your sensory skills by taking a trip across campus to stimulate your senses by asking What are the predominant smells, sounds, and touches of buildings, hallways, open spaces, transportation, libraries, parking lots, recreation areas, student hangouts, and so forth?

TABLE 9-6

Sense Appealing Words

Sight	Sound	Touch	Taste	Smell
massive	cracking	abrasive	bitter	antiseptic
miniature	ear-piercing	fluffy	buttery	putrid
opaque	crushing	gritty	doughy	citrusy
mountainous	grating	matted	nutty	rancid
rectangular	hissing	leathery	brackish	piney
shapeless	pulsating	coarse	creamy	briny

Create reader interest by switching senses. For example, if you're writing an essay about NIL (name, image, and likeness) on social media, what is the taste of reaching a hundred thousand subscribers? What is the sound of celebrity? What's the smell of disparaging comments? At the academic level, what's the sound and sight of earning an A on an essay? What's the sound of a disappointing grade?

Employing compact words

Some of life's greatest joys come in small packages: a smile, a thank you, a complimentary text, a high five, and free food. Does college offer a more satisfying gift than a capital A? The power of the English language also includes the strength of two- and three-letter words: *no, yes, stop, life, hope, we, act, old, zoo, eat,* and *tax.*

Other words contain more letters, and also pack a mountain of meaning, words such as *capitalize, precision, acclimate, orientation, workshop, curriculum, tradition, persuade, summa cum laude, finalize,* and *adapt.*

REMEMBER

Compact words tell a story because of their long-history of meaning. They save you additional words of explanation. Include compact words in your essays to communicate your message concisely and crisply. For example, *orientation* describes the events designed to acclimate you to college, opportunities to meet your peers, explanations of procedures for adding and dropping courses, and upcoming campus events and activities.

REMEMBER

Compact words eliminate longer explanations; specific nouns and action verbs are compact words.

Here's an academic sentence with compact words defining humor:

Humor is the intellectual apprehension of the juxtaposition of incongruities.

The story behind those compact words includes the following:

>> **Intellectual:** Knowledge and analysis at a high academic level, consciousness of limits of information beyond what most people think

>> **Apprehension:** The understanding or grasping information at an academic level, based on intellectual experiences

>> **Juxtaposition:** A coming together of experiences for the purpose of being compared and contrasted

>> **Incongruities:** Not in harmony, events and experiences not expected to exist together

How do you learn these words? Read. Read with an awareness of words that tell a story, including the story of *degree*.

Using familiar words

When I taught SAT preparation, I taught vocabulary words by the terabyte, most of which weren't engrained in my listening vocabulary. They were unfamiliar words and words that never appeared in my writing and speaking.

But that was decades ago when the purpose of writing was to impress rather than to communicate. Today's familiar words are the foundation of memorable writing. Write with words that rush to the brain — sense words, compact words, and active verbs and specific nouns. See "Knowing Who's Doing What: Active Verbs and Specific Nouns" at the beginning of this chapter.

Take a look at familiar words in the messages that follow:

"It always seems impossible until it's done." —Nelson Mandela

"My life is my message." —Mahatma Gandhi

The most complex word among the sentences is the four-syllable *impossible*. All words are familiar to third-grade students, most words are one or two syllables, and the messages generate discussion among college students.

Said is a familiar word. Avoid synonyms for *said* like *exclaimed*, *stated*, and *touted* that distract from what is being said.

Considering content words

Some unfamiliar words and words that require context in your college writing include those related to your content topic. For example, if you're writing about self-driving cars, content vocabulary likely includes *autonomous systems, robotic, hands-free driving, radical change, adaptive cruise, super cruise, Levels 0-5,* and *artificial intelligence.*

Your content word choice highlights your background reading, research, and content knowledge. Also, identify content vocabulary your professor uses in class to discuss readings and essay topics.

Every college writing project requires content words — nouns, verbs, and technical language related to your topic. Prewriting strategies in Chapter 12 show you how to generate content words for your writing, words that play a major role in the success of your assignment.

TIP

If your writing project requires terminology unfamiliar to readers, technical terms may be defined in an optional glossary (Chapter 12 also discusses glossaries).

Staying away from style-buster words

Another collection of words diminish your style. They include tired, overworked, wordy, and sometimes unnecessary words. Some words are too familiar and their overuse destroys style, so make sure you don't use them. Table 9-7 lists some you can delete from your writing. Chapter 14 offers more information.

TABLE 9-7 **Style-Buster Words to Avoid**

Category	Examples
Adjectives	very, really, truly, tremendous, super, nice, a great number of, a large amount of, amazing, beautiful, pretty, incredible
Adverbs	clearly, honestly, simply, really, quite, actually, just, possibly, essentially, literally, truly, totally, probably
Nouns	things, stuff, factors, ways, implements
Verbs	got, have got, gotten, have gotten, could of (have), should of (have), would of (have), wonder, looked, amazed
Spoken language fillers	well, basically, fundamentally, in my opinion, if you ask me, from my point of view

Simplifying the complicated

Successful writing takes complicated ideas and explains them simply and clearly. Here's a couple of paragraphs on a complex topic written in simplified language. It's from *Law For Dummies* by John Ventura, J.D. (John Wiley & Sons, Inc.):

Our laws reflect society's standards, values, and expectations. They establish "the rules of the game" in our personal interactions and in our business dealings, helping to ensure that we're treated fairly and that we treat others fairly, too. Laws establish our responsibilities and our rights and help us both avoid problems and resolve problems.

The laws that govern our lives come from six basic sources: the U.S. Constitution, the Bill of Rights, stature law, administrative law, common law, and case law.

Ventura's simplified verbs include *govern, measured, established*, and *applies*.

Sentence meaning requires clarity in your mind as a writer before meaning is clear to your reader. Some high school students write with the belief that their writing isn't clear to them, but their teachers are smarter and will figure out what they intend to write. High school teachers are smart, but most haven't yet taken courses in mind reading.

When your writing ideas become confusing to you, return to simplified language, such as the preceding example.

Feeling Risky: Styling with Figures of Speech

Figures of speech engage readers' interest with language that appeals to the non-logical part of the brain. Think of figures of speech as visual and emotional surprises the sustain reader interest. Use them like a mild sweetener, but remember that too much sugar is unhealthy for your writing.

The tools that follow offer time-tested strategies for maintaining reader interest. Use them to garnish your writing, but they aren't the entrée.

Comparing and contrasting

College life is overloaded with comparisons and contrasts, such as professors, courses, programs, and performances. Fewer comparisons and contrasts belong on campus and more belong in your writing. Study the following examples of comparison and contrast:

"You can discover more about a person in an hour of play than in a year of conversation." —Plato

The Greek philosopher compares learning about a person through *play* and *conversation*. He offers the surprise that play is more revealing. Also note the dominance of familiar and compact words such as *discover*, *person*, *play*, and *conversation*.

Here's another example of comparison and contrast:

"Science is what you know. Philosophy is what you don't know." —Bertrand Russell

The British philosopher contrasts science and philosophy with *what you know* and *what you don't know*. Both sentences total nine single-syllable words, and all words are familiar.

Repeating

No other figure of speech adds rhythm to writing more than repetition. Imagine the quality of music without repetition. Think of that song that's stuck in your head.

The classic example of repetition is the famous first sentence of Dickens' *A Tale of Two Cities*:

"It was the best of times, it was the worst of times, it was the age of wisdom, it was the age of foolishness, it was the epoch of belief, it was the epoch of incredulity, it was the season of light, it was the season of darkness, it was the spring of hope, it was the winter of despair."

In addition to repetition, Dickens' also includes contrast (*best* and *worst*, *wisdom* and *foolishness*, *belief* and *incredulity*, *light* and *darkness*, *spring* and *winter*, and *hope* and *despair*).

Here's an example of repetition that also includes contrast:

"Great minds discuss ideas; average minds discuss events; and small minds discuss people." —Eleanor Roosevelt

The famous first lady repeats *minds* with three degree-descending adjectives (*great*, *average*, and *small*), ending with the surprising *small minds discuss people*. Also note the use of semicolons to slow the reader and force concentration on each independent clause.

Adding surprise

When ESPN personality Sal Paolantonio spoke to my Rowan University classes a few years ago, he offered the advice that good writing informs, entertains, and occasionally surprises. Here's a sentence with repetition and a generational message that includes a surprise ending:

> "In this life we cannot do great things. We can only to small things with great love."
> —Mother Teresa

Mother Teresa offers two fast-paced sentences using familiar words with repetition and contrast (*we cannot* and *we can only*; and *great things* and *small things*). She surprises the reader with *small things with great love*.

The following example is from one of the most creative people who ever lived. He uses understatement and surprise:

> "If you really look closely, most overnight successes take a long time." —Steve Jobs

The inventor of the iPhone uses surprise to tell us *overnight success* takes time.

Eyeing additional style builders

Building style is like growing up. Almost all life experiences in your formative years contribute to the adult you are today. Your writing style developed similarly. Your style is the product of your literary experiences from your first childhood book to your last college paper.

Table 9-8 provides some additional figures of speech you can implement in your writing:

TABLE 9-8   **Additional Figures of Speech**

Figure of Speech	Explanation: Example
Anaphora	Repetition of key words and phrases: Our school's cross country coach said, "Run far, run fast, and hurry back."
Euphemism	A less offensive word choice: Our friend passed away.
Hyperbole	Overstatement: Comp class requires enough writing to fill a library.
Irony	Opposite the literal meaning: Writing essays is easy; you can write an A essay in an hour.
Onomatopoeia	Words that sound like their meaning: A crush of students attended the concert.
Personification	Human qualities attributed to inanimate objects: Active verbs are a writer's best friend.
Synecdoche	Part of the whole is representative of the whole: During recent history the sword has been mightier than the pen. (The sword represents violence; the pen represents the written word.)
Understatement	Making a situation seem less important: Essay writing is easy. Hemingway could easily earn a B in the course.

Avoiding Tragedy: Sabotaging Your Style

Developing a writing style is a use-it-or-lose-it skill. Style thrives with regular practice and deteriorates with lack of practice. Style development strategies include active verbs and specific nouns, sentence variety, rhythm awareness, and figurative language. It dies with lack of writing practice and lack of style development.

Here's a look at practices that sabotage development of style.

Overrepeating words

Most forms of intentional repetition add to your style, but unintentionally repeating words in close proximity diminishes style. Here's an example:

> Poor modeling by parents and other adults influences children's decision not to wear bicycle *helmets*. Children wearing *helmets* needs to be a no tolerance rule to prevent *catastrophic* injury: no *helmet*, no bicycle. But what parents do (wearing a *helmet* or not) speaks louder than what they say. Bicycle *helmets* rank as important as baseball and football *helmets*. Studies show little difference between moderately- and expensively-priced *helmets*, and both prevent *catastrophic* injury.

The paragraph includes seven uses of *helmet(s)* and two uses of *catastrophic*. Excessive word repetition destroys sentence rhythm that distracts the reader.

Self-referencing

The satisfaction of dessert is in the eating, not in the baking and certainly not in the cleaning. The satisfaction of your writing is the message, not the thought process or ingredients that produced it. As a writer, avoid references to yourself doing the job of a writer.

Avoid self-references such as the following:

>> As I see it

>> From my perspective

>> I also considered

>> I believe

>> I discovered that

- » I feel
- » It seems to me
- » My mother suggested I include
- » The idea came to me when
- » When I was talking to . . . about . . .
- » When I researched my topic
- » When I thought about

Writers telling readers about their creative process is like artists telling their audience how they mixed paint. When you self-reference, you self-destruct your writing style.

Writing (exactly) like you talk

The write-like-you-talk advice is frequently misinterpreted to mean verbatim — write the exact words you talk. Because most people speak at least ten times more words as they write, writing like you speak would produce an unmanageable text size, in addition to paragraphs of uninteresting conversation.

The advice refers to writing in the patterns you speak, primarily using the subject-verb-object pattern, the simple declarative right-branching sentence (see Chapter 8 for more information). Use these patterns as the foundation of written language, but not as the exclusive structure.

TIP

The ear and mind thrive on language rhythm that offers opportunity for reflecting, slowing down, and speeding up. The reading process requires continuous flow of information. Unlike a conversation, your readers can't interrupt and ask questions. Writer's anticipate readers' questions and answer them in the text. Write like a writer; talk like a talker.

Overexplaining

More than likely you've experienced conversation with someone who not only talks incessantly, but also talks in endless loops of repetitive stories. Overexplaining in writing is just as uninteresting as endless conversation.

Readers need detail, but not detail of the details. For example, if you're arguing the advantages of autonomous vehicles, readers don't need the history of alternative-energy sources, and they don't need detail of your personal interest in buying a self-driving vehicle.

The dominant characteristic of an essay is focus on one thesis. Avoid overexplaining yourself and undermining your grade. Use compact words and concise language to show your details. Enough is enough.

Stacking adjectives

Stacking adjectives is like stacking pancakes. Two are usually satisfying. Occasionally, after a good workout you may crave a third, but rarely a fourth.

A two-stack of adjectives is almost always acceptable, as seen in the following example:

> The multilingual personable student lives on the West Coast.
>
> The tall, lean soccer player scored two goals.

But three-stacked adjectives are usually one too many, as these examples show:

> The multilingual personable music student lives of the West Coast.
>
> The tall, lean, intelligent soccer player scored two goals.

Use commas to separate adjectives in the same category, such as physical appearance: *tall, lean*.

Extending quotations

Extended quotations are like a ten-minute speech before the last two minutes of a movie. It destroys pace. Quotations of four or more lines are almost never appropriate for essays. They're unacceptable because of the following reasons:

>> They occupy too much essay real estate in proportion to essay length.

>> They present too much information for the author to engage with.

>> They appear visually unbalanced in the essay.

The principles of extended quotations also apply to research papers where five or six lines is appropriate for a block quotation. Don't use more than three or four blocks in a seven-to-ten-page paper. As the length of research papers increases, acceptable lines for quotations increases.

Professors see excessive quotations as padding to fulfill requirement length.

Chapter **10**

Showing Sensitivity: Language That Builds Better Societies

P lay fair and play by the rules — one of the first lessons parents teach their children. The importance of playing fair and respecting people exceeds playing childhood games. It includes the game of life and practicing sensitive and respectful language when you reference race, ethnicity, gender, sexuality, age — and almost 15 percent of the world's population who experience disabilities.

The words people choose to reference that 15 percent (and the other 85 percent) represent their beliefs and how they feel about one another as a world community. People show sensitivity and respect for each other by choosing respectful language in their speaking and writing.

In this chapter I illustrate guidelines for respectful language; explain sensitivity for talking about race, age, gender inclusiveness, and sexual orientation; and review current thinking for language referencing age and disabilities.

Your generation has championed respect for all people, especially those marginalized by a segment of society. The advancements in this chapter reflect your generation's efforts to improve society by respecting all its members.

Raising Standards: General Guidelines for Respectful Language

Just as rising tides lift all boats, rising standards of respectful language lift respect for all people. Language is power, but disrespectful language builds wall rather than bridges and weakens the strength of a unified society.

The APA, MLA, and organizations that advocate for bias–free language offer guidelines and recommendations for respectful language. Because language lives and evolves, these organizations don't set standards, but offer preferences. Most people and groups generally accept the language recommended in this chapter, but some people and groups may disagree.

You'll be reminded throughout this chapter that the most respectful language is the language preferred by the people you are communicating with. Ask them the language they prefer.

TIP

Choose language that's positive, respectful, and sensitive to your readers. If you question your language's sensitivity, seek a second opinion.

Guidelines for respectful language suggested by those advocacy organizations include the following:

REMEMBER

>> **Prefer people-first language.** Use language that references the person first, such as "person with the disability," rather than "the disabled person." Prefer "person with diabetes" rather than "diabetic." Language of disabilities is explained later in this chapter.

Recognize that some people with disabilities embrace their condition by preferring disability-first language, such as "the blind," rather than "people with vision loss." The choice of preferences is a personal decision.

>> **Use gender-neutral language.** Gender-neutral or gender-inclusive language shows gender respect and doesn't associate a gender with occupations, positions, or affiliations, such as assuming teachers are female and construction workers are male. Examples of gendered language include the titles "Mr." and "Mrs." and "Miss." The female references identify marital status, whereas the male reference doesn't. Refer to the later section, "Being inclusive with gender and sexual orientation," for more about gender-neutral language.

TECHNICAL STUFF

Associating genders with occupations represents early 19th century world-wide thinking that women couldn't perform in occupations such as the military, government, construction, business management, and so forth.

>> **Avoid irrelevant references.** Steer clear of referencing a person's disability, race, gender, age, and so forth when it's not related to the writing or conversation. Avoid, for example: Johnathan, *an older Irishman*, will visit us Saturday. Johnathan's visit is unrelated to his age and nationality.

>> **Exercise topic sensitivity.** Some topics elicit emotions among some people that prevent respectful and logical language and encourage emotional language. Exercise language sensitivity when writing or speaking about topics such as politics, religion, and marital status.

Your words form connections you share with others. When your words are thoughtful and respectful, you build relationships with people and improve society. Unfortunately, sometimes insensitivity toward the words you choose shows disrespect, and you create obstacles that denigrate the shared human experience. The following topics require attentiveness to the words you write and speak. Sometimes your words require a step back and reflection such as: How would I feel if were hearing those words?

Referencing Race and Ethnicity

Language referencing race and ethnicity evolves as meanings change from acceptable to unacceptable. In professional sports, for example, team nicknames once acceptable to franchises in Washington D.C. and Cleveland became unacceptable in recent years and evolved to names such as Washington Commanders and Cleveland Guardians. Here I examine racial and ethnic terminology accepted by many (but not all). I also review spelling and capitalization of those terms.

Using preferred racial and ethnic terminology

According to the APA, race refers to "physical differences that groups and cultures consider socially significant." Names of races include Native American, Indigenous, First Nation, or Alaska Native; Asian; Black or African American; and White or Caucasian.

Words such as "Negro" and "Afro-American" are outdated and may be considered offensive.

REMEMBER

Respectful language includes listing races with a purposeful design, rather than listing names randomly, which shows preference from first to last. The previous list of races is structured alphabetically. Other structured designs include population and geographical location.

Language continues to change with the intent to respect all populations of people. For example, "minority" has evolved into a negative term. Prefer "underrepresented." Also, prefer "Native American" to "American Indian." Here's an example in a sentence:

> The dancers at the North American Cultural Heritage Festival wore authentic Native American Iroquois Indian designs.

Avoid racial and ethnic stereotypes of associating race and ethnicity to foods and customs. Also avoid describing individual people of a race as "well-mannered," "intelligent," "behaved," and "articulate." The adjectives imply that the individuals were formerly the opposite of the adjective, for example, the individual described as "intelligent" was "not intelligent."

REMEMBER

Two other offensive racial and ethnic expressions are "those people" and "your people." When communicating with individuals about their identify group, the terms imply judgment about group behavior.

REMEMBER

Offensive stereotypes also include "jew" and "gyp" as verbs.

Spelling and capitalizing racial and ethnic names

Capitalize racial and ethnic names because they are proper nouns. Examples of racial and ethnic terms include the following:

>> Arab

>> Asian

>> Black

>> Caucasian

>> Jewish

>> Muslim

>> Polish

>> Ukrainian

APA excludes hyphens in expressions such as "Mexican American traditions" and "Italian American athletes." For example:

> The celebration included a selection of Polish American foods.

Here's a list of tips for discovering more about cultures:

>> **Explore community resources.** Local communities frequently celebrate cultures with exhibits, monuments, and plaques.

>> **Read.** Read about cultures at your local bookstore or library.

>> **Attend cultural events.** Large and small cities regularly celebrate various cultures with parades and festivals, and the celebrations usually include tasty food.

>> **Study the language.** Language is unique to cultures, including variations of the same language. Begin by learning "hello" and "goodbye."

>> **Try cultural foods.** Taste the culture with a visit to an ethnic restaurant and absorb the full experience.

>> **Travel.** You can find a lot out about the culture when you visit the geography. Initiate conversations with the people you meet.

>> **Avoid stereotypes.** Every culture has the spectrum of personalities. Avoid stereotyping all with the characteristics of one.

Making Age References

Age and disability represent two areas frequently referenced with biased language. This section focuses on age; the next section addresses disability. Exercise sensitivity in your writing and speaking on these topics. When you question your language, seek a second opinion.

Be specific when describing the age you're referencing. If a specific age is unavailable, use a term such "adolescent." Avoid large group definitions such as "older than 18" and "younger than 65."

For individuals 12 years of age and younger, APA suggests terms that include "infant," "child," "girl," and "boy." For individuals 13 to 17 years of age, APA suggests terms such as "adolescent," "youth," "young woman," "young man," and so forth. For 18 years of age and older, APA suggests terms such as "adult," "woman," and "man."

WARNING

Two age references that offend many people over 65 are "seniors" and "senior citizens." In contrast to seniors in high school or college, "seniors" for an older person carries the meaning that the end is near. "Senior citizens" offends because of its finality of citizenship. The over 65 group, many of whom are more physically fit than some of the under 25 group, object to terminology that identities them as ancient or feeble.

Currently acceptable terms describing older adults include "older people," "older adults," and "persons 65 and older." Terms discouraged because of stereotypes include "the aged" and "the elderly."

Here are some tips for learning about older adults:

>> **Share meals with them.** An ideal day for many older adults is eating a meal with a family member or friend — or both.

>> **Visit them.** They enjoy seeing the younger people in their lives — which includes almost everyone. Have a day with them.

>> **Talk and text with them.** Like people of all ages, they enjoy talking and texting. Yes, most of them can text — just go easy on the emoticons, slang, and abbreviations.

>> **Value their history.** They lived through the times you studied in history books. They saw sports legends and performing artists you never heard of.

>> **Avoid stereotypes.** Treat each one as an individual. Not all older adults experience hearing loss, but be patient with ones who have.

Making Disabilities References

APA explains that the purpose of disability language choices is to "maintain the integrity of all individuals as human beings," which is achieved with language emphasizing the person first.

When relevant, use the name of the disability, such as "person with cystic fibrosis" and "child with autism."

Consider this example:

Avoid: The cancer patient was admitted first.

Prefer: The person with cancer was admitted first.

Here I guide you more through writing and speaking about guidelines explain how you can show respect through the words you use.

Writing about disabilities

Most professors recognize that respectful language may result in an awkward sentence structure. The topic of respectful language and sentence structure offers rich classroom discussion. Raise the issue in a classroom discussion.

Here are some guidelines for writing and speaking about disabilities:

WARNING

» **Avoid stereotypes and labels.** Avoid perpetuating stereotypes with language that labels groups as "the disabled," "the aged," and "the handicapped." These labels diminish individualism of people in the group and aren't representative of all people in the group.

Avoid negative language that denigrates people with disabilities such as the following:

- Crippled
- Deaf and dumb
- Deranged
- Freak
- Idiot
- Imbecile
- Lame
- Mentally ill
- Physically challenged
- Psycho
- Retarded

The term "special needs" is uniquely positioned within the language of disability, especially when referencing children. "Special needs" communicates to nondisabled people the complexity of the world to the family of a child with disabilities. Those "special needs" frequently include education, transportation, accommodations, socialization, and additional support systems. Some members of the disability community prefer the term "functional needs." Refer to the section, "Showing Inclusion," later in this chapter for terms to use.

WARNING

Avoid coining words such as "handicapable," offensive to some people with disabilities because it minimizes the disability.

» **Steer clear of patronizing language.** Some people with disabilities prefer not to be patronized with language such as "inspirational," "survivors," or "fighting a battle." They don't manage their disabilities to inspire others.

People with disabilities are representative of all people who share diverse opinions of language preferences. Some people are "inspirational" and "survivors;" and some people aren't.

>> **Keep away from extreme comparisons.** Avoid bias comparisons of groups. For example, comparing people with disabilities with "normal people" implies that people with disabilities are "abnormal people."

Showing respect through words

All disabilities aren't illnesses, and all people with disabilities aren't patients.

Here are tips for respectful language when referencing people with disabilities to ensure you're respectful with your words:

>> Avoid obvious insulting terms and advocate for discontinued use of such terms.

>> Communicate with a friendly welcoming tone.

>> Steer clear of language intended to minimize the disability.

>> Treat people with disabilities as you would treat any other person.

>> Use names of people.

Because of individual sensitivity and preferences, ask the primary source their preferences for referencing disabilities.

Showing inclusion

Words matter, especially words used to reference people with disabilities. The discourse of disabilities requires understanding its specialized meaning, such as the following:

>> **Accessible:** Make usable for disabled and able-bodied people

>> **Accommodations:** Adaptions to programs and facilities to make accessible to people with disabilities

>> **Access barriers:** Obstructions that prevent people with disabilities from using standard facilities

>> **Adaptive technology:** Hardware and software products accessible by people with disabilities

CHANGING THE LANGUAGE OF DISABILITY — AMERICANS WITH DISABILITIES ACT (ADA)

The language of disability developed from the Americans with Disabilities Act (ADA). The ADA, enacted in 1990, was passed to ensure that people with disabilities are granted equal access (along with able-bodied people) to employment, public services, buildings, telecommunications, and mass transportation.

Title II of the ADA prohibits discrimination against people with disabilities by public entities. Colleges support providing accommodations to all services and buildings for all people with disabilities.

The ADA has changed the lives of people with disabilities by providing opportunities such as the following:

- Improved access to buildings through accommodations such as curb cuts and ramps
- Increased employment opportunities
- Provided access to educational opportunities
- Provided access to recreational opportunities
- Permitted access to mass transportation
- Permitted digital accessibility

>> **Biased language:** Language considered offensive, hurtful, and demeaning to people

>> **Captioning:** Text included with video that shows the audio portion of a visual presentation

>> **Disability:** A physical or mental impairment that limits a major life activity such as self-care, walking, seeing, hearing, and so forth

>> **Impairment:** Loss or reduced function of a body part

>> **Mobility impairment:** Disability that affects movement

>> **Twice exceptional:** Term that describes students with disabilities who are also gifted

Many disability terms originated in the medical field and weren't considered offensive. The language at the time represented terminology used to describe medical conditions. As language evolved and the terms became offensive, they were obviously changed. The offensive terminology at the time, introduced in the 18th and 19th centuries, contributes to its sporadic use today. Efforts to eliminate use of those terms remains a challenge.

Language lives and evolves. Table 10–1 shows outdated and preferred phrases related to disabilities.

RETIRE THE R-WORD

An offensive word commonly heard on campuses today, and occasionally seen in college essays is the R-word. "You're such a retard" and "That's such a retard grade" are common uses of the R- word as synonyms for "stupid" and "dumb."

The word "retarded" first appeared as a medical term around 1900 meaning slow in mental development. It was introduced to replace two other medical terms at the time: "idiot" and "imbecile." The term was introduced by the American Association on Mental Retardation in 1961 and was adopted by the American Psychological Association. The R-word replaced the non-offensive description at the time, "intellectual disability."

"Retard" and variation of the root "tard" are highly offensive words used indiscriminately to describe people today. It's casually used by adolescents, especially those who have had no experience with mental disabilities.

The mental disability community is offended by the insensitive use of the word because they experience everyday life with a person affected with mental disability.

Over a decade ago, the Special Olympics campaigned against use of the word. In 2010 President Barack Obama signed Rosa's Law that deleted use of the words "mental retardation" from federal law. The movement to change the language was inspired by a nine-year-old.

A recent study of online media showed that almost 30 million people posted negative comments related to mental disabilities and used forms of the R-word.

As college students and readers of this book, advocate for eliminating the R-word, not only in essays, but also in everyday life. It's one of the most offensive words in the language today and a major enemy against the fight for respectful language.

TABLE 10-1

Outdated and Preferred Disability Phrases

Outdated Phrases	Preferred Phrases
Abnormality	Condition
Asylum	Hospital for mentally ill
Birth defect	Congenital disability
Chronic lunatic	Person with mental illness unlikely to recover
Confined to a wheelchair	Wheelchair user
Crippled, crippled	Person with physical disabilities
Feeble minded	Person with mental disabilities
Fits, attacks	Seizure
Handicapped parking	Accessible parking
Idiot	Person with lowest level of functional ability
Normal, able-bodied	Person without disabilities
Slow learner	Person with learning disabilities
Suffers from, afflicted with	Has a disability

Being Inclusive with Gender and Sexual Orientation

What is written and spoken is important. Conversely, what's excluded from writing and speaking is less important. For example, if a family of five is recognized individually for community service, excluding the name of one member is offensive and insensitive to that member. Inclusion of gender-neutral references requires similar sensitivity. A person's use of gender language reflects their thinking about gender.

REMEMBER

When gender is unnecessarily emphasized, it's offensive to other genders. When gender is inappropriately ignored, it's also offensive.

The use of gender in language has evolved worldwide in the past hundred years from a time when language reference was male centered with words such as human, management, mankind, manmade, manufactured, freshman, chairman, and so forth.

Worldwide language of gender and sexual orientation has rapidly evolved in recent years and continues to change. For example, the English adopted gender-neutral "they" as singular and plural (see Chapter 11). Advocacy groups in Argentina are supporting eliminating gender references in their language. German and French are prioritizing gender-neutral language. Sweden adopted the gender-neutral pronoun "hen."

Advocacy groups recommend using the terms people use to describe themselves. Just know that terms may vary from individual to individual.

Using gender inclusiveness

APA describes gender as "inherent sense of being" male, female, or nonbinary. Gender identity, exclusive of sexual orientation, includes transgender men and cisgender women. Examples of gender terminology is included in Table 10-2.

TABLE 10-2   **Gender Terminology**

Term	Definition
Agender	A person who doesn't identify with any one gender or who doesn't identify with any gender
Androgynous	A person identifying a neither distinguishably masculine or feminine
Bigender	A person who identifies as two genders
Cisgender	A person whose sense of identity aligns with their birth sex
Genderfluid	A person who identifies as shifting genders
Gender nonconforming	A person whose actions don't conform traditional expectations of their gender
Genderqueer	A person who rejects characteristics of standard gender behaviors
Nonbinary	A person's whose gender identity can't be described as exclusively male or female
Omnigender	A person who identifies as possessing all genders
Polygender	A person who identifies as possessing multiple genders
Queer	An all-inclusive term to describe people with fluid identities and orientations
Transgender	A person whose sense of identity doesn't align with their birth sex

TIP

Avoid the expression "opposite sex" and "fair sex," terms popular in the '50s and '60s.

Nonbinary gender doesn't correspond to a gender at birth and blends elements of being male or female, such as genderqueer, agender, and bigender.

Referring to gender: What to do

Guidelines for referencing gender include the following:

>> **Use parallel references.** Utilize parallel gender forms such as male and female, ladies and gentlemen, boys and girls, and so forth.

> **Biased:** The girls prepared the lab for the presentation; the men prepared the library.

> **Respectful:** The women prepared the lab for the presentation; the men prepared the library.

>> **Avoid gender stereotypes for occupations.** Keep away from stereotyping occupations with a gender.

> **Biased:** The nurse prepared her patient for surgery.

> **Respectful:** The nurse prepared their patient for surgery.

>> **Avoid irrelevant gender references.** Avoid gender references when they're not related to sentence meaning.

> **Biased:** The female teachers discussed plans for online classes.

> **Respectful:** The teachers discussed their plans for online classes.

> See Chapter 11 for additional explanations of pronoun use, including gender-neutral pronouns and use of all-inclusive "they."

Avoid the awkward use of "he or she," "she/he," and alternating male and female pronouns. Table 10-2 shows language of gender.

Finding out you need to know about gender

This book is about college writing, so make sure that before you write about someone, you take some time to know more about their gender. Tips for learning about gender include the following:

>> **Educate yourself.** Learn the language of gender.

>> **Ask people their identified pronouns.** Merely asking the question demonstrates respect and support.

WARNING

>> **Use their pronoun.** After learning their pronoun, use it in conversation.

Don't misgender someone, especially on purpose. If a person identifies as nonbinary and uses the they/them pronouns, don't refer to person as he or she. Again, it's about respect.

>> **Respect their identity.** Initiate respectful conversation.

>> **Tell them your pronoun.** Begin a welcoming conversation by introducing yourself with your preferred pronoun.

>> **Ask their preference of compliment.** The language of personal compliments includes strong binary references. Language continues to evolve.

>> **Practice neutral pronouns.** It takes practice. Prefer gender-neutral pronouns in everyday speech. Begin by emphasizing all-inclusive they and their.

Table 10–3 lists outdated and preferred gender–neutral references.

TABLE 10-3

Outdated and Preferred Gender-Neutral References

Outdated	Preferred
Freshman	First-year student
Man-made	Machine made
Chairman	Chair
Gender noun	Gender-neutral noun
Mailman	Mail carrier
Steward, stewardess	Flight attendant
Congressman	Congressional representative
Salesman	Salesperson
Waiter, waitress	Server
Spokesman	Spokesperson

Making sexual orientation references

APA describes sexual orientation as a person's "sense of identity" based on their patterns of feelings. Terms for sexual orientation include lesbian, gay, heterosexual, straight, asexual, bisexual, queer, and polysexual. When writing about sexual orientation, use specific terms such as "bisexual people" and "straight people." Avoid group labels such as "the gays," and "the straights."

The abbreviation LGBT is outdated and replaced by LGBTQ+. If you use the latter, be sure it's representative of the group you're referencing. If you have questions, ask your friends who are LGBTQ+. *Remember:* Sexual orientation and gender identity are two different parts of a person.

Considering Socioeconomic References

General guidelines for socioeconomic references include the following:

>> Focus on what people have, not what they don't have.

>> Avoid denigrating stereotypes.

Use economic language such as "experiencing homelessness," rather than "the homeless," and "opportunity gap" to "achievement gap." Also prefer more specific language such as "federal poverty thresholds" rather than "low income."

Socioeconomic conditions are improved by education. A number of landmark studies show that increasing education increases income and improves socioeconomic factors.

Use language emphasizing attainments. Table 10-4 shows examples.

TABLE 10-4 ## Language Emphasizing Attainment

De-emphasizing Attainment	Emphasizing Attainment
High school dropout	Eighth-grade education
College dropout	High school plus college
Graduate school dropout	College degree

Chapter **11**

Scrutinizing Your Paper for Sneaky Grammar Errors

This chapter is sponsored by the people who inspired my passion for the rules of grammar that have been part of my life for almost three-quarters of a century — the nuns at St. Rose of Lima Grammar School (Eddystone, Penn.) and John Mooney, my most influential English teacher at St. James High School (Chester, Penn.). John and I frequently email discussing grammar.

I share the belief of many language educators that good writing is much more than correct writing. But I also recognize that readers lose interest when errors abuse the message. This chapter isn't a grammar handbook, but an overview of grammar, usage, punctuation, capitalization, and spelling errors that I've seen throughout my decades teaching college writing. The spirit of this chapter is that you don't need to learn hundreds of grammar rules, but you can master a few principles with each essay.

This chapter shows you language rules that sneak up on you and bite you in the jugular. I discuss priority parts of speech and positioning of words and help you correct issues that crash your essays. I spare you from diagramming sentences, a visual display of sentence parts that was common practice decades before the birth of Steve Jobs and the iPhone.

Don't underestimate the value of mastering these rules by reading quality materials. If you learn rules primarily through reading, you'll own strategies to repair issues — even though you may not understand them technically. No problem.

TIP

Refer to Chapter 9 for condensed definitions of parts of speech and grammar terminology applicable to this chapter.

Making Pronouns Agree

Pronouns share virtual spaces with nouns and verbs. They abound on Facebook, Twitter, and Instagram, and have been seen together on Tinder. Pronouns and nouns are compatible because they value agreement, but they often have their disagreements.

When relationships are good, pronouns agree with their *antecedent* (the noun or pronoun they replace) as follows:

>> **Person:** First, second, and third (speaker, person spoken to, and person spoken about). See Chapter 6 for more information on person.

>> **Number:** Singular (refers to one) or plural (refers to two or more).

>> **Gender:** Male, female, and nonbinary.

>> **Case:** Subject, object, and possessive.

Here's an example of how pronouns and antecedents remain in agreement:

The mother of a *son* is the major influence of *his* educational attainment.

The pronoun *his* agrees with the antecedent *son* in person (third), number (singular), gender (male), and case (objective).

The following sections take a closer look at what you need to know about pronouns, all in plain English.

Recognizing the types of pronouns

Table 11-1 shows common types of pronouns, definitions, examples, and reminders specific to each type. The following sections examine these characteristics in greater detail.

TABLE 11-1 **Pronouns' Extended Family**

Type	Definition	Examples	Reminder
Personal	Refer to people, groups, or objects.	I, you, he, she, it, we, they, them, ey, em, ze*	*You* is singular and plural; *they* is all-inclusive.
Indefinite	Refer to an unknown number of people or objects.	someone, all, none, no one, both, few, many, several	*Both, few, many,* and *several* are usually plural.
Demonstrative	Point out specific references.	this, these, that, those	Used as nouns or adjectives.
Interrogative	Ask questions.	who, whom, what, which	Who is used as a subject; whom is used as an object.
Possessive	Show possession or ownership.	his, my, her, their, its	Possessive *its* is spelled without an apostrophe.
Reflexive	Refer back to someone or something in the sentence.	myself, himself, herself, ourselves, yourselves, themselves	A reflexive pronoun is used as an object, and the antecedent is used as the subject.

** **Note:** Ey, em, and ze represent gender-neutral pronouns accepted by most communities.*

Number agreement

Pronouns and antecedents agree in number. Rules for that agreement include the following with an example for each:

>> **Two singular nouns connected by *and* require a plural pronoun.** *Cantaloupe* and *pineapple* have *their* unique flavors.

>> **Course names require a singular pronoun.** *Mathematics* has *its* unique vocabulary.

>> ***Both, few, many,* and *several* require a plural pronoun.** *Both* listed *their* required readings.

>> **If one of the compound subjects joined by *or* or *nor* is singular and the other is plural, the pronoun agrees with the closer word.**

  • Either the laptop or the *phones* lost *their* connection.

  • Neither the iPads nor the *television* lost *its* connection.

REMEMBER

Pronouns agree with their antecedent, not the object of a prepositional phrase positioned between the pronoun and its antecedent.

USING THE ALL-INCLUSIVE "THEY"

The plural pronoun *they* (inclusive of all people) has been endorsed as singular (and its singular forms) by the APA, MLA, Chicago, as well as the Merri*on-Webster Dictionary* and advocacy groups. It's also required for a person who uses *they* as their identified pronoun.

Here are examples:

- A patient must submit *their* forms before *they* are operated on.
- The doctor performed *their* surgery.

When referencing people, your easiest and less clunky writing option is using *they* and *their* as singular and plural. *They* and *their* eliminate the need to know the gender of the doctor, teacher, race car driver, and so forth.

Here's an example of a prepositional phrase (*of the boys*) positioned between the pronoun (*None*) and its antecedent (*his*):

None of the boys is exempted from *his* final exam.

None is a singular pronoun and agrees with the singular *his*. Avoid agreeing the singular antecedent *his* with the plural object of the preposition *boys*.

Case agreement

Many pronoun errors result from misuse of subject and object case pronouns. Before determining the pronoun, determine the pronoun's sentence use as subject or object. Subject case pronouns include *I, she, it, ze,* and *they*. Object group pronouns include: *me, us, zim,* and *them*. Here are examples of incorrect and corrected case pronouns:

>> **Incorrect case:** This was *me*. These are *them*.

>> **Correct case:** This was *I*. These are *they*.

In the incorrect case example, *me* and *them* are objective case pronouns, where the subject case is required. The rule for the subject case following a linking verb is challenging. *Was* and *are* are "to be" verbs (see Chapter 9) and don't require the objective case, even though they're positioned after the verb where the objective case is commonly located. The subject case is required because of a term called a *predicate nominative*, a reference to the subject — but that term isn't important.

When the main verb is a "to be" verb (*am, is, are, was, were, be, been, seems,* and *appears*), the pronoun that follows requires the subject case. Here's another tip to remember it; shout out ten times: *This was I. These are they.*

Here's another incorrect and corrected case pronouns example:

>> **Incorrect case:** *Him* and *me* jogged home. *Me* and *him* jogged home.

>> **Correct case:** *He* and *I* jogged home.

In the incorrect example, *him* and *me* are object case pronouns, but the pronouns are the subject of the sentence and require subject case pronouns (*he* and *I*). Remember that any time you're writing or talking about yourself and another person doing something, the pronoun combination is almost exclusively *he* (or *she) and I.* Give a big shout out for *he and I.*

Avoid beginning a sentence with *me* in your writing and speaking.

The reason for the shout-out is that language is learned by ear. When you're conditioned to hear correct language, incorrect patterns sound awkward.

Possessive case

Here's a pronoun case rule that most English speakers are negligent of and that you'll frequently see incorrect in print: The possessive case immediately precedes a gerund (an *ing* word formed from a verb). Possessive use applies to nouns and pronouns.

Here are examples of each:

>> I dislike *your* speaking in that tone.

>> The *president's* announcing the award pleased the students.

In the examples, *your* and *president's* are possessive forms immediately preceding the gerunds *speaking* and *announcing.*

Reflexive pronouns

Reflexive pronouns reflect or refer back to someone or something previous in the sentence. Standard usage for reflexive pronouns includes use of the reflexive pronoun as an object and its antecedent used as the subject of the sentence.

Here are examples:

>> *Caroline* ordered take out for Barbara and *herself*.

>> *Jason* grilled salmon for Carter and *himself*.

>> *Ophelia's* horse injured *itself* on the rail.

The reflective pronouns *herself*, *himself*, and *itself* are used as objects and refer back to their respective subjects *Caroline*, *Jason*, and *Ophelia's horse*.

REMEMBER

When referencing yourself and another person, position the other person's name first, as in the example of *Barbara* and *Carter* referenced before the reflexive pronouns *herself* and *himself*.

Tackling problem pronouns

Some pairs of pronouns are frequently confused in college writing. Here's a look at problem–pair pronouns:

>> **That, which:** *That* introduces clauses essential to sentence meaning. *Which* introduces clauses nonessential to sentence meaning. Nonessential clauses are marked off with commas. **Examples:** The building *that* houses the Writing Department is located on the North Campus. The Writing Department, *which* is the newest department in the university, is located on the North Campus.

>> **Who, that:** *Who* refers to people; *that* refers to ideas, objects, and organizations. **Examples:** The doctor *who* performed the surgery also taught psychology. Universities endorse policies *that* respect all people.

>> **Who, whom:** *Who* is a subject pronoun; *whom* is an object pronoun. **Examples:** *Who* wrote the *For Dummies* book about playing the guitar? *Whom* should I speak with to attend the conference?

>> **Who's, whose:** *Who's* is a contraction for *who is*; *whose* is a possessive pronoun. **Examples:** *Who's* attending the writers' conference? Whose responsibilities include monitoring first-year courses?

Positioning Prepositional Phrases

A *preposition* begins a prepositional phrase, which shows a time, place, direction, or manner relationship with another word in the sentence. Prepositional phrases function as adjectives (primarily describing nouns) and adverbs (primarily describing verbs). Prepositional phrases should be positioned in close proximity to the word they describe.

Here's a list of common prepositions: *above, across, at, before, below, beside, down, during, for, from, in, into, of, off, on, over, through, under, with, within,* and *without.* For those of you counting, the English language contains approximately 150 prepositions.

Prepositions combine with a noun or pronoun (called its *object*) and form prepositional phrases. Here are some samples:

>> Above the water

>> Across the park

>> Around the corner

>> After the game

>> Under the house

>> Without the facts

>> Within the guidelines

For clarity, position prepositional phrases within proximity of the word they describe. Prepositional phrases distanced from the word they describe often distort meaning, such as these examples:

>> **Distorted:** The *house* was recently listed for sale *between the two trees.*

>> **Clearer:** The *house between the two trees* was recently listed for sale.

The prepositional phrase *between the two trees* (used as an adjective) describes the noun *house.* When the phrase and noun are distanced, the meaning is compromised.

ENDING SENTENCES WITH PREPOSITIONS

One of the great debates for grammar nerds is the question: Can sentences end with a preposition? The origin of the issue is unknown, but it may trace to early grammar books titled with the word Latin and the Latin language prohibiting ending sentences with a preposition.

(continued)

(continued)

Prepositions may end sentences that sound natural. Prepositions may not end sentences where deletion creates awkward language. Here are examples where sentence-ending prepositions are natural and needed:

- I asked him where he was *from*.
- This is the researcher I was communicating *with*.
- This isn't the problem I am concerned *about*.

Chop off prepositions in sentences such as the following:

- Where is the idea heading *to*?
- What time is class *at*?
- Whom did you buy lunch *for*?

Writing sentences like these for an assignment will cost you style points because you can easily eliminate the ending prepositions, resulting in smoother structure.

The question of sentence-ending prepositions becomes complicated when you ask an inhabitant from Australia where they come from and they respond with three sentence-ending prepositions: "I come *from down under*."

For your amusement only, here's a sentence that ends with six prepositions. First, the back story: Little Johnny's father rewarded him for eating his vegetables by reading to him after dinner just before bedtime. On one occasion Johnny didn't finish his vegetables, and his father brought his book to his room to read to him. Johnny asked: "Why did you bring me that book that I shouldn't have been read *to out of up for after*?" The sentence-ending propositions could have been avoided if Johnny ate his vegetables. Eat your vegetables and end sentences with prepositions when necessary.

Connecting Conjunctions

Conjunctions graduate your writing from simple sentences with simple ideas to complex sentences with complex ideas. Reach for a conjunction when you need sentence variety that includes a main idea combined with a dependent thought (complex sentence), multiple independent ideas (compound sentence), and multiple ideas with a dependent thought (compound–complex sentence).

Here I examine how to use the different types of conjunctions and what common conjunction problems you can avoid.

Understanding what conjuctions are

Conjunctions connect words, phrases, and clauses. The absence of conjunctions is like stranded motorists at a malfunctioning draw bridge. The alternative route requires many additional miles and words.

Conjunctions are used in three flavors, which I discuss in the following sections, and all three appear regularly in college writing. If they don't appear regularly, your writing may lack complex ideas and sentence structure variety (see Chapter 9).

TECHNICAL STUFF

If you need a nerdy activity, review past writing assignments and correlate the number of conjunctions with grades. It's also data for your portfolio reflection statement (see Chapter 4). Your professor will be impressed.

Coordinating conjunctions

Common *coordinating conjunctions* include *and*, *but*, *nor*, *for*, and *or*. They connect two or more equivalent words, phrases, or clauses. Here are the three coordinate conjunctions and an example:

>> **And:** We worked on the laptop for two hours, *and* we completed most of the assignment.

>> **But:** Jamie and I searched for causes of poverty, *but* we were discouraged by unstable connectivity.

>> **Or:** Education worldwide needs to improve, *or* we accept the consequences.

Here's an example of how to use coordinating conjunctions by combining sentences:

>> **String of sentences:** Chantel worked on her essay in the library. She asked the reference librarian for help. The librarian helped her with searches on JSTOR. Chantel felt confident with JSTOR after working with the reference librarian.

>> **Revised with conjunctions:** Chantel worked on her essay in the library *and* asked the reference librarian for help. The librarian helped her with JSTOR, giving her confidence to include quality sources in her essay.

The string of sentences contains three simple sentences and one complex sentence. The first two sentences are combined into one complex sentence connected with the conjunction *and*.

Grammar terminology, such as defining coordinating conjunctions, isn't your priority. Correctly using grammatical elements to enhance your writing is.

Correlative conjunctions

Correlative conjunctions are used in pairs. They connect statements of fact with qualifications of that statement, an excellent tool for college writing (see Chapter 8). Include correlative conjunctions in your sentence–variety packages as the following list suggests (I also include an example):

>> **Either . . . or:** *Either* colleges improve the dropout problem, *or* we accept an unsuccessful level of higher education.

>> **Neither . . . nor:** *Neither* time commitment *nor* work ethic should prevent you from earning your degree.

>> **Not only . . . but also:** *Not only* is reading a strategy for academic success, *but also* writing is similarly important.

>> **Both . . . and:** *Both* visiting the writing center *and* meeting with a reference librarian are habits of successful first-year college writers.

>> **Whether . . . or:** *Whether* you work in the library *or* work in retail, you are gaining workplace experience.

Subordinating conjunctions

Subordinating conjunctions connect an independent thought with a dependent thought. Examples include *after, since, because, before, when, while, as though, if, unless, whenever, though, even if,* and *in order that.* The following list identifies five with examples:

>> **After:** *After* the reports were returned, our team meet to evaluate our feedback.

>> **Because:** *Because* Megan was prepared for the test, she was disappointed that severe weather cancelled class.

>> **In order that:** *In order that* academic standards are maintained, library databases are vetted.

>> **Whenever:** *Whenever* academic integrity is compromised, the value of degrees declines.

A word's part of speech is determined by its use in a sentence. In this list, *after* is used as conjunction. In the nearby sidebar, *after* is used as a preposition, such as the sentence . . . *by reading to him after dinner.*

Noticing conjunction problems

Conjunction problems for college students include the following:

>> Correlative conjunctions aren't used in pairs.

>> Introductory subordinate clauses aren't followed by a comma (see the section, "Profiting with Punctuation: Common Punctuation Errors" later is this chapter).

>> Compound sentences don't include a comma before the coordinate conjunction.

>> Conjunctions aren't used to combine simple sentences.

REMEMBER

When your language instinct says you're losing control of your writing, default to simple and complex sentences and include a subject–action verb sentence pattern.

Following Parallel Structure

Parallel structure, one of grammar's logical concepts, is the principle that similar ideas require similar structures. It benefits not only the writer to construct ideas logically, but also the reader to anticipate content logically. It's as good as Google predicting readers' search needs.

For example, if the writer writes, "My favorite activities include swimming in the pool, running in the park," the reader expects a third item ending with *ing* followed by a three-word phrase.

REMEMBER

Parallel structure is not only a structural tool, but also a rhythmic tool. Unparallel structures are like driving a road with wheel-size potholes. Unparallel structure sounds like this:

My favorite activities include college football, pizza, writing on the beach, when the mountains are covered with snow, and, of course, family time.

That unparallel sentence is filled with peaks and valleys. Written with parallel structure, it looks like this:

My favorite activities include watching college football, writing on the beach, staring at snow-covered mountains, eating pizza, and, of course, spending time with family.

Use parallel structure for the following:

» Ideas connected by *and* and similar coordinate conjunctions:

- The first two requirements of essay writing are *addressing the audience* and *writing with a purpose*.

- Grammar construction on either side of *and* includes *ing* words (*addressing* and *writing*) and their objects (*audience* and *purpose*).

» Items in a series:

- The challenges of college include *academics, socialization, independence,* and *finances.*

- Each of the parallel items is a one-word noun. The parallel items don't include language such as *social life* in place of *socialization* and *financial stability* in place of *finances.*

» Lists following a colon:

- College students are successful when they perform the following:

  - Meet with their academic advisor

  - Visit professors during office hours

  - Attend every class prepared to participate

  - Complete assignments before deadlines

- The first word of each item is a present tense verb (refer to the section, "Improving Page Accuracy: Spelling Plurals," later in this chapter).

Placing Description

Sentence word order is as important as spelling your name in the correct letter sequence. In addition to positioning related words in proximity, follow these guidelines to avoid misplaced description (I provide some examples, too):

» Position the subject of the sentence immediately after introductory participle phrases (*ing* and *ed* words used as adjectives):

- **Misplaced:** Injured by the fall, the play was postponed until the main character recovered.

- **Revised:** Injured by the fall, the main character's recovery determines when the play resumes.

>> Logically position awkward adverbs such as *only, unusually, almost, hardly,* and *scarcely*:

- **Misplaced:** If I *only* revised my essay, I would have scored higher.

- **Revised:** If *only* I revised my essay, I would have scored higher.

>> **Position description to clarify meaning:**

- **Misplaced:** I could see the professor looking through the door.

- **Revised:** I could see the professor as I look through the door.

- **Revised:** I could see the professor as they looked through the door.

The description in question is who was looking through the door, thec professor or subject (*I*). *They* in the last example sentence is representative of the all-inclusive pronoun.

Remembering Verb Forms

What's similar about cell phone numbers and verb forms? Both require memorization. How many phone numbers can you recall from memory? One? Your own? How many irregular verbs can you recall from memory?

Recalling principal parts of verbs from memory frustrates some college writers. Verb properties include three principal parts: present, past, and past participle.

TIP

Chapter 9 focuses on action verbs as tools creating style, and Chapter 6 explains verb tense and tone consistency. This section focuses on technical properties of verbs to help you avoid incorrect verb constructions.

Correctly using regular verbs

Most verbs are regular and form the past and past participle by adding *d* or *ed* to the present form as in Table 11-2.

Being familiar with irregular verb forms

Another group of verbs, called *irregular*, have principal parts that require memorization. If you don't memorize them, you can't correctly write a sentence in the past tense. Table 11-3 lists some common irregular verbs.

TABLE 11-2

Principal Parts of Regular Verbs

Present	Past	Past Participle
argue	argued	(have, had) argued
ask	asked	(have, had asked)
talk	talked	(have, had) talked
walk	walked	(have, had) walked

TABLE 11-3

Principal Parts of Irregular Verbs

Present	Past	Past Participle
begin	began	(have, had) begun
bring	brought	(have, had) brought
built	built	(have, had) built
choose	chose	(have, had) chosen
come	came	(have, had) come
get	got	(have, had) got / gotten
let	let	(have, had) let
lose	lost	(have, had) lost
run	ran	(have, had) run
wear	wore	(have, had) worn

Making friends with the past participle

Past participles (and its cousin the present participle that ends in *ing*) are used as adjectives and nouns.

Here's an example of a past participle used as an adjective:

The *determined* student submitted an A portfolio.

The past participle *determined* describes *student*.

Here's an example of a present participle used as a noun:

Skating on thin ice can be hazard to your health.

The present participle *Skating* is used as the subject of the sentence.

Here's an example of a series of present participles used as nouns:

> My favorite activities include *writing* on the beach, *solving* mechanical problems, and *eating* pizza.

The three present participles are used as compound objects of the verb *include*.

Comparing Incompletely

Almost every college writing project includes comparisons such as the following:

>> Does recycling cost more than not recycling?

>> Do proficient college writers have a job advantage over average college writers?

>> Are online courses better than hybrid courses?

Comparisons in these examples contain two items, such as recycling compared with not recycling. But frequently readers remain uninformed when a comparison isn't compared to another element and remain incomplete.

Here are examples of incomplete comparisons:

>> Does recycling cost more?

>> Do proficient college writers have a job advantage?

>> Are online courses better?

Incomplete comparisons leave reader questions, for example: Are online courses better than independent study courses? Better than zoom course? Better than study abroad courses?

REMEMBER

To ensure your comparisons are complete, ask: Than whom? Than what? Be sure your comparisons contain a second element.

Confusing Adjectives and Adverbs

Hemingway had a reason for telling writers to use more verbs and nouns rather than adjectives and adverbs. The latter part of speech experiences anxiety, not knowing their identity or purpose. They don't know if they feel *good* or *well*.

» **Adjectives describe nouns and pronouns.** They tell appearance, number, size, and classification. Examples of adjectives describing nouns include *expensive* tuition, *approachable* professor, and *confident* senior.

» **Adverbs, which frequently end in *ly*, describe verbs, adjectives, and other adverbs.** They tell when, where, how, and to what extent. Adverb examples include the following:

- Maria answered *confidently*. (*Confidently* describes how Maria answered.)

- They walked *briskly*. (*Briskly* describes how the subject (they) *walked*.)

Some adjective and adverb combinations are especially challenging for college writers, including the following:

» **Good and well:** *Good* is an adjective; *well* is an adverb. You feel *good*, an adjective; and your play games *well*, an adverb.

» **Bad and badly:** *Bad* is an adjective; *badly* is an adverb. Adjectives describe nouns; adverbs primarily describe verbs. So how do you feel about criticizing your friend? You feel *bad*, an adjective describing the pronoun *you*.

The reason is confusing. *Feel* acts like the linking verb *am* and doesn't take a direct object. *Feel* links the word that follows it back to the subject, and adjectives (*bad*) describe subjects. If *feel* refers to the sense of touch, your response is *I feel badly*. Use of feel as a verb is extremely unusual.

And how do you drive? Bad or badly? You drive *badly*, an adverb describing the action of driving. Drive safely; and don't text and drive.

Most adverbs end in *ly*, describe verbs, and usually follow verbs.

REMEMBER

Profiting with Punctuation: Common Punctuation Errors

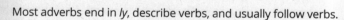

Writing a textbook before digital technology, I asked my publisher's preference on use of the serial comma (also called Oxford or Harvard) positioned before *and* in a series. His response showed me that money drives punctuation. He said, "I can save a million dollars a year on ink costs if I avoid the serial comma and all other optional marks of punctuation."

Punctuation rules that follow won't save you money, but they will save you from a poor grade on a writing assignment. Punctuation and capitalization in this section focus on rules that college students sometimes misuse. Master them and study their use in your reading. And for the record, regardless of ink costs, the serial comma represents standard use in academic writing. It's endorsed by APA, MLA, and Chicago/Turabian.

Commas: Taking a short break

A *comma* is like a short drink of water during a workout. If you need a longer drink of water, use other types of punctuation like a semicolon, dash, or period. You're probably familiar with comma rules such as separating dates, addresses, items in a series, and numbers.

Comma uses that challenge some college writers include the following (I add an example):

>> **Following a conjunction in a compound sentence:** Harry walked along the river in the morning, and he planned to visit the museum in the afternoon.

>> **Separating parenthetical interrupters:** The twins, however, planned to visit the library in the afternoon.

>> **Following an introductory dependent clause:** Since the fall semester started her senior year, Paula renewed her excitement for graduation.

>> **Following a four-word or longer introductory prepositional phrase:** During the early morning hours, many students complete their heavy studying.

>> **Following identifying a person by name:** Charlene, is this your book?

>> **Separating the author and date in an in-text citation:** First-year students who visit the writing center earn higher grades than those who don't (Lu, 2021).

>> **Following the words *yes* and *no* at the beginning of a sentence:** No, your professor does not accept the excuse that your Golden Retriever ate your essay.

>> **Separating all items in a series:** My favorite sports authors are Ray Didinger, Bill Lyon, and Red Smith. (See the nearby sidebar for more about the serial comma.)

TAKE A BOW FOR THE SERIAL OR OXFORD COMMA

The serial (Oxford or Harvard comma) is placed before the *and* in a series of three or more elements (attending class, participating in class, and meeting deadlines). The frequently unwanted comma is required in almost all academic writing. If you hear your professor say, "Don't use the serial comma under penalty of walking the plank," you have a bigger problem than punctuation.

In some settings the serial comma is necessary for clarity such as the following:

My idols are my parents, Frank Sinatra, and Queen Elizabeth.

As the example reads with the comma before the *and*, I'm the son of Angie and Johnny, and I admire the crooner and the Queen. Without the comma I'm the son of musical royalty and the sentence would read:

My idols are my parents, Frank Sinatra and Queen Elizabeth.

I continue to admire the Queen, even though the comma is generally omitted in British writing. News writers also agree with the Queen, thinking the extra comma breaks sentence rhythm. Business writers support the serial comma, and it's also endorsed by the APA, MLA, and *Chicago Manual of Style*.

The birth of the Oxford comma is allegedly attributed to its endorsement by Oxford University Press, who required it, at the end of the 19th century. The serial semicolon also aligns with the serial comma.

Colons and semicolons: Taking a deep breath

The semicolon is my wife's favorite punctuation mark. She likes it because it clarifies complex ideas. It's like her mixer; it simplifies complex processes. Me, I dislike colons and semicolons because they remind me of my least favorite medical procedure. Here I break down these two in greater detail.

Colons

Common uses of *colons* that most college students are familiar with include displaying time and separating minutes, hours, and seconds. Colons' most common use in college writing includes introducing lists. Here's an example:

Habits of successful college students include the following:

>> Attend every class.

>> Prepare for active participation in class.

>> Complete assignments before deadline.

>> Participate in campus activities.

Semicolons

Many college students lack a strong relationship with semicolons. They're minimalists and prefer using only the bottom half of semicolons.

Think of a semicolon as a comma on steroids. The *semicolon*, a super separator, separates words, phrases, and classes that are separated with commas.

Here's an example:

> Topics for writing a senior thesis include causes of reading disorders in children who experience trauma, separation, and anxiety; academic advantages of children who read early, wrote early, and traveled extensively; and chronic class disruptions by children who experienced light and sound sensitivity and allergic reactions to food.

Dashes and slashes: Politely interrupting

Dashes and slashes are my favorite rhyming punctuation marks. The dash is like a rude interruption during a conversation. The slash has appeared on best-selling punctuation lists because of its renewed use in technology. Here I delve deeper into these two.

Dashes

Dashes like to change sentence flow and sometimes change topics. They come in the following two lengths (I also include examples):

>> **En dash (-):** The en dash separates equal terms: I regretted seeing Villanova lose to Connecticut 79-77. The story appears between pages 2-3.

> » **Em dash (—):** The em dash digresses and offers further explanation: Homework proves its value — especially reading — for students reading below grade level. Remember that most college professors don't require spaces before and after dashes. *For Dummies* style is to use a space before and after em dashes.

Slashes

Growing up I never learned that slashes were *bi-directional* — forward and backward. *Slashes* are sometimes necessary, but they do more harm than good when they're overused and extend in the wrong direction. The two-thousand-year-old forward slash (/) is used to separate lines of poetry and music, fractions, dates, close relationships, and URL addresses. Here are examples of the forward slash:

> » The recipe required ¾ cup of walnuts.

> » Class included the nature/nurture debate.

Avoid forward slash abuse in sentences such as the following:

> Shanta dedicates one computer for video games/graphics/play/trouble shooting.

WARNING

Avoid the "and/or" expression. When possible, replace it with "and" or "or."

Ellipses, parentheses, and brackets: Adding afterthought

Ellipses, parentheses, and brackets are the politeness police of punctuation. Parentheses and brackets gently interrupt conversation with a whisper, and ellipses thrive on leaving it unsaid, as they quietly sail into the sunset.

Ellipses

Ellipses, three periods separated with single spaces on both sides (. . .), show omission and represent using your imagination to fill in the dots. The priority use of ellipses in college writing includes omission of content in quotations. It looks like this:

> The Hallinger Report said, "About 40% of college freshmen underutilize campus writing centers as a resource for improving their writing . . . resulting in more freshmen underperforming in their composition course."

When an ellipses ends a sentence, it includes a fourth period (or other end punctuation). Writers assume ethical responsibility (see Chapter 13) to avoid using ellipses to delete information that changes meaning.

Parentheses

Parentheses always appear in pairs and their uses include the following (I include examples):

>> **Minor sentence interruptions:** Use parentheses to identify minor sentence interruptions such as the following: Living at the beach has its disadvantages (I can't currently think of one), and it feels like year-round vacation.

>> **Citations:** Enclose citations in parentheses like this: Most first-year students experience a successful composition course (Baille, 2021).

>> **Uncommon abbreviations:** Use parentheses for abbreviations following the name of a group or organization, such as the following: The Library of Congress (LOC) celebrates Black History Month.

After the abbreviation is identified, successive uses require the abbreviation only.

Common abbreviations don't need explanations. They include NATO, Dr., FBI, APA, MLA, ASAP, RSVP, N, BA, vs, CEO, IQ, and Ave.

REMEMBER

Brackets

Brackets ([ ]), parentheses who play the angles, are used to insert editorial comment in a sentence or quotation. Their use looks like this: The report explained that the researcher [Dr. Hackage] is not affiliated with the laboratory in question.

End punctuation and spacing: Finalizing thoughts

Style guides such as APA require one space following a sentence-ending period, question mark, exclamation point, and quotation marks. One space also follows a colon.

This rule change represents the change in spacing appearance between a typewriter and word processor. Colon spacing is used as follows:

The College Essay: A Path to Success

When a sentence-ending question appears within quotation marks, position the question mark inside the quotation. It looks like this:

The professor asked, "Who has questions?"

Avoid overuse of exclamation points. Also avoid multi-exclamation points that look like this!!!!!

Quotation marks: Calling out the word

Quotation marks represent high-priority punctuation for college students because they signal understanding plagiarism. If you invest time mastering quotations, you'll save time defending plagiarism accusations.

The following rules for quotation marks (accompanied by an example) improve quality of life for college students:

>> **Sources' exact words (direct or partial quotation):** Enclose exact words in quotation marks: "Nothing great was ever achieved without enthusiasm," said American writer and philosopher Ralph Waldo Emerson.

>> **Titles of periodical articles and book chapters:** Enclose periodical articles in quotation marks: The required essay article was "Causes of Academic Anxiety."

>> **Minor works of art**: Enclose minor works of art in quotation marks: The assigned poem was Frost's "The Road Not Taken."

Proper nouns, titles, and headings: Avoiding capital offenses

Capitalization shows readers visual importance of priority words. It helps distinguish between chemistry and Introduction to Chemistry. Basic capitalization rules, such as the first word of a sentence and people's names, represent basic literacy. Such rules require 100 percent accuracy.

The capitalization rules that follow represent rules that college students should be familiar with.

Academic terms

Academic terminology requiring capitalization includes official names of courses (Writing 101, Advanced Accounting) and official names of degrees (Bachelor of Arts, Master of Education). Don't capitalize fields of study or majors (science, management major).

Titles

Capitalize titles when mentioned with names (President Farrish, Dean Johnston). Capitalize official names of departments (Writing Arts Department, Music Department). Capitalize *university* and *The* when it's part of the official name (*University* of Pennsylvania and *The* Ohio State University). Capitalize titles of academic organizations (Society of Electrical Engineers, Honor Society).

Headings

Capitalization of headings varies with style guides. As a general rule, capitalize the first word, the first word following a colon, and nouns and verbs. Notice varied headings in this book. Chapter headings require capitalization of the first word, the word following a colon, and all major words. APA requires distinct punctuation for five levels of headings.

Italics, abbreviations, and numbers: Punctuating words

Some words and numbers stand out among their peers and require special attention features, which are common to college writing.

Italics

Italicize book titles (*The Red Badge of Courage*), periodicals (*Psychology Review*), court cases (*Marbury v. Madison*), and major pieces of art (*Mona Lisa*).

Abbreviations

Abbreviations in formal academics are determined by style books, primarily APA, MLA, and Chicago. These style guidelines frequently differ from The Associated Press Stylebook, a guideline for journalists. APA abbreviations include a.m., EdD, IQ, MSW, and RN.

Numbers

APA guidelines for numbers include the following (with examples):

> >> **Reword sentences to avoid beginning a sentence with a figure:**
>
> - **Avoid:** 1927 was the year Charles Lindbergh flew solo from New York to Paris.
>
> - **Revised:** Charles Lindbergh flew solo from New York to Paris in 1927.
>
> >> **Prefer words to express fractions:** Who ate *two-thirds* of the peach pie?
>
> >> **Form plurals by adding *s* or *es*:** *Fives* and *sixes* are needed for the sign.
>
> >> **Prefer figures for dates, ages, scores, and sums of money:** January 14, 2023, 22 years old, 21-14, and $235.

Apostrophes and possessives: Owning up

Apostrophes and possessives challenge college writers and many educated people. It's an area of language that requires study and review at the writing center. These guidelines are especially challenging for students who are studying English as an additional language.

Apostrophe

In addition to omissions in contractions (they're), *apostrophes* are used for plurals of numbers and letters (*4's* and *A's* — which is different in this book), and possessives. Possessives represent a major challenge for many students.

Possessives

Possessive forms of nouns are written in the singular and plural. Forming the possessive singular requires a two-step process.

1. **Write the singular.**

For example, *man, woman, boy, girl*

2. **Add the apostrophe *s*.**

For example, *man's, woman's, boy's, girl's*

Forming the possessive plural requires a three–step process:

1. **Write the plural.**

   For example, *men, women, boys, girls*

2. **If the plural ends in s, add an apostrophe.**

   Such as *boys', girls'*

3. **If the plural doesn't end in s, add apostrophe s.**

   For example, *women's, men's*

REMEMBER

Some plurals are exceptions to the rule and require memorization similar to irregular verbs. Table 11-4 shows exceptions for possessives.

TABLE 11-4

Forming Irregular Possessives

Singular	Possessive Singular	Plural	Possessive Plural
child	child's	children	children's
deer	deer's	deer	deer's
lady	lady's	ladies	ladies'
ox	ox's	oxen	oxen's

WARNING

Be sure to distinguish between possessives (The *essay's* thesis lacked an argument) and plurals (The course required three *essays*). Check out "Improving Page Accuracy: Spelling Plurals" later in this chapter.

Hyphenation: Making connections

Hyphenation has been simplified with word processing, but familiarization with these rules will add to your literacy skills (I include some examples):

>> **Hyphenate for sentence clarity.** A hyphen distinguishes between language such as "two-student dorms" and "two student-dorms."

>> **Hyphenate related adjectives preceding a noun.** Hyphenating related adjectives adds clarity in sentences such as: A banquet is honoring *award-winning* seniors.

>> **Hyphenate some references to age.** Here are standard uses of hyphenation in age references: A *twenty-two-year-old* offered the first donation. He's *twenty-one* on September 23. The party is for two five-year-olds. Most juniors are *twenty years old*. Look at this *hundred-year-old* house.

Locating, Locating, Locating: Common Usage Errors

These word problems are easier than ones you solve in math class. Word problems are frequently disguised. Here's a list of word pairs confused by some college students. They need further (not farther) explanation. Frequently they need extra sets of eyes.

TIP

File the following usage misuses with misspelled words. List correct uses for future reference. Writers tend to repeat errors until they are recognized and corrected.

The following word combinations are confused by some college writers:

>> **Assure, ensure, insure:** *Assure,* a verb, means to make a promise of support. *Ensure,* a verb, means to make certain. *Insure,* a verb, means to provide compensation. **Examples:** I will *assure* my students that the test will include essay responses. Please *ensure* that you revise your essay. Delivery companies *insure* packages.

>> **Cite, sight, site:** *Cite,* a verb, means to reference a source. *Sight,* a verb, means to locate visually. *Site,* a noun, means a location. **Examples:** *Cite* accurate sources in your essays. Did the Coast Guard *sight* the plane? We visited the *site* of the scheduled conference.

>> **Farther, further:** *Farther,* an adjective, means a measurable distance. *Further,* an adverb, means to a greater degree. **Examples:** Pennsylvania is *farther* from Alaska than Michigan. Alex is *further* advanced in chemistry.

>> **Fewer, less:** *Fewer,* an adjective, refers to a countable number. *Less,* an adjective, refers to quantity. **Example:** *Fewer* students enrolled in accounting this semester than last semester. Today's students have *less* technology patience than their parents.

>> **Former, latter:** *Former,* a noun or adjective, means the first of two items referenced. *Latter,* a noun or adjective, means the last of two items referenced. **Examples:** I can survive winter or summer, but I prefer the *latter* (summer). The *former* (winter) requires more heavy clothing.

>> **Loose, lose:** *Loose,* an adjective, means not firmly positioned. Lose, a verb means to misplace. **Examples:** Patrick's tooth became *loose.* Did Rebecca *lose* her phone?

THE WAY YOU APPROACH GRAMMAR

Avoid approaching grammar with a fixed mindset (Chapter 5) that you're good or bad at grammar. A fixed mindset says you don't need to work to improve grammar. The good news for you is that no study correlates knowledge of parts and speech and ability to write successfully. You've obviously been successful at grammar and language skills as evidenced by your college acceptance. You've been writing well and demonstrating language proficiency to achieve the academic success you have today.

Approach grammar that challenges you as rules you haven't yet learned. No one knows all grammar rules. Commit yourself to learning grammar rules that you misuse in your writing and rules that will add sentence variety to your writing.

Follow these rules all the time: agreement, comma use, verb forms, usage, italicizing titles, and apostrophes.

Challenge yourself to learn a few additional grammar principles with each essay. When you read, analyze the author's grammar use. If you're looking for a few laughs about punctuation, read Lynn Truss' bestseller *Eats, Shoots, and Leaves.*

Sounding Smart: Similar-Sounding Words

If you're a writer by name, words are your game. If you hear an echo, it's the word novelties that help build vocabulary and word precision. This section takes a deep dive into similar-sounding words. Approach this section with your ears wide open.

Similar sounding words appear in this section in twos and threes and are often confused in spelling and meaning. Their accuracy needs a little love as they travel from the brain to the screen.

The following word lists are identified as similar sounding, but word pronunciation varies among geographical locations. For example, the three words that follow are pronounced similarly in some geographical locations: *Mary, marry, merry.*

Word pronunciation includes subtle variations. Listen for slight variations in pronunciations of these words: *I scream* and *ice cream.* Distinguish tongue and teeth formation of *I scream* and the back-of-throat formation of *ice cream.* The word pronunciations that follow may vary slightly; meanings and spellings are often confused.

Table 11-5 includes frequently confused trios.

TABLE 11-5 | **Similar-Sounding Trios**

band: a ring	band: musical group	banned: prohibited
Chile: a country	chilly: cold	chili: stew
cite: document	sight: visually locate	site: a location
desert: abandon	desert: dry land	dessert: food treat
I'll: I will	aisle: a path	isle: island

Table 11-6 includes frequently confused pairs.

TABLE 11-6 | **Similar-Sounding Pairs**

advice: guidance	advise: recommend
bite: cut into	byte: digital data
complement: complete or enhance	compliment: praise
eminent: distinguished	imminent: impending
foreword: book introduction	forward: advancing
precede: to come before	proceed: to go forward

Improving Page Accuracy

An entrée shouldn't be judged by its appearance, and neither should an essay be judged by its spelling — but unfortunately both are. Spelling of some words challenges almost every educated person, except 12- and 13-year-olds who compete in the National Spelling Bee (note how this book handles ages differently than I discuss in the section, "Italics, abbreviations, and numbers — Punctuating words," earlier in this chapter).

Google identifies as the most frequently misspelled words. You can locate the complete list at www.khon2.com/news/national/google-reveals-list-of-most-misspelled-words-in-us.

This section offers categories of words that are frequently misspelled by college students and other educated people, including yours truly.

Plurals: Making it more than one

If you doubt that English is a difficult language to learn, ask an English second-language learner. Their list of learning challenges includes inconsistent rules for spelling plurals.

Proper-noun plurals

Rules for spelling plurals of proper nouns include the following (with an example):

>> **Add *s to names*.** The general rule for pluralizing proper nouns is add *s*: *Dakotas, Toyotas, Carolinas,* and *Josephs.* Also add *s* to italicized words: *Grapes of Wraths, The Great Gatsbys.*

>> **Add *s* to abbreviations.** To pluralize an abbreviation, add *s*: PhDs.

Common-noun plurals

Rules for spelling common nouns include the following:

>> **Drop *f* or *fe*, and add *ves*.** If a singular noun ends in *f* or *fe*, drop the *f* or *fe*, and add *ves*: wife-wives, loaf-loaves, life-lives, and half-halves.

>> **Change *us* to *i*.** If a noun ends in *us*, change *us* to *i*: syllabus-syllabi.

>> **Similar forms.** Some nouns use the same form for singular and plural: aircraft-aircraft, shrimp-shrimp, trout-trout.

>> **Add *s* or *es* to *o*.** If a noun ends in o, add *s* or *es*: tomato-tomatoes.

>> **Pluralize principal words in compounds.** With compound words, pluralize the major word: *time-out* becomes *times-out.*

Misspelling: My personal gremlins

Everyone has a list of spelling words that challenge them. Recognition is the first step for recovering mis-spellers. File misspellings and refer to them when you question a spelling.

When I write, I dedicate one device to asking Siri how to spell. She is never too busy to help me with spelling. If I can pronounce it, she can spell it. Here is my gremlin list with my mnemonics, my memory aids:

>> **Cincinnati:** 3 *i*'s, 3 *n*'s

>> **Familiar:** ends with *liar*

>> **Foreign:** *e* before *i* exception

>> **Honorary:** middle *nor*

>> **Knowledge:** *d*

>> **Occurring:** 2 *c*'s, 2 *r*'s

>> **Pittsburgh:** ends with *h*

>> **Supersede:** ends with *sede*

>> **Tattoo:** 2 *t*'s, 2 *o*'s

>> **Wisconsin:** ends with *sin*

4

Rehearsing for Success: Planning, Writing, and Revising

Prepare to write the essay by analyzing the assignment question asked, determining the audience and purpose, surveying the rubric, and brainstorming prior knowledge.

Complete your first draft by following steps that include planning and focusing, reading background information, writing body paragraphs, drafting the opening and closing, and revising.

Avoid plagiarism by planning time wisely, detailing research, citing sources as you write, and using plagiarism detection software.

Discover a three-level approach to revising: the global level, the sentence and paragraph level, and the word level.

Finalize your writing projects for submission by reviewing the title, coordinating the opening and closing, standardizing page appearance, reviewing level headings, applying editing strategies, verifying information, and asking that final question: What's missing?

Analyze genres used in writing projects across the curriculum such as essays in other courses, reaction papers, reports, literature reviews, and research papers.

Chapter **12**

Preparing Your Persuasion: Planning, Gathering, and Organizing Information

Thomas Edison said he found 10,000 ways the lightbulb didn't work. I lack knowledge about how lightbulbs work, but I can offer you one way your essay doesn't work — don't have a plan for its success. A plan doesn't guarantee you essay success, but lack of a plan will almost ensure you essay failure.

Your essay plan includes analyzing the assignment, gathering information, studying the rubric, and answering the essay question.

This chapter explains the organizational process for planning and generating ideas for your essay. I help you choose a winning topic, unlock hidden storage in your right-side brain, and reduce the unknown in assignment requirements.

Organizing Yourself — and Your Essay

Recall your first day on a new job. You may have experienced the frustration of getting lost or the helplessness of unfamiliar procedures. But you learned quickly and developed a set of lifetime skills — and possibly became a trainer of new employees.

You're facing another new challenge with your college assignments. But you aren't writing your first essay, and you bring a wealth of experiences for organizing yourself and your essay. You have a professor who wants you to succeed. You have your past successes and opportunities to add new skills to help you with future projects. Preparation for your essay is a two-step process: organizing yourself and organizing materials before writing your essay. The following sections examine these two in greater detail.

Preparing yourself

College success is a team effort, but you're the point person and the one accountable for your academic performance. You have support to refine your skills and save you time. Your past academic performances represent your strengths to build on as you face new challenging assignments in your writing course.

Here's a look at questions to address to prepare yourself for the new challenges in your college writing course (you can use these pointers for your other college courses as well):

>> **What study skills need improving?** Evaluate your proficiencies such as studying efficiently, organizing material, preparing for tests, comprehending reading, and meeting deadlines.

>> **What assignment parts challenge you most?** Review past essays and evaluate strategies needing improvement such as organizing structure, developing a thesis, researching, presenting evidence, creating opening and closings, and documenting.

>> **What assignment-related technology skills challenge you?** Technology saves you time or drains your time. Evaluate your technology skills such as storage and retrieving, sending large files, backing up, organizing, and formatting. Are you confident using your course-management platform?

>> **How efficient are your self-maintenance skills?** Academic performance requires physical and emotional stamina. Evaluate yourself in areas such as exercising, managing stress, and controlling emotions.

>> **What are your contingencies?** Plan your backups and reduce deadline pressure caused by computing problems. Plan your off-hours sources of

information when campus resources are unavailable. Who's your contact for a tech question or a course question? What's your comfort source when you need a quick pizza or a something sweet?

On-campus resources are available — as part of your tuition — to help you in all of the referenced areas. Chapter 2 explains these resources in greater detail. Don't approach resources as optional; consider them as necessary time-savers and skill builders for improved academic performance. These resources deposit hours into your time management budget.

Preparing your essay

Legendary NFL coach Vince Lombardi, for whom the Super Bowl trophy is named, allegedly said, "Luck is preparation meeting opportunity." Improve your opportunities for luck by applying the following essay preparation strategies:

>> **Create a paper trail.** Consider a dedicated notebook for all notetaking from sources and record keeping for documentation. Date the entry for each session. Keep accurate records for documentation of summaries, paraphrases, and quotations.

>> **Identify feedback sources.** Coordinate with peers who will serve as sources of feedback (see Chapter 14). Your writing center also provides feedback as well as your professor. Feedback with your peers is a give and take process.

>> **Plan your writing schedule.** Work backward from the assignment due date to schedule completions of major sections. Plan two days for content revision and one day for editing and presentation preparation. Coordinate your writing schedule with major requirements due in other courses.

>> **Schedule resources.** When you complete half your essay, schedule dates to visit the writing center, academic success center, and library.

>> **Create your essay outline.** After completing your research and working thesis, create an outline of the body section. Include supporting evidence and counterevidence.

>> **Study models of assignments and class notes.** Study course materials related to the project, especially model assignments available, focus on content, structure, and writing style.

>> **Visit your professor during office hours.** Go during the early part of the writing for the purpose of clarifying the major question and addressing any concerns you have. If a rubric is unavailable, ask which assignment part represents the highest point value.

Meeting Expectations: Analyzing Assignments

Think of assignment analysis as a game, but a game without rules. Your professor determines the purpose of the game — to write an essay that earns an A, but you as the student determine the path to achieve that purpose. You ultimately win the game by submitting a document that demonstrates writing skills that align with the professor's expectations.

REMEMBER

Those last two words "professor's expectations" represent the elephant in the assignment. Translating the assignment is as easy as dissecting an elephant. Your ability to analyze the assignment gives you confidence to begin the assignment with a direction.

Assignment analysis begins answering general questions about the relationship among the assignment, the professor's objectives, and course goals. Here's what those questions look like:

>> What do you anticipate as the professor's purpose for the assignment?

>> How does the assignment align with course content?

>> What do you anticipate as the assignment learning goals?

>> What learning activities are occurring in the classroom in conjunction with the assignment?

The purpose of an assignment analysis is to clarify the major question in the assignment and isolate individual requirements whose omission can destroy your grade.

The following sections explain assignment details and approaches for addressing them.

Comprehending the assignment prompt

You may receive an assignment sheet, sometimes called an *assignment prompt*, that usually contains information such as the following:

>> The assignment name and purpose

>> Assignment parameters (length, requirements, due date, sources, documentation style)

- » Learning objectives
- » Portfolio application
- » Submission requirements
- » Grading criteria (rubric)

TIP

Focus on information identified with graphic design such as bold, highlight, or underline.

ADDRESSING OPEN-ENDED AND VERBAL ASSIGNMENTS

Some professors strongly believe that the college assignment game should require reading professors' minds to determine what they want. They believe students show academic adaptability by creating a specific solution to their general requirement. Their thinking contains academic merit, and they're entitled to their academic freedom.

Here are suggestions for addressing open-ended and class dictated assignments:

- Apply your best notetaking skills, including abbreviations, recording assignment information as accurately as possible.

- Apply question marks to information needing immediate clarification. The assignment preview is usually followed by the professor asking for questions.

- If you know in advance when the assignment will be previewed, prepare for class with questions related to assignment information in this section, information that includes purpose, sources, document style, optional sections, and so forth.

- As soon as possible after class, review your notes, add information, and identify questions that need verification.

- Coordinate a meeting with peers to validate and update assignment information, especially dates and mission requirements.

- Follow up group validation by meeting with your professor to answer additional questions.

Analyzing the approach: The how-to

After processing general information on the assignment, follow these steps to understand the assignment in depth:

1. Survey the assignment.

Read through the assignment for the purpose of identifying an overview and becoming familiar with the assignment.

2. Read actively.

Read again with a pen for the purpose of identifying (underline, circle, highlight) grade-influencing information such as the major question, research requirements, objectives, purposes, writing tips, requirements, supporting materials, feedback requirements, rubric, and documentation style. Identify logistical data such as due dates, page length, presentation requirements, point value references, a not-to-do list, and so forth.

3. Annotate.

Follow identifying information with annotating and engaging that includes asking questions, noting need for clarification, marking priorities, and identifying content that needs exploration. See "Annotating Reading" later in this chapter.

4. Take a preliminary approach.

With the assignment in your head, randomly list suggestions for an approach to the topic such as comparing and contrasting, connecting with course discussions, and connecting with required readings.

5. Create lists.

Begin a to-do list and a not-to-do list.

As you gather additional information, focus toward understanding the following specifics about the assignment. Your list may include requirements such as expectations related to the following:

>> **Major question:** What's the primary question your assignment requires you to answer?

>> **Minor questions:** What additional questions are asked, questions that represent content that should be included in the essay?

>> **Content:** What additional content is required, such as readings, class lectures, discussions, and handouts?

>> **Writing:** What writing skills are required, such as active verbs and specific nouns, sentence variety (see Chapter 9), and concise language (see Chapter 14)?

>> **Thinking:** College requires critical thinking such as analyzing, synthesizing, prioritizing, and evaluating.

>> **Source engagement:** Does your assignment include specific sources that you're required to engage with in the body paragraphs?

>> **Submitted materials:** What are you required to submit?

>> **Presentation:** What are you required to submit in what form (see Chapter 15)?

WARNING

Professors have their quirks, strange behaviors, and expectations that may filter into grading. These idiosyncrasies are usually referenced frequently in the classroom and may include omitted hard-page breaks, nonstandard margins, or multiple sentence-ending exclamation points. Identify them, learn them, and avoid them.

Zooming In: Assignment Requirements

The body of the assignment is a continued game of questions. Your professor asks you questions to address, and you ask your professor questions about the questions.

Here I help you identify assignment details, assuring that you're answering the assignment's major question and prioritizing rubric point values.

Noting the deliverables

Before beginning the assignment, identify required tasks, sometimes called *deliverables*. Post this list of requirements in your study area. They represent your completion goals and may include the following:

>> 650-word essay formatted in APA with informal citations (see Chapter 7)

>> Annotated Works Cited

>> Cited references from three required sources

>> Title page

>> One revised draft with feedback

>> One-file PDF submission with hard-page breaks

WARNING

Avoid line-space games that will sabotage your grade and your professor's assessment of your academic commitment. Yes, your professor will recognize your attempt to inflate your word count with technology deceptions such as a slightly larger font size, slightly increased margins, and slightly increased line spacing. Word count deceptions are a form of academic dishonesty. The thought to increase font size indicates your essay needs development.

Answering the ask

This section is important. The major focus of your essay is answering the question asked in the assignment. If you fail to identify the question and answer the question, your grade is toast. In addition, be sure your understanding of the ask is the same as your professor's understanding. If you have doubts on interpreting the question, meet with your professor during their office hours.

The language identifying the major question and the purpose of your essay asks you, for example, to analyze, argue, prioritize, and so forth. See Chapter 6 for an explanation of purposes. Your approach to answering the question, your writing purpose, determines the structural framework of the essay (refer to Chapter 5).

Surveying the rubric

Rubrics, a description of performance expectations, represent the standard of achievement for various parts of the assignment. They tell you point values of essay elements. Before the widespread use of rubrics, completing writing assignments was described as bowling with a curtain in front of the pins. Students didn't know what they were aiming for. You were asked to reach an unknown destination.

TECHNICAL STUFF

Rubrics became popular in the field of composition in the 1990s, and research continues to show they improve writing by specifying point values of assignment parts. Rubrics contributed to nearly eliminating writing being judged by personal opinion.

The following sections explain how rubrics determine assignment priorities and planning be coordinating time allocation with point values of assignment sections.

Understanding what's in the rubrics

Rubrics may be as general as telling you your essay will be scored on audience, purpose, tone, focus, evidence, and organization. Or it may be as specific as telling you "audience" represents 20 percent of your grade and prorated levels of "audience" include "Excellent," "Good," and "Needs improvement." Rubrics are created by your professor or by the college English Department. Your professor may post a rubric or apply one from general knowledge.

Table 12-1 shows an example of a rubric defining levels of achievement for one rubric — organization.

TABLE 12-1 **A Rubric Example: Levels of Organization**

Writing Element	Excellent	Good	Needs Improvement
Organization 25 percent	Includes a clearly defined opening, body, and closing with appropriate transitions. Opening engages and closing leaves thoughtful message.	Includes an identifiable opening, body, and closing. Transitions are adequate and opening adequate.	Differentiation of organizational elements need clarification.

Rubrics show point values of essay elements and explain the level of performance expected.

Using the rubrics to your advantage

You can take the information in the rubrics and use it to your advantage in the following ways:

- >> Recognize what the professor values important for your writing and grading.
- >> Identify point values of essay elements.
- >> Allocate your time management according to point values of assignment sections.
- >> Improve grading communication between you and your professor by using similar rubric language.
- >> Contribute to your understanding of where you lost points.

If your professor doesn't reference a rubric in class or post one, ask if one is available. Professors are happy to discuss rubrics during office hours.

Being aware of other rubrics

Your essay-writing process may include a variety of rubrics for different parts of the writing process. For example, your professor may include a rubric for researching, building an argument, or documenting sources. Table 12-2 is an example of a revising rubric. In place of a point value, the revising rubric identifies what's "acceptable" and "unacceptable."

TABLE 12-2   **Rubric Sample: Revising**

Revising Strategy	Acceptable	Unacceptable
Action verbs	Pattern of active and specific verbs	Pattern of inactive verbs, linking verbs, and passive voice
Concise sentences	Pattern of revising unnecessary and overused words	Pattern of unnecessary and overused words, and weak verbs
Varied sentence structure	Pattern of similar structured sentences and right branching	Excess of similar structured sentences and right branching

The rubric in Table 12-2 identifies acceptable revising for active verbs, concise sentences, and varied sentence structure. For example, "acceptable" active and specific verbs include *earned*, *recommended*, *coordinated*, and so forth as explained in Chapter 9. The rubric language, such "active and specific verbs," correlates with language used by professors in the classroom.

Starting Strong: Beginning with Background Reading

College students are frequently asked to provide background, and it's usually for a good reason such as being considered for a job or promotion. Providing background in the form of reading on the assignment topic may also help you promote your essay grade.

REMEMBER

Background reading helps you become familiar with your topic and learn topic language, limits, and liabilities. After reading your assignment and identifying related topics, read for additional background information.

TIP

Take a field trip to your local bookstore and browse newspapers and magazines for information related to your topic.

REMEMBER

Begin your background reading search with key terms from Chapter 5 and 6 and terms you identified analyzing your assignment prompt. Start with general information databases, and ask your reference librarian for search help. Also perform a general Google search, and note what Google suggests for additional topics. And don't forget to ask Siri or Alexa.

Read background materials for purposes that include the following:

>> **Topic overview:** Determine the broad extent of the topic. What's the extent of the who and what related to the topic? What's its history? What's the good news and bad news? Why is the topic important enough to be identified with an essay topic? What's the when, where, how, and why of the topic?

>> **Topic definition:** Define the topic in one sentence within the context of your essay. If you can define the topic in one sentence, you have a clear understanding of it.

>> **Topic implications:** What are topic implications socially, culturally, legally, historically, and economically? If your topic has a political implication, choose words objectively.

>> **Key terms:** What additional key terms are revealed by your background reading? Focus on terms related to your topic.

>> **Recent events and related dates:** What recent events does the topic reveal? What past events were related to it? What is topic relevance in various time periods?

>> **Associated names and organization:** Who and what are associated with the topic? What are names and organizations related to the topic? What nouns and verbs are related to the topic?

>> **Problems related to the topic:** If your topic didn't have a rap sheet, it wouldn't be assignment worthy. What's the questionable history of the topic that makes it an arguable issue?

Brainstorming Strategies: Surfacing the Unknown

Many college students fear the academic unknown, especially when the unknown includes information needed for a major assignment. But you have more knowledge than you're aware of, and you can easily cure your fear of the unknown by surfacing information, especially information in the creative right side of your brain.

Your brain's long-term memory stores a wealth of experiences and information for writing college essays. It's readily available to come forward, but it needs a prompt — the same word your professor uses to encourage information to answer the essay question. Brainstorming is a strategy to release information from your memory and generate ideas to answer your question. Brainstorming is especially effective for retrieving information stored in the right-side of your brain.

REMEMBER

Your brainstorming began during the analysis and annotation of your assignment (refer to the section, "Meeting Expectations: Analyzing Assignments," earlier in this chapter). Here's an example how brainstorming works. Think of names of careers. Now think of names of careers prompted by letters of the alphabet:

A: accounting	D:	G:
B: biology	E:	H:
C: chemistry	F:	I:

How many careers did you think of that you didn't know were in your memory? The initial letters were prompts that generated the response. Additional brainstorming strategies follow.

A-Z sentence generators

Another use of A–Z prompts includes generating phrases or sentences. What follows is a list of ideas on the topic of energy conservation on campus:

A: Awareness of daily uses of energy on campus (transportation, building utilities, technology)

B: Better energy management benefits for the campus community.

C: Create a challenge to reduce consumable energies and use savings to reduce tuition.

Freewriting

You're probably familiar with ten minutes of uninterrupted writing to discover what you're thinking. This strategy is similar to speaking in public and revealing information you didn't want to say. The subconscious is unstoppable. Freewriting works. Here's a freewriting example on the topic of consumable energies on campus:

People go hungry at night and college students, like people in many large-group food settings, waste food during large-group dining. Look at food wastes where dishes and silverware are returned. We can better manage community food supplies. We need to implement strategies for reducing food waste. We know that plate size correlates with self-serving portions of food. Does calorie display correlate with food portions? What conditions influence food consumption? What conditions correlate with food waste?

Freewriting reveals topics applicable to the essay and topics requiring further exploration. The previous example of freewriting revealed questions for further research that may be applicable to the topic or may lead to relevant information.

Asking What if . . .

Applying "what if?" questions to your writing forces you to think about additional approaches to your topic. Here are examples of "what if?" applied to the topic of government partial-repayments or loan forgiveness for student loans:

>> What if the amount of loan forgiveness were coordinated with earned income?

>> What if loan forgiveness were offered in the form of a tax credit?

>> What if partial repayment were coordinated with a community service obligation?

The answers to "what if?" force you to think about new information related to the topic.

Give it five

With this brainstorming method, analyze your topic from five positions.

Compare it: How do other campuses address their consumable energies?

Refute it: Consumable energies are part of the cost of doing business in higher education.

Argue it: Internet connectivity to public spaces should be provided by communities.

Apply it: What alternate energy resources are easily adaptable for campus use?

Personalize it: What can I do to reduce my energy footprint?

Contemplating other strategies

Here are some other brainstorming strategies you can use:

>> **Visualize it.** Create a stick drawing of each side of your argument. Use thought bubbles to identify what each side is thinking.

>> **Interrogate it.** Ask your topic questions. Begin with the five Ws (who, what, where, where, and why) and how. Additional types of questions (see Chapter 9) to ask your topic include

- Why are you important?

- What are some of your dark secrets?

- How did your childhood influence you?

- How did you end up in a college writing assignment?

- What should I know about you?

- Who are your relatives?

- How have you changed during your lifetime?

>> **Draw circle spiders.** Circle spiders visualize relationships among topic details. Enclose a topic inside a circle (spider body). Write topic details on lines extended legs from the circle.

>> **Use Google.** Take advantage of Google's suggestion to help you. As you enter search terms in Google, check out topics related to you topic that Google is suggesting you may be interested in.

>> **Ask Siri or Alexa.** These artificial intelligences know a little about everything and extensive knowledge about some topics. Their information is yours for the asking — at the speed of thought.

Taking Time for R & R: Reading and Recording

Recording notes is the who, what, and when of reading; annotating notes is the how, why, and so what of reading.

REMEMBER

Reading, notetaking, and annotating are the tools of information gathering. They have a better reliability performance than your internet connectivity. They're better than Siri or Alexa because they create knowledge. Your essay loves them. The following sections delve deeper into the basics of notetaking and annotating.

Recording notes

What your professor says in class is important. How you intellectually process what your professor says is more important.

Recording notes is a passive activity of listening or reading information and transcribing it for the purpose of future reference. Voice-to-text software can perform the recording, but you add the intelligence of prioritizing importance — another example of college students outperforming software.

REMEMBER

The purpose of notetaking includes reducing information to meaningful chunks applicable for integrating into writing and class discussion. Notetaking requires very little filtering or interacting, but it's a first step for engaging the annotating.

Notetaking lacks the academic celebrity of an essay or presentation, but your notetaking skills are displayed whenever you submit an assignment. Common notetaking strategies include outlining.

Sequential outlining

Sequential outlining from a lecture or text captures major concepts. Listen and look for sequential ideas that follow signal phrases such as "another reason," "additional cause," and "equally important." Major concepts are followed by supporting details and evidence. Use your abbreviation language during notetaking and identify content that needs clarification.

From a lecture, listen for details of each category and record significant details. For example, a major notetaking concept may appear as follows:

> Shakespeare wrote comedies, tragedies, and histories.

TIP

Professors frequently speak approximately 150 words per minute, while you can record notes at a pace approximately 20-words-per-minute. If your professor permits questions during lectures, ask for clarification. Don't ask your professor to slow down, because college students are expected to develop notetaking skills necessary for their academic success. You may ask a question about content such as: "Can you clarify which category represented his best writing?" The question allows you time to reorganize your notetaking. Also, your campus resources can help you streamline your notetaking skills. Refer to Chapter 17 for some resources.

Descriptive outlining

Descriptive outlining, exclusively for texts, includes more detail than lectures because you control the notetaking pace with your reading. Descriptive outlines may also be written in sentence format in your own words, a process that begins internalizing information for integration into your writing.

Descriptive outlines provide depth of information needed for writing assignments and test study. They can be further developed by applying annotation strategies.

Mapping

Mapping, sometimes called *mind-mapping,* allows more coordination of information than outlining. Create a map by drawing content circles about the size of a beverage can and record details of the topic into the circle. For example, topics in a circle may include Shakespeare's "comedies," "tragedies," and "histories."

The mapping strategy includes connecting lines between similar topics in different circles. Mapping notes offers a visualization of connected ideas.

Annotating readings

Annotative active reading is the process of interacting with readings and performing higher-order thinking such as evaluating, interpreting, analyzing, synthesizing, questioning, and applying. Annotating is a career-changing skill. It's a strategy for high-achieving college students and trend-setting career leaders. These sections focus on what you need to know about annotation.

Figuring out what the author wants you to take away

Annotated notes parallel your thinking process and seek to answer the question: "What does the author want me to understand?" The process results in a more thorough knowledge of text and deepens understanding of why, how, and so what.

The advantages of annotation include the following:

>> Creates a record of key ideas and your reactions

>> Encourages analyzing and synthesizing ideas

>> Promotes deeper understanding of content

>> Prepares information for inferences and conclusions in writing

>> Integrates reader's thinking into text

>> Prioritizes information

>> Organizes ideas for writing, studying, and class participation

Concentrating content to support your thesis

When you take notes and annotate for an essay or other writing project, focus content on your thesis.

Annotation includes identifying information in the text such as the following:

>> Patterns of information

>> Agreements and disagreements

>> Outliers

>> Information biased or unsupported

>> Information related to class and other sources

>> Profound information

TIP

Annotating isn't crafting sentences in formal language. The goal is to sustain flow of thinking. If necessary, use college-speak, such as "Sick idea," "No way," and OMG.

Making annotation easier with abbreviations

Using abbreviations for lecture notetaking isn't a suggestion, it's a necessity. You can't write at the speed of sound. Ask for an annotation demonstration at the writing center or academic support center. Table 12-3 lists examples of notetaking abbreviations created and used by some students.

TABLE 12-3 **Suggested Notetaking Abbreviations**

Abbreviation / Symbol	Meaning	Abbreviation / Symbol	Meaning
→	Connects with	Res	Research
Otl	Outlier	CLa	Class applicable
*****	Highest rating	*	Lowest rating
EX	Example	Circle	New word or term
Double underline	Major idea	?	Question information

Not Showing or Placing: Selecting Winning Topics

Choosing a topic may be the most important grade-influencing decision you make concerning your essay. *Outlier topics* are the high-achieving grade-guzzlers of academic performance. Average topics may earn average grades, and cliché topics earn cliché grades — grades similar to the first letter of the word cliché.

Topic selection should be as thoughtful a process as developing your argument and organizing your essay. Sources of developing winning topics come from the following:

>> Assignment prompt

>> Books

>> Class content

>> Crossing disciplines

>> Other courses

>> Other written projects

>> Technology

Make sure the topic you choose, including outlier topics, is related to the assignment prompt and answers the prompt question.

The following sections help you figure out what does and doesn't make a good topic.

Knowing what makes a good topic

Your topic may be passionate to you, but you aren't assigning your grade. Think of a topic that attracts the passion of your professor, addresses the prompt, and includes language that attracts attention. Think of topics that argue against the grain.

Here's an example, not an example I'm advocating, but an example of an untraditional approach to a topic. Many students and organizations effectively argued against smoking, an important topic and a cliché topic. But arguing against the grain is unique and effective and represents an outlier. A pro-smoking topic, arguing economically, takes the approach that smoking saves the healthcare system billions of dollars because smokers die an average ten years earlier and saves costs during the ten years of life when healthcare is most expensive.

Recognizing when a topic isn't good

A not-so-good topic results from an incomplete thought process, shutting down thinking before average and cliché topics develop into outlier topics.

Here's a list of categories of topics that need more thought:

>> Defends values or non-concrete ideas, such as dependability is more important than honesty

>> Lacks connection between the prompt and course

>> Exceeds the audience and professor's general knowledge

>> Argues topics that lack application to the prompt

>> Includes too much personal obsession

If your topic is cliched or gimmicky and unlikely to earn an A, don't give up. Frequently an average topic can be converted to an outlier topic as seen in Table 12-4:

TABLE 12-4 **Converting Cliché Topics to Outlier Topics**

Cliché Topic	Outlier Topic
College students should graduate with as little student loan debt as possible.	Colleges should share student loan debt with students who aren't provided a path to graduate.
Gun registration should be mandatory.	Gun manufacturing should include technology that traces ownership.
Athletes' salaries exceed sensibility.	Should capitalism have a salary cap that includes mandatory financial responsibilities?

Ordering a La Carte: Optional Assignment Sections

Plain lacks popularity. When did you last see a sports team or your favorite musical performers in plain attire? And when was the last time you ordered plain pizza?

Plain also lacks popularity with your essays and writing projects. Just like accessories can pop your wardrobe and pizza, accessories such as a title page, table of contents, glossary, and appendix can pop your writing grades.

REMEMBER

Some optional features that follow are exclusive to essays, some are exclusive to other writing projects, and some apply to all college projects. I identify compatibility with each option.

Accessories not only complement wardrobes, they also complement writing projects.

Title page

Title pages make a good first impression for all your college writing projects and tell your professor that what's enclosed is important and deserves special packaging.

Some professors require an adaption of a formal title page (see Figure 12-1), with formatting that includes the following:

>> One-inch margins on four sides

>> Bolded title centered just above mid-page

>> Contact information single-spaced in upper left corner that includes student's name, course name and section, professor's name, assignment name, and essay due date

Michael P. Touhey
College Writing 101-2
Sustainability essay
Dr. Ludlow
January 5, 2023

To Sustain or Not to Sustain: A Game Changer

Essay begins here.

FIGURE 12-1:
An example of a title page.

© John Wiley & Sons, Inc.

Because title page requirements vary among professors, ask your professor for a model of their specific requirements.

WARNING

Spelling errors aren't created equally, especially when they appear on the title page and include misspellings such as your professor's name and the name of the course. Misspelling words in titles and headings doesn't receive a dispensation because they are featured words.

Some professors require a formal title page. Figure 12-2 shows a formal APA formatted title page for essays and almost any other college project. The page formatting also includes one-inch formatting on all sides. APA formatting includes page numbering in the upper right corner on all pages, including the title page.

To Sustain or Not to Sustain: A Game Changer Michael P. Touhey Department of Rhetoric and Writing College Writing, 101-2 Sustainability essay Dr. Ludlow January 5, 2023 [The remaining three-quarters of the page is blank.]

FIGURE 12-2: A formal APA title page.

(c) John Wiley & Sons, Inc.

Formal title page information includes the paper's title, student's name, university affiliation, course number, professor's name, and date due.

Table of contents

Think of a table of contents as a highlight of the paper's contents. The reader's relationship with the topics begins with the table of contents, including what's excluded. Tables of content aren't usually required for essays, but they're necessary for organization of papers that require subheadings and exceed five pages. Some style guides refer to the table of contents as "Contents." Figure 12-3 shows a sample table of contents that almost all professors will accept.

Contents

Introduction	1
Research Background	3
Argument	5
Refutation	7
Works Cited	9
Appendix A: Figures and Tables	10

FIGURE 12-3: A sample Contents page.

(c) John Wiley & Sons, Inc.

Appendices

You may or may not have your appendix, and if you don't, you don't miss it. When professors require an appendix, they'll miss it if you don't include it. The following is list of common uses of an appendix (it's an appendix of appendices):

An appendix includes supplementary information for topics related to any writing assignment. Common appendix topics for essays include the following:

>> A diary entry of your revising strategies for your project

>> A list of topics you recommend for further study

>> Notes of an interview with a person referenced in the paper

>> A description of survey results for a survey referenced in the paper

>> A description of your searches

>> A diary entry of your major activities writing your essay

>> A description of what you learned about writing through your essay writing project

REMEMBER

Appendices don't exceed one page.

Glossary

If your college paper requires extensive use of specialized terms that require definition beyond their contextual use on the body of the paper, include those terms and definition in a glossary.

Glossaries aren't usually required or necessary in essays, but they may be necessary for essays across disciplines. Glossaries are more common in larger college writing projects.

Abstracts and executive summaries

An *abstract* is a summary of a research paper that's positioned before the introduction. It's common to longer research projects, but not essays.

An *executive summary* is preliminary information in a business document. If you're required to write one, your professor will provide specific guidelines.

Taking One for the Team: Team Projects

One of your most memorable college experiences — for better or for worse — will be your numerous opportunities (and catastrophes) working on collaborative writing projects. Dickens couldn't have described it better with his "best of times . . . worst of times" opening. Group projects are as much part of the academic fiber as textbook buyback day.

Working with others, you'll experience the best and worst of academic behavior. But the challenges offer opportunities. If you can motivate the reluctant, you have a skill highly valued in the workplace, the ability to improve performance. In addition, team projects offer an opportunity to practice leadership with your peers and test your problem-solving strategies.

TECHNICAL STUFF

How do teams differ from groups? Teams coordinate efforts to complete a project. Group members complete their individual parts and submit them to the group member responsible to compile parts. Team members work toward a shared common goal, collaborate with each other, and motivate other members to improve performance. Team members care about their team first, whereas group members care about their grade first.

The advantages of collaborative writing projects include the following:

>> Experience peer styles of writing, collaborating, achieving, problem-solving, and diplomacy

>> Capitalize on team members' strengths

>> Learn writing skills in a reduced stress environment

>> Observe team members display interpersonal skills such as negotiating, problem-solving, collaborating, and motivating

When you're required to participate in a collaborative writing project, here's a list of tips for being a good team member:

>> Build a friendly working relationship with all team members.

>> Greet members at meetings with a relationship-building: "Hi, how's your day going?"

>> Be inclusive of all team members, especially those who appear marginalized.

>> Accept the challenge of improving the performance of other team members.

>> Be a model of encouragement, optimism, and exceeding expectations.

>> Compliment team members for their contributions; offer help with their shortcomings.

>> Communicate with team members and discuss issues before they become problems.

» **Preventing procrastination**

» **Delivering draft one**

» **Ensuring academic integrity — no plagiarism allowed**

Chapter **13**

Getting One Done: Completing Draft One

Writing develops the brain like exercise develops the body. Both require long-term planning and regular commitment and physical and mental stamina, and both offer the satisfaction of accomplishment.

Writing and exercising frequently begin with rituals. Observe the spider-like stretching of swimmers and the arm-flailing gyrations of runners as they approach their respective starting points. Rituals prepare the mind and body for the demanding activity that follows, including the activity of writing.

This chapter explains rituals and prerequisites for writing, which neutralize procrastination and other writing impediments. I prepare you for accomplishing the first two steps of writing readiness: preparing yourself and your essay. I walk you through six easy-to-follow steps for completing a successful first draft, the foundation of your final submission. I also explain guidelines for writing ethically and objectivity, while avoiding plagiarism.

Awakening Inspiration: Composing Environments and Writing Rituals

Your writing time and location may be insignificant to you, but they're important to your brain — an organ that prefers inspirational writing conditions. You can maximize your creative time and writing time by reflecting on the writing environment you're most productive.

The importance of identifying your ideal conditions is that your brain requires one set of conditions and you may prefer other conditions. Listen to your brain, as well as your preferences, and identify conditions that result in successful writing. Here I delve deeper into the location and what you do to get ready to write.

Location, location, location — college composing environments

Two of your most important writing-preparation decisions are when to write and where to write. The sections that follow explain how to make those decisions and why your brain is counting on you to make good choices.

Your brain needs disengagement from your devices, both sound and sight. Mute your phone and place it face down. It also needs its space from looking at you all day. Your brain also needs focus. Brain science has refuted the value of multitasking, explaining that the brain functions like broadband data transmission with one pipeline of information.

REMEMBER

Brain power that diverts into texting, talking, gaming, posting, and viewing, reduces brain power available for writing. If you avoid distractions by multitasking, you'll reserve 100 percent of the brain's data for your writing. You'll produce better writing in less time.

Here are brain-friendly considerations to determine a brain-happy writing environment:

>> **Time of day:** Determine when you're most creatively productive — early morning, late afternoon, early evening, or late night. When your schedule allows, plan your writing during your most productive hours. When that's not possible, adapt a growth mindset (see Chapter 5) and make it work.

>> **Ambiance:** Your brain doesn't like competition during writing. Figure out what kind of environment you prefer — possibly passive activity or isolation, a coffee-shop atmosphere with background activity, or isolation with

inspirational views. Figure out what motivates you — nature or indoor comforts. Is your style a cubicle in the library, a bench in the park, a table in a quiet room, a beach chair on a lawn, or just a lawn?

>> **Music:** Your brain dislikes music with words that beg to be listened to. Instrumental music sooths brain cells — maybe easy listening or light jazz. Overstimulated brains thrive on the sound of silence. They've heard it all.

>> **Variety:** Vary your writing environment based on your mood and assignment. If one setting isn't productive, try another.

>> **Goals:** Schedule a weekly number of hours for writing and revising, such as two hours writing and two hours revising. If your writing time frame remains productive, continue writing. If your writing brain needs rest, continue with a writing-related activity such as organizing or planning.

>> **Rewards:** Reward yourself for a successful writing session, such as text time, social media time, or gaming time.

REMEMBER

Writing may be your brain's most demanding intellectual activity. Expect your writing to require intellectual effort. Ideas you create while writing remain in your brain for a lifetime. Recall your early writing projects. The harder you work to download writing into your brain, the easier the retrieval when you want to recall it.

Ritualizing writing

Rituals are brain science–supported procedures that prompt the brain to transition to performance activities. You may have noticed professors' rituals before starting class, similar to the following:

>> Walk into the classroom and boot the computer.

>> Hang a jacket on a chair and look out the window.

>> Place notes and a bottle of water on the podium.

>> Answer student questions as the computer boots.

>> Comment about a song or recent sporting event.

>> Say "Hi, everyone" and take attendance.

Life is full of rituals. Your classroom-entering ritual may include sitting in the same seat, saying hello to the same person, and positioning your backpack in the same location. The ritual begins the process that transitions into the beginning of class.

TIP

Student writing rituals include writing while wearing a favorite cap or sitting in a favorite chair.

My ritual before beginning a morning writing session includes turning on a YouTube loop of beach scenes, strategically positioning piles of notes on the floor, placing my hazelnut coffee to my right, booting my computer, and beginning writing from my last stopping point. The ritual tells my brain to begin delivering action verbs.

Establish your writing ritual by determining materials you need, your location, and your emotional needs, such as a stare into space, a good-luck charm, and a comfort beverage.

Table 13-1 examines rituals from writers you may recognize.

TABLE 13-1 **Rituals of Famous Writers**

Writer	Ritual
Jane Austen	Wrote during early morning hours; scribbled notes secretly during the day
Charles Dickens	Wrote daily from 9:00 a.m. to 2:00 p.m.; took long walks for breaks
Ernest Hemingway	Began writing during early morning hours and wrote until empty of ideas; allegedly wrote standing up
Stephen King	Sits down every morning with a cup of tea or glass or water, positioning papers in the same location every day
Herman Melville	Wrote daily; worked as a farmer to clear his writing mind
Mark Twain	Wrote daily; locked in a private room designated for writing
Kurt Vonnegut	Began writing during early morning hours; took breaks for swimming and push-ups

Destroying Delays: Procrastination and Writer's Anxiety

Imagine you have a choice: a week vacationing at your favorite tropical resort or a week cleaning an abandoned warehouse. You're human if you choose pleasure over pain, comfort over discomfort, the beach rather than the building — and a Netflix binge over starting an essay.

REMEMBER

Procrastination is the enemy of many college students, an enemy rarely defeated but always controlled by successful students. Procrastination becomes detrimental when the delays affect class preparation time, result in missed deadlines, and cause descending grades.

Causes of delaying assignments include expectations of perfectionism, performance anxiety, and poor planning. Here I examine the obstacles to writing and how to overcome them.

Focusing on procrastination and delays

If you're reading this book, you're most likely accepted into college where an admissions committee validated your ability to perform college work. They believe in you. The committee members are confident in your academic ability, especially your proficiencies to read and write. The following sections show you how to manage your high expectations and remain optimistic on your path to success.

Looking at the connection between perfectionism and delays

The ability of some students to achieve is delayed by uncontrolled *perfectionism* — unrealistic and obsessive expectations to produce perfect text. The quest for perfectionism can be a destructive liability when they compare themselves to others, set unreasonable standards, or reach for unreasonable goals, such as earning the highest GPA in a class, an achievement reached by only one person.

TECHNICAL STUFF

Some students' unreasonable academic expectations neglect to consider that students mature academically at different paces. Research supports the academic advantage of starting school at an age closer to seven, rather than the traditional five or six.

Channeling perfectionism

A body of research supports the value of controlled perfectionism. The aim for perfectionism benefits students who learn from their setbacks and remain optimistic during their failures.

The student health center and the writing center help students adapt perfectionism by teaching them to perform as follows:

>> Excel for themselves and not for an external measurement or designated recognition.

>> Separate self-worth from self-achievement.

>> Set reasonable goals focused on improvement.

>> Recognize failure as a step toward success.

>> Celebrate their successes and accomplishments.

A healthy emotional perspective includes working hard and utilizing resources with the goal of accepting the results of your best effort. High-level career success results from above-average work habits and average intelligence.

Preventing and controlling procrastination

Almost all college students experience writing and assignment procrastination, but they develop tools to control it. Incorporate some of the following procrastination prevention strategies in your writing plan:

>> Recognize the challenge of college writing projects.

>> Identify the importance of organization, preparation, planning, and a supportive study environment.

>> Plan academic projects and schedule them into a weekly and long-range planner.

>> Prepare for assignments analyzing the assignment, reading background information, determining a focus, and organizing information (see Chapter 12).

>> Hold yourself accountable for completing the assignment.

>> Reward yourself upon completion.

Reducing writer anxiety

Writing anxiety, similar to writer's block, is an emotional attitude toward writing that can prevent writing performance. It's usually driven by fear of failure and inability to meet personal expectations.

Writing anxiety may occur with a specific writing genre, such as fiction or poetry, or with a specific discipline such as scientific writing. Writing anxiety may also result from an experience of negative criticism.

Strategies for adapting to writing anxiety include the following:

>> Write assignments with the supervision of the writing center.

>> Set goals to complete assignments in sections, such as the body, closing, and opening.

>> Identify and address specific parts of the writing process that cause anxiety.

>> Celebrate small writing successes, such as completing a first draft well before deadline (see Chapter 13).

>> Form a study group with peers to work on assignments.

>> Practice healthy self-maintenance such as exercising, good nutrition, and good life balances.

Your campus health facility and writing center provide resources to help you with writing issues.

Research supports the practice of reducing stress with ten minutes freewriting describing your stresses. Chapter 12 explains how to freewrite.

GETTING STARTED AND TAKING RISKS

The status quo represents a comfort zone for some people and the satisfaction of "same old, same old." But comfortable wasn't satisfying for innovators and barrier-breakers such as Jane Austen, Wilber and Orville Wright, Anne Frank, Steve Jobs, Rosa Parks, Thomas Edison, Harriet Tubman, Malala Yousafzai, and Amelia Earhart.

College isn't the environment for status quo. It's an opportunity to initiate and ignite new ideas — frequently articulated in writing projects. And because you're in college, you expect more than status quo, and you're ready for the academic risk of college writing.

Like the legends mentioned in the "Ritualizing writing," section in this chapter, you want more for yourself and the society you live in. Dreams begin with self-starting, especially your writing projects. Think of yourself as the product of your rituals and habits — your writing preparation habits.

Beginning an essay requires confidence and discipline, shutting down the ritual world of and opening the imaginary world of arguing a theoretical statement in three or four typed pages. Professional writers struggle with starts also, and they sometimes experience a false start and need a restart. The steps in the section, "Completing a Draft in Six Easy-to-Follow Steps," in this chapter can help.

Completing a Draft in Six Easy-to-Follow Steps

A first draft is like a first date, the beginning of a relationship you want to develop into a forever essay. Your goal with a first draft is to develop an essay for better or for worse. Your purpose isn't to write a perfect draft, but a completed draft that will create a foundation for a successful essay.

The steps that follow help you improve your essay; however, they won't help you improve a failed first date.

Step 1: Plan and focus

Planning is the foundation step of your essay; your essay can't survive a faulty foundation that lacks a plan and lacks focus. Tips for planning include the following:

>> Put on your writing face, and adapt a frame of mind for two weeks' writing.

>> Create a timeline that accounts for life's interventions, revising, and editing (head to Chapter 14).

>> Gather notes, the assignment, materials, and your laptop.

>> Analyze the assignment and identify the major question (see Chapter 12).

>> Review past writing assignments for special focuses.

>> Establish writing goals and content goals.

>> Coordinate writing priorities with rubric priorities.

Step 2: Read for background

Background materials provide an overview of the topic and include additional terminology and implications beyond the assignment prompt. The purpose of background reading includes the following (see Chapter 12):

>> Familiarize yourself with the extent of the topic.

>> Identify names and events affiliated with the topic.

>> List working arguments and working theses.

>> Annotate readings to visualize your thinking on the topic and your interaction with the content.

>> Identify evidence and counterevidence.

Step 3: Organize information

Essays are built on the information you gather. As you increase knowledge on the topic, organize information as follows:

>> Finalize a working topic and thesis (see Chapter 6).

>> Determine a framework (refer to Chapter 5).

>> Structure your argument (check out Chapter 7).

>> Identify counterarguments (flip to Chapter 7).

>> Isolate information for the opening, body, and closing (see Chapter 5).

>> Outline the essay (head to Chapter 12).

>> Organize body paragraphs (refer to Chapter 5).

Step 4: Write the body paragraphs

The body section contains the key points of your essay. Draft the body section of your essay, focusing on the following:

>> Write with awareness of your word count, estimating 10 percent for your opening and 15 percent for your closing.

>> Begin your argument paragraphs with your evidence (go to Chapter 7).

>> Apply brainstorming strategies, such as A-Z prompts (see Chapter 12).

>> Begin evidence paragraphs with topic sentences that introduce evidence (refer to Chapter 8).

>> Document citations as you write (see Chapter 7).

REMEMBER

As you write, apply good writing principles and practices such as the following:

>> Write in the Word file, formatting and documenting the style required to submit your essay (see Chapter 7).

- » Compose paragraph lengths approximately six to seven lines of text (see Chapter 8).

- » Vary sentence length and structure (see Chapter 9).

- » Prefer nouns and verbs to adjectives and adverbs (refer to Chapter 9).

- » Write primarily in the active voice (check out Chapter 9).

- » Back up your work regularly, including emailing drafts to yourself (see Chapter 15).

- » Default to the subject-action verb sentence pattern (see Chapter 9).

- » Avoiding writing to impress your professor with big words (see Chapter 9); write to develop your argument.

- » Write with an awareness of academic honesty, ethics, and objectivity (see Chapter 13).

Step 5: Draft opening, closing, and title

The body paragraphs transition from the opening and to the closing. Follow draft-ing the body section with writing the opening, closing, and title. Focus on the following as your write (refer to Chapter 5 unless otherwise directed):

- » Consider an anecdotal opening.

- » Transition the opening into the thesis statement.

- » Introduce the thesis with the thought or wording, "The purpose of this essay is to argue that . . ." (flip to Chapter 6)

- » Follow the opening with a background paragraph.

- » Write the closing.

- » Write a title.

- » Add the reference or works cited (see Chapter 7).

Step 6: Revise

After completing the first draft of your essay, rest it for 24 hours. Begin revising your draft with attention to the following:

- » Validate your file format (see Chapter 15).

- » Double-check that you answered the assignment question (refer to Chapter 12).

- >> Review accuracy of citations (check out Chapter 7).

- >> Overwork your feedback team (see Chapter 14).

- >> Ensure that your structure contains a clearly defined opening, body, and closing (head to Chapter 5).

- >> Revise at the sentence and paragraph levels for conciseness, cohesiveness, flow, and transitions (refer to Chapter 14).

- >> Revise at the word level for unnecessary and overused words.

- >> Write additional drafts as needed.

- >> Finalize your paper for submission (see Chapter 15).

Ensuring a Night's Sleep: Plagiarism Protection

Successful families are built on trust, with each member feeling valued, respected, and loved. Academic institutions are built on the same trust that assignments were completed within the guidelines of academic honesty. Each member of the academic community shares the trust that what is learned is earned fairly.

When academic trust is compromised, members lose confidence in the system and degrees are devalued.

When you practice academic integrity and responsible representation of sources, you're endorsing scholarship and protecting against *plagiarism*, failure to credit the work and ideas of others and passing them off as your own. (flip to Chapter 13). Good sound documentation practices are as relaxing as a good night's sleep.

Accepting academic integrity

Academic integrity is the belief that the teaching and learning process is flawless and that grades are earned fairly. Academic integrity is the foundation of a university's beliefs. University policies support elimination of academic dishonesty to ensure degrees are earned fairly through the exchange of intellectual properties.

REMEMBER

Your contribution to academic integrity as a student includes accepting responsibility to educate yourself by reading, writing, thinking, satisfying curiosities, and deriving meaning from classroom content — within the guidelines of academic honesty. Students accept responsibility to voice support of academic integrity as an uncompromised value.

Honor codes and academic integrity

Some institutions institute an *honor code,* obligating students to disclose others who commit academic dishonesty. The earliest honor codes were established by U.S. military academies who strongly supported a code not to lie, cheat, or steal — or tolerate anyone who does. Students' obligation to disclose honor code violations has become controversial at many universities today.

Another honor code controversy is prohibiting collaboration, a learning theory supported by many universities and practiced in many workplaces. Current research on college honor codes fails to show their effectiveness.

Teams and academic integrity

Collaboration is an accepted practice working on team projects, and individual members accept responsibility for all team members practicing academic integrity. Plagiarism by one team member, such as falsifying a source, implicates all team members.

Many professors require each team member to complete a form acknowledging their academic integrity responsibilities for team projects. Many professors also require teams to discuss plagiarism before beginning assignments, and formulate a set of team guidelines.

Faculty responsibilities

Faculty responsibility toward plagiarism includes the following:

>> Build student trust in the shared responsibility of academic integrity.

>> Offer a variety of student assessments for demonstrating their proficiencies.

>> Design assignments that reduce opportunities for plagiarism.

>> Introduce plagiarism into classroom discussion.

>> Provide students with the support that makes them feel academically confident.

Academic integrity is a value requiring endorsement by all members of the university community.

A BRIEF LOOK AT SOME HISTORY OF PLAGIARISM

Protecting academic integrity has an issue for more than 2,000 years. The term plagiarism dates to the first century when poets accused other poets of stealing their lines. It reached epidemic proportions during Middle Ages when documenting practices varied among geographical regions and genre.

Attitudes protecting literary creations were strengthened during the 18th century with the implementation of copyright laws. In today's world of academia, the simplicity of plagiarism has been expedited by technologies such as copy and paste. Plagiarism will become a greater challenge in the near future with artificial intelligence, which now provides software to invalidate plagiarism-detection software.

Researching plagiarism

Studies in the past few years revealed the following concerns for protecting academic integrity:

>> A plagiarism-detection software company reported student plagiarism increased 10 percent when classes moved online during the pandemic.

>> A recent study of 60,000 college students showed more than 50 percent admitted to plagiarizing an assignment.

>> A study at a leading Eastern university revealed that more than 60 percent of its students admitted cheating.

>> On the high school level, plagiarism detection increased 10 percent during Covid.

The good news is that a survey between 2005 and 2015 showed plagiarism decreased where students were made aware of plagiarism and its consequences.

Noting the consequences of plagiarism

Most universities post an academic integrity policy that includes examples of plagiarism, usually examples that the university has personally experienced. Policies include students' responsibilities for academic honesty and consequences of plagiarism. Infractions are generally classified into levels ranging from unintentional violations to systematic cheating.

Alleged violations are presented to a sitting review board composed of students, faculty, and administrators. Consequences range from a one-grade scoring deduction for minor infractions to expulsion for serious infractions or multiple violations.

Policies also encourage faculty to teach responsible documentation and discuss plagiarism consequences with every assignment.

Recognizing forms of academic dishonesty

Academic dishonesty has many faces and nuances and ranges from unintentional references without documentation to purchasing papers online. Here's a look at variations of plagiarism:

>> **Cheating:** Violations of cheating include presenting works of others as one's own, copying or collaborating during tests, and premature knowledge of test information.

>> **Self-plagiarism:** Referencing an unauthorized previously written paper represents a form of plagiarism, such as submitting a paper you wrote in philosophy for class as an original assignment for a composition course — without permission from your professor.

>> **AI based writing:** Uses of artificial intelligence to write papers or manipulate text to avoid software recognition is a form of plagiarism.

>> **Unauthorized collaboration:** Assignment parameters may or may not authorize collaboration. When guidelines don't approve collaboration, use of it constitutes cheating.

>> **Falsification:** Various forms of falsifying sources are considered plagiarism, such as creating fictional sources.

>> **Source stuffing:** Use of unnecessary sources is plagiarism, such as sources irrelevant to your paper.

>> **Patchwriting:** *Patchwriting* is the practice of changing a few key words in a copy and paste assignment.

Avoiding plagiarism: Helpful strategies

Plagiarism violations frequently result from time mismanagement and the need to shorten assignment preparation time.

Strategies for avoiding plagiarism include the following:

TIP

» **Managing time:** Efficiently budgeting time represents the most reliable strategy to ensure academic honesty. When preparation is compromised, academic honesty is also frequently compromised.

A frequently overlooked time management strategy is starting assignments sooner, preferably soon after they're introduced in class when requirements are fresh in your mind.

» **Detailing research:** Source organization requires detailed records of bibliographical information as well as summaries, paraphrases, and quotations. Many students keep paper and electronic copies of their sources, especially for essays that required limited sources.

» **Citing as you search and write:** To ensure documentation accuracy, insert citations as you draft. Also, as you write, distinguish between your words and source words.

» **Using plagiarism-detection technology:** Many universities and professors require submitting writing assignments to plagiarism-detection software, such as Turnitin, as plagiarism defense.

» **Annotating assignment records:** If you're accused of unintentional plagiarism, your best defense is detailed record-keeping of your notes, planning, and drafts of the assignment from planning through submission.

» **Reviewing your draft with the writing center:** As an additional redundancy and learning experience, review your sources and documentation with your writing center.

Understanding plagiarism and nonnative English students

Learning English as an add-on language and learning plagiarism as a new culture is like learning to drive in a foreign country — in reverse. The clash of cultural beliefs on crediting sources challenges almost every student from an Eastern culture.

The protection of scholarship, the pillar of belief in Western cultures, is viewed as a gift to be shared among Eastern cultures. Their access to information includes using sources without reference to the author. The highest form of academic respect in many Eastern cultures is inserting memorization of source information into the essay. Memorizing is considered a higher priority than writing.

Many universities provide resources to help nonnative English students to learn the concepts of engaging with and crediting sources to avoid plagiarism. Chapter 18 is another place to look.

Strategies for adapting practices of Western culture scholarship to nonnative English–speaking students include the following:

>> When you read from a source, transform the information as a summary, paraphrase, or quotation.

>> When you apply information from your sources, do so as a summary, paraphrase, or quotation.

>> Following writing the information with source credit is called an *in-text citation*. Write the citation in the style required by your professor, APA, MLA, or Chicago/Turabian.

>> List every source you use in the reference or works cited at the end of the paper.

>> As you write your paper, record in-text citations, avoiding the confusion of identifying citations when you've finished your paper.

Additional tips for learning documentation include the following:

>> Study documentation and references in other student papers.

>> Study documentation and references in research you read.

>> Before submitting your paper, have it reviewed at your writing center.

Remember that many first–year writing instructors require informal citations and references for essays, similar to the style of Eastern cultures.

Recalling Olden Rules: Ethics and Objectivity

Ethics and objectivity should be as simple as distinguishing right from wrong and fair from unfair — but it isn't and writers need care with word choices to represent their work accurately and fairly. Their responsibility includes author credibility, credible sources, accurate documentation, inclusive language, and fair representation of ideas. Ethical writing also includes distinguishing between author's words and source's words.

Ethical writing is objective — not subjective — which requires fairness of facts, not influenced by personal opinion or bias. To insure objectivity, first person pronouns (I, we, me, and my) represent personal opinion, and are generally avoided in formal nonfiction academic writing — with the exception of occasional use in the essay.

You as the writer practice ethical responsibility to your reader by distinguishing objective information from subjective information and by presenting information fairly and accurately. The skills to distinguish and present objectively is a challenge of college writing.

Here's an example of first-person subjective writing that's infrequently used in formal academic writing:

> I feel that smoking is unhealthy for you.

The use of "I" eliminates objectivity, offering opinion rather than factual information supporting the unhealthiness of smoking.

That statement may be written objectively as follows:

> Numerous studies show the harmful effects of smoking.

Table 13-2 looks at the differences between objective and subjective writing.

TABLE 13-2: **Comparing Objective versus Subjective Writing**

Objective	Subjective
Fact-based third person	Opinion-based first person
Hard to disagree with	Easy to disagree with
Today is 60 degrees.	Today is too cold.
Statistics, health data	Diaries, blogs
Research papers and textbooks	Essays and novels
Analysis	Interpretation

Both objective and subjective writing offer value to the academic community. Accounts of experts' opinions represent a valued source of subjective writing and an opinion for the reader to agree or disagree with.

Essays represent a genre of subjective and objective writing. An essay thesis is a subjective opinion on an assigned topic. Support of the thesis is argued with facts — objective writing.

» **Giving and taking feedback**

» **Revising at three levels**

» **Designing a college revising plan**

Chapter **14**

Rethinking and Repairing: Three-Level Revising Plan

With more than a half-century experience teaching writers from K to grad school, I offer two conclusions about academic writers:

» They're the best readers.

» They're the best rewriters.

The reading–writing connection is obvious to college students. The writing–revising connection is less obvious to students — but very obvious to professional writers who have been championing the importance of revising for generations. Here's what a couple of experts said:

» "The greatest pleasure in writing is rewriting. My early drafts are always wretched." —Ernest Hemingway

» "The beautiful part of writing is that you don't have to get it right the first time, unlike, say a brain surgeon. You can always do it better . . ." —Robert Cromier

One lesson is that you have three opportunities to excel as a writer:

>> Learn to be a good writer (which includes revising).

>> Learn to be an exceptional rewriter.

>> Read obsessively.

Combine all three and you're dean's list material.

This chapter explains feedback in the revising process and interpretations of professor comments on your paper. It shows revising at three levels and offers a plan for approaching revising as a college writer.

You can improve your writing by improving your revising; you can improve your revising by improving your feedback.

Feeling Loopy: Feedback and Revising Loop

Would you consider having brain surgery from doctors who performed one operation, never reviewed their procedure, never studied how to improve, and never accepted feedback from their peers? Although writing isn't brain surgery, submitting a one-and-done draft is as risky for your grade as an inexperienced brain surgeon is for your health. Think of your first draft as your first try. The following sections delve deeper into why revising is important and the different forms of revisions you'll encounter as a college writer.

Understanding why you revise

If Ernest Hemingway, mentioned on the first page of this chapter, couldn't produce successful first drafts, you're not going to produce successful first drafts either. Revising in inherent to improving writing. Revising improves the following higher-order skills:

>> Writing and reading

>> Prioritizing and evaluating

>> Analyzing and synthesizing

>> Critical thinking

Revising requires collaboration with a team who offers you feedback to evaluate for improving your writing. A good feedback partner is like a coach who can suggest adjustments to improve your game.

The value of receiving feedback includes the following:

>> Suggests where writing needs clarification

>> Identifies strengths and weaknesses

>> Provides suggestions from a reader emotionally unattached from the writing

>> Reads without an investment in the grading process

Giving and receiving peer feedback

Your parents may have taught you that giving is better than receiving. But if they were teaching you about feedback, the lesson would have been that giving and receiving feedback is better than not giving and receiving feedback. These sections explain feedback and its role in improving your writing.

Focusing on feedback and revising

Writing improves with feedback from trial readers, sometimes an emotional experience for developing writers. You invite readers into your emotional space and risk their negative evaluation of your writing.

When your professors and other feedback sources negatively criticize your writing, they aren't criticizing you personally. Thank them for an honest evaluation of your work and analyze the validity of their comment. As you grow as a writer, you'll value feedback partners who identify a writing idea that needs clarification.

Your writing improvement depends on your professor objectively evaluating your writing, good or bad. If your professor comments that your margins are perfect and that your indentations are intriguing — your writing is bad. If your writing receives an unsatisfactory review, reaffirm that you're a good person and camp outside your professor's door for the next office hours for clarification on how to revise the assignment. The issue frequently is a student misunderstanding of the assignment.

REMEMBER

Feedback remains an integral part of the revising process. You're writing to connect with readers, and test peer readers can tell you if you're successful. If a pattern of feedback tells you your thesis is vague — your thesis is vague.

The value of feedback is that your nonthreatening peers, who lack influence on your grade, offer you an opinion that you can evaluate as helpful or unhelpful. If your feedback readers are correct that your thesis is vague, you have an opportunity to improve your thesis.

Coaching peers' feedback

You need to have a talk — with your peers who provide feedback — and your talk needs to improve instructions for providing feedback. Tell them the level of feedback you prefer: warm and fuzzy, friendly, or brutally honest. The latter includes telling you weaknesses in structure, ideas that lack relevance, language that's unclear, sentences that make no sense, and paragraphs that seem to have parachuted into your essay.

If you're not ready for old-fashioned, bloody red-pen brutality (ask your grandparents), choose warm and fuzzy that will puff your personality. If you want a mixed bag, go for friendly.

Ask your peers to briefly offer feedback to questions such as the following:

>> What's your understanding of what I'm arguing?

>> What part of my argument needs clarifying?

>> What do you see as the purpose?

>> What language do you see that identifies the audience I'm writing to?

>> What's the good and bad of my evidence?

>> What do you see as the purpose of each body paragraph?

>> How well did I answer the major question in the assignment?

>> How successful do topic sentences connect to the thesis?

REMEMBER

Clarify with your feedback peers that you aren't interested in editing at this time and prefer feedback related to structure and content.

Accepting peers' feedback

When you receive feedback from your peers, respond with two words — thank you — followed by silence. This response is especially important if you asked for brutally honest feedback. Silence allows your peers to offer more feedback and prevents you from defending your writing.

Evaluate all sources of feedback and identify patterns of suggestions. Carefully consider feedback of content identified as "not sure of purpose," "not convincing," and "thesis not clear."

Getting professor feedback and comments

Your most important feedback comes from your professor, the person who awards your grade. Some school's portfolio requirements include an opportunity to revise your essay after professor feedback and prior to inclusion into your portfolio. It's like having a second chance to make a good first impression. If you don't have that opportunity to revise before final grading, professor comments afford you a path to improve your upcoming essays. The following focuses on how to decipher and tackle your professor's feedback.

Interpreting professor feedback

When professors give you essay feedback, their goal is to provide you with their best two or three pieces of advice to improve your essay. That advice is usually organizational and structural and expressed in short phrases such as "needs a stronger thesis," "lacks organization," or "needs more evidence."

If comments are local to a paragraph or specific to content such as "needs a better example here," "clarify source," or "needs a citation here," your professor likes your essay, and your revisions offer an opportunity to earn a B or better.

Professor feedback comments identify issues your professor recommends for improvement. Table 14-1 shows professor comments and how to address them.

TABLE 14-1   **Professor Comments and Interpretation**

Comments	Addressing Comments
Needs development	Develop connections between evidence and the thesis statement. Evaluate evidence quantity and quality (see Chapter 7).
Lacks focus	Evaluate thesis for application to the assignment (see Chapter 6), evidence supporting the thesis (see Chapter 7), or transitions connecting body paragraphs (see Chapter 8).
Organization	Evaluate distinguishable opening, body, and closing sections (refer to Chapter 5).
Please see me	Don't assume the worst. You could have an issue such as misunderstanding the assignment, documentation errors, not answering the question, or a pattern of language issues.
Language issues	Revise sentence structure (see Chapter 15) and edit for grammar, usage, spelling, and punctuation (refer to Chapter 11).

Addressing professor feedback

Avoid confusing peer feedback with professor feedback. Your professor isn't suggesting revisions. The revisions are a requirement to earn a good grade. Don't question the professor's feedback and comments; revise your essay.

When professors receive your revised draft addressing their feedback, they look first at their comments and how you addressed them. They aren't happy when you neglect to address issues they identified in your essay.

Your essay revisions and your essay success depend on understanding your professor's feedback. If you need clarification, meet with your professor to discuss it.

If you're meeting with your professor to discuss feedback, be sure your tone says you're asking for clarification, not questioning.

TIP

Offering peer feedback

This is a time to be selfish. You can learn from your peer's essay, in addition to evaluating questions they ask you to address.

Study your peer's essay by asking yourself questions such as the following:

>> How do they approach answering the assignment question?

>> How do they address other requirements such as incorporating readings, engaging with sources, and annotating a bibliography?

>> How do they write key sentences such as the thesis statement, topic sentences, and thesis-connecting sentences in the body paragraphs?

>> How do they connect topic sentences to the thesis statement?

>> How do they identify with their audience?

>> How do they connect evidence with the thesis?

>> How do they transition from idea to idea?

Analyze language choices, evidence, opening, closing, and formatting.

When you provide their feedback, ask them their preferred level of honesty (warm and fuzzy, friendly, or brutally honest). Compliment them on at least two examples of content ideas. If you want to exceed expectations, compliment them on their use of writing style tools (see Chapter 9).

Providing self-feedback

Your third source of feedback, yourself, represents the best of feedback or the worst of feedback. You can be your worst source if you fall in love with your thesis, argument, approach, paragraphs, sentences, and words — in other words, everything about your essay including your font selection is nonnegotiable. Love may be blind, and it may easily blindside you by compromising your essay objectivity.

Begin self-feedback by divorcing yourself from your essay and setting it aside at least 24 hours. Read your essay as a ruthless doubter and question everything: the answer to the question, thesis, argument (see Chapters 6 and 7), transitions, organization and framework (refer to Chapter 5), evidence (flip to Chapter 7), opening and closing (see Chapter 5), and sentences and paragraphs (see Chapter 8).

The advantages of objective self-feedback is that you know your essay better than anyone, and you're available at your convenience.

Focusing on the Global Level: Organization and Structure

The big picture isn't complete without the encompassing frame. Your essay requires framing with organization and structure. If the global view of your essay lacks coherence, your essay will crumble — your grade with it.

Essay revision begins with a global review of key elements such as organization, thesis, argument, structure, framework, audience and purpose, and style. The following sections offer questions to consider for revising at the structural level.

Allocate a majority of your revision time at the structural level. That strategy will ensure you address major requirements in the assignment and that your information flows from the thesis statement to the closing. Structural elements earn you the most essay points — or lose you the most essay points.

Revising organization and structure

Revising your essay's structure is like reviewing a team presentation before delivery. Your presentation review includes identifying who's delivering primary sections, who's referencing special sections, and who's coordinating technology. Your essay requires a similar global overview.

As you write and rewrite college projects, study assignments and recognize major structural elements: the opening, body, and closing. Readers need to distinguish those three parts to understand your message. For example, you'll confuse your reader if you explain the importance of the topic in the body paragraphs or introduce new evidence in the closing.

TIP

Revise with Track Changes, giving you a record of changes.

Organization

Organizational elements include your mental approach to the assignment and understanding the assignment purpose. Here are questions to consider for revising at the organizational level:

>> Did you begin the assignment with a mindset (refer to Chapter 5) required to sustain a multiweek project?

>> Does the assignment meet the expectations of yourself, your professor, and the academic audience (see Chapter 6)?

>> Does it fulfill the assignment requirement (check out Chapter 12)?

>> Does it say what you intended to say?

>> Can you identify writing strengths to build on and writing weaknesses to improve?

>> Did you evaluate feedback relevant to organization?

Thesis

The thesis statement determines the success of the essay and requires early consideration for revising. If your professor approved your thesis, and no feedback readers questioned it, consider only minor wording changes to improve focus. Here are questions to consider for revising the thesis (refer to Chapter 6):

>> Does the thesis align with the question in the assignment?

>> Does the thesis align with the argument?

>> Does the thesis offer the reader value?

Argument

The thesis statement identifies the debatable issue your essay is arguing. Here are questions to consider for revising the argument (refer to Chapter 7):

» Is the debatable issue in your argument a position acceptable to reasonably thinking people?

» Does your argument include supporting synthesized data?

» Does the essay refute counterevidence or identify any common ground?

» Does your argument avoid logical fallacies?

Structure

Fundamental structure of your essay includes an opening, body, and closing. Here are questions to consider for revising structure:

» Does the essay include a distinguishable opening, body, and closing (see Chapter 5)?

» Are lengths of the opening and closing proportionate to the length of the body paragraphs?

» Does the essay flow from the opening to the body to the closing?

» Does the closing include a reference to the opening?

Framework

Various framework or genres (persuasive, analysis, cause and effect, and so forth) in Chapter 5 help you develop your argument. Here are questions to consider for revising framework:

» Is an exclusive framework required in the assignment?

» Does the essay sell the argument?

» Is narration used to apply background on the topic?

» Is comparison and contrast used to differentiate ideas?

» Is analysis used to evaluate, distinguish, and draw conclusions?

» Is synthesis used to reveal relationships among and between ideas?

Audience and purpose

Audience identifies the readers you're writing to, and purpose identifies the reason you're writing to them. Here are questions to consider for revising audience and purpose (refer to Chapter 6):

>> Do the thesis and argument align with the audience and purpose?

>> Does the essay address the audience?

>> Is the complexity of information compatible with the audience's background on the topic?

>> Is the purpose valued by the audience?

Style

Your writing style represents your voice or writing personality. Here are questions to consider for revising style:

>> Is your writing style compatible with standards of academic writing (refer to Chapter 1)?

>> Does your writing include an emphasis of active verbs and specific nouns?

>> Do sentence structures vary?

>> Do you write with an awareness of rhythm?

>> Does your word choice include sensory words, compact words, and familiar words?

>> Does your writing avoid repetition, self-references, overexplanation, and extended quotations?

Chapter 9 can help with the last questions.

Opening: Working title, first sentence, and introduction

You've heard the expression you get one opportunity to make a good first impression. Fortunately, the expression doesn't apply to essay writing where you get unlimited revision opportunities to make a good impression with your revisions. But the expression emphasizes the importance of writing a good opening impression, connecting with readers, and beginning your essay.

Title and first sentence

The title and first sentence are like pre–Covid handshakes opening the relationship of your essay–meeting audience. Here are questions to consider for revising the title and first sentence (refer to Chapter 5):

>> Does the title preview the topic and suggest the thesis?

>> Does the title include a figure of speech such as rhyme, repetition, or literary reference?

>> Does the first sentence entice the reader to read the second sentence?

>> Does the first sentence include a strategy such as surprise information or an expert quotation?

>> Did you evaluate feedback relevant to the title and first sentence?

Introduction

The purpose of the opening or introduction is to symbolically represent the thesis before identifying the thesis statement. Here are questions to consider for revising the introduction:

>> Does the opening include a strategy, such as an anecdote or series of questions that symbolically represents the thesis (see Chapter 5)?

>> Does the opening transition into the thesis statement?

>> Does the opening end with the thesis statement?

Supporting middle paragraphs

The body paragraphs, the most important part of the essay, offer evidence that develops the argument. The elements of the body paragraphs include topic sentences, sources, and evidence. Here are questions to consider for revising the elements of the body paragraphs.

Topic sentences

Topic sentences introduce evidence in the body paragraphs. Here's a list of questions to consider for revising topic sentences (see Chapter 8):

>> Do topic sentences introduce evidence that connects to the thesis?

>> Do topic sentences preview the content of the paragraph?

>> Do topic sentences reference source attribution such as the author and title?

>> Are topic sentences supported by paragraph sentences?

>> Can you delete any supporting sentences?

Sources

Sources provide information used for evidence. Here are questions to consider for revising sources (Chapter 7 examines sources in greater detail):

>> Are sources relevant, current, accurate, specific, and unbiased?

>> Do sources meet expectations of your professor?

>> Is source information appropriately presented as paraphrase, summary, and quotations?

>> Are sources documented according to the required style?

>> Is documentation formal or informal as required?

Supporting evidence

Evidence from sources support the argument. Here are questions to consider for revising supporting evidence (refer to Chapter 7 for more information):

>> Is evidence specific to the topic?

>> Is evidence adequate for the argument?

>> Is evidence presented in topic sentences (see Chapters 6)?

>> Does evidence connect to the thesis?

>> Is evidence analyzed and synthesized?

Closing

The closing convinces your reader, especially your professor, that your evidence supports the argument and that the argument fulfills assignment requirements. Here are questions to consider for revising the closing (Chapter 5 discusses closings):

>> Does the body transition into the closing?

>> Does the closing reference the opening?

>> Does the closing synthesize evidence (Chapter 7 explains synthesizing)?

>> Does the closing reference main points of the evidence?

>> Does the closing explain the broader application of the evidence?

>> Does the last sentence include a poignant reader message?

Addressing the Middle: Sentences and Paragraphs

Growing up frequently requires navigating situations described as "caught in the middle," an unpleasant position. The middle level of your writing (sentences and paragraphs) frequently experiences the unpleasant ripple effect of requiring revision when structure is revised. A thesis revision frequently necessitates topic sentence revisions, and topic sentence revisions frequently require supporting sentence revision — all which the following discuss.

In addition, some first draft sentences fail on their own as a result of improper word positioning. Revising at the middle level requires considering sentences as they connect with other sentences and as they stand of their own.

TIP

Revising is brain intensive at the sentence level where wordiness is more specific than global issues. Take breaks during sentence–level revising. Don't try to revise more than two or three sentence–level issues during one session, the maximum focus level of the working memory.

Eyeing sentence-starter patterns

Daniel's Kahneman's *Thinking, Fast and Slow* describes thinking as instinctively (System 1) and deliberately (System 2), with System 1 the default thinking. *It is* as a sentence starter delays the subject–verb pattern and exemplifies the brain's System 1 thinking.

Avoid starting sentences with instinctive constructions such as *there are, it is, it seems,* and *it becomes.* Think deliberately (System 2) and revise *it is* patterns by identifying the doer of the action (subject), followed by the action performed (verb). Almost any sentence can begin with subject delaying constructions, which delay reader comprehension.

Here's what sentence starters look like and how they're revised:

Sentence starter: *There are* many reasons why first-year college students avoid revising essays.

Revised: *First-year college students avoid* revising essays because they start their assignment late and neglect quality revising.

You revise the sentence starter *There are* by identifying the doer of the action (*First-year college students*) and following it with the action performed (*avoid*).

When you consider revising sentence patterns, answer questions such as the following:

>> Is the subject pattern identifiable to the reader (see Chapter 9)?

>> If the subject is a noun, is it a specific noun?

>> If the verb an action verb, is the action specific?

>> Are most verbs written in the active voice?

>> Are the subject and verb located within proximity?

Avoiding spoken-language wordiness

The spoken language can be a writer's worst friend, especially when spoken expressions allow speakers time to think. Here are examples of spoken language expressions that require deletion from your writing:

>> By the way

>> Give me a minute

>> I believe

>> If you ask me

>> In a minute

>> It must be remembered

>> It's no wonder

>> Let me think

>> Permit me to say

Here's an example:

> **Spoken language wordiness:** *If you ask me,* college students prefer reading hard copy books to reading on electronic devices.
>
> **Revised:** College students prefer reading hard copy books.

TIP

If language sounds like talking, revise it.

Steering clear of wordy expressions

Spoken language lacks the conciseness filter of written language, and wordy expressions infiltrate writing. Like other forms of wordiness, patterns are common to each writer. Recognize your wordiness expressions, file them for future revisions, and revise them (refer to Table 14-2).

TABLE 14-2

Wordy Expressions to Avoid

Wordy Expression	Revision
A large number of	Many
Because in all instances	Always
Because of the fact that	Because
During that time	While
For the simple reason that	Because
Has the ability	Can
In the near future	When
When the time comes	When

Here's an example in a sentence:

> **Wordy phrase:** *Because of the fact* that the sun is readily available, solar power is a reliable source of energy.
>
> **Revised:** Because the sun is readily available, solar power is a reliable source of energy.

Here's an example of a wordy clause:

Wordy clause: The person *who was a talented vocalist* performed at the outdoor venue.

Revised: The talented vocalist performed at the outdoor venue.

Concentrating on the Local Level

Writing is continuous decision making, and decisions begin with word choices to create sentences. Word choices determine a sentence's success or failure. Avoid patterns of words that contribute to cloudy sentences. These sections discuss areas to look out for wordiness.

Recognizing overused words

Choosing words is like eating at the buffet. Words are plentiful, but don't expect pedigree choices. Table 14-3 is a list of overused words that contribute little to your daily word menu.

TABLE 14-3 **Overused Words**

Part of speech	Overused Words
Adjectives	fabulous, nice, amazing, tremendous, fantastic, awful, horrible, awesome, outstanding, terrible
Nouns	thing, gadget, factor, way, stuff, aspect
Verbs	claims, seems, appears, impacts, went, got, do, fix
Adverbs	very, really, truly, extremely, fine

Another category of overused words includes cliches. Here are a few clichés I see regularly in college writing:

>> A prime example

>> On pins and needles

>> For all intents and purposes

>> Proof is in the pudding

>> Searched high and low

Revise clichés with specific language such as the following:

Cliché: We *searched high and low* for essay evidence.

Revised: We searched library databases and Google Scholar for essay evidence.

Identifying unnecessary words

Unnecessary words contribute to readers' one-star ratings and should be aligned with delete keys. Test the need for every word; if it's unnecessary, delete it. Here's an example:

Unnecessary words: Don't use words that you don't need in a sentence.

Revised: Avoid wordiness.

The unnecessary words *that you don't need in a sentence* can be reduced to *wordiness*. *Don't use* can be reduced to *Avoid*.

Reducing redundancies

Some word patterns that have high opinions of themselves think they're worth repeating. Avoid the following redundancies identified by the italicized words in the list that follows:

>> **A *time* of two weeks:** Prefer *two weeks* exclusively. *Time* and *two weeks* are repetitious.

>> **Absolutely *certain*:** Prefer *certain*. *Absolutely* and *certain* are repetitious.

>> **Actual *decision*:** Prefer *decision* exclusively. *Actual* is unnecessary.

>> **Baby *puppies*:** Prefer *puppies*. All puppies are babies.

>> **Circle around:** Prefer *circle*. All *circles* are around.

>> **Close proximity:** Prefer *proximity*. *Close* and *proximity* are redundant.

>> **Collaborate together:** Prefer collaborate. *Collaborate* and *together* are redundant.

>> **Definite decision:** Prefer *decision*. All decisions are definite.

>> **End *result*:** Either word is acceptable individually. Together they're redundant.

>> **Estimated about:** Prefer *estimated*. *Estimated* and *about* are redundant.

>> **Infiltrate into:** Prefer *infiltrate*. *Infiltrate* and *into* are redundant.

>> **Must** necessarily: Either word is acceptable individually. Together they're redundant.

>> **Revert** back: Either word is acceptable individually. Together they're redundant.

>> **Saw** with my own eyes: Prefer *saw*. Together they're redundant.

>> **Two** *twins:* Prefer *twins*. Together they're redundant.

Taking care of fragile qualifiers

Qualifiers or intensifiers add to your writing what an extra pair of shoes adds to your feet — nothing but awkwardness. Overuse of qualifiers weakens arguments and dilutes readers' confidence in your information. Hers's an example:

I am quite sure the best college readers are the best college writers.

Here's a look at that sentence without the qualifiers:

The best college readers are the best college writers.

Qualifiers also increase informality in your academic writing. Refer to this sentence and eliminate the qualifier:

Unnecessary qualifier: I am pretty sure that a bit more reading would help with school stuff.

Revised: Increased reading improves academic performance.

The revised sentence also reduced word count from 14 to 5 words. Readers appreciate more meaning with fewer words.

Here's a list of qualifiers to avoid in your academic writing:

generally	pretty	undoubtedly	extremely	completely
essentially	most likely	especially	definitely	literally
virtually	very	quite	totally	almost
probably	really	rather	amazingly	only
clearly	pretty	fairly	somewhat	slightly

You can also increase writer confidence and clarity by revising negatives to positives such as the following:

Negative: Alexandra was not usually accustomed to reading fewer than three books a month.

Revised positive: Alexandra reads at least three books a month.

Negative: Good writers don't use unnecessary words.

Revised positive: Good writers avoid wordiness.

DIFFERENTIATING BETWEEN EDITING AND REVISING

Avoid equating revising with editing. Editing is like eating pizza. Revising is like immersing yourself in Italian culture. Here's a look at the differences.

Editing	Revising
Correcting paragraphing	Clarifying boundaries of major sections
Correcting punctuation	Replacing inactive verbs and general nouns; eliminating unnecessary words and replacing overused words
Correcting spelling	Choosing words consistent with audience, purpose, and tone
Eliminating an awkward word	Repositioning description near words they're associated with
Replacing *is* with a synonym	Replacing a verb that tells action with a verb that shows action
Enforcing rules	Applying tools

Zooming In: Designing a Doable Revising Plan

College academics for successful students is a timed game, similar to the last two minutes of a college basketball game. You have a finite number of weekly hours to complete your school work and earn your As and Bs. You can't put time back on the clock.

As a freshman you may write B and C essays, and you may adopt a fixed mindset (see Chapter 5) that you don't have the time to write better essays. But you can write better essays within your study hour budget, and here's a three-step plan to do it.

Step 1: Start essays promptly

Beginning essays soon after they're assigned is a time saver and time management skill. The requirements are fresh in your mind, and your subconscious has more time to continue delivering impromptu ideas. An early start also adds flexibility scheduling writing time, revising time, and editing time. Allocate approximately 15 percent of your time for planning, 35 percent for drafting, 40 percent for revising, and 10 percent for editing. Review earlier sections of this chapter for questions to consider revising those elements.

Step 2: Revise in layers

Concentrate initial revising at the structural level, establishing the thesis, audience, purpose, framework, opening, body, and closing. Revising those elements in your first draft provides the foundation for a B or A essay. The grading points are in the specific details.

Step 3: Revise in short sessions

With structure established, begin revising at the sentence and paragraph levels (see the section, "Addressing the Middle: Sentences and Paragraphs." earlier in this chapter). Because this level revising is intense, work in 15-minute increments focusing on two revising elements such as action verbs and specific nouns. Continue revising for argument development, supporting evidence, topic sentences, and documentation. Then revise inactive verbs, general nouns, and wordiness.

After mastering organizational and structural revising, focus revising at the word choice level, eliminating wordiness and improving conciseness.

Chapter **15**

Finalizing for Shipment: Format and Presentation

P arents tell their children not to judge by appearance. Parents are correct about judging people, but incorrect about judging an assignment. In academics, appearance matters. And don't think appearance only matters for hard copy assignments.

For example, imagine your professor receiving an assignment with the filename "assignment." And opening it, grading it, dragging it into a folder, and then searching for the student's assignment. Not the best way to make a memorable impression. This chapter shows you the importance of filenames.

Furthermore, this chapter explains the assignment submission process that includes finalizing titles, formatting pages, and completing the title page. It also details approaches to editing, verifying information, and asking that final question: What's missing? Time for a tour through the packaging department.

REMEMBER

In other words, this chapter focuses on presenting and formatting the essay prior to submission, not content. You can find information on revising content in Chapter 14.

Making Ends Meet: Finalizing Titles, First Sentences, Openings, and Closings

Presentation points are like free cookies — they're available for the taking. But unlike free cookies, not taking the presentation points will cost you more than a quick snack. Deductions for presentation are in the details and require avoiding point losses rather than earning point gains.

Creating a first impression and earning your presentation points begins with the four firsts: first page, first words, first sentence, and first paragraph. Here's a closer look.

Starting on the right foot — The first page

The first page begins your essay's first impression. Here are questions to guide you through your first page presentation:

>> Is the page appearance aesthetically pleasing?

>> Does it pass the eye test of near-perfect appearance?

>> Is the print clear, crisp, and perfectly aligned? Does it lack print head and paper alignment issues?

>> Does the first page include required contact information positioned in the upper left corner?

>> Is the first page formatted with one-inch margins on all four sides?

Standing out — The title

The title (see Chapter 5) is your first eye contact with your reader. Here are questions to guide you through presentation of your title:

>> Is the title positioned about one-third down the page?

>> Is the title written in title case with major words capitalized?

>> Is the title bolded and centered?

Formatting the words — The first sentence and first paragraph

The first sentence and first paragraph (see Chapter 5) are like the first bite into a snack with memory. Here are questions to guide you through presentation of your first sentence and first paragraph:

>> Does the first sentence begin one double line space following the title?

>> Does the first sentence begin with an indentation?

Figure 15-1 shows what a first page should look like.

Cheryl Likens
Writing 101
Essay #2
Professor Daily
July 17, 2023

Driverless Vehicles: Risk or Reality?

    Begin the first paragraph indented here and continue text to the bottom of the page. Format one-inch margins of all four sides. APA requires page numbering on the title page, many professors don't want the first page numbered. Avoid right-side justification.

© *John Wiley & Sons, Inc.*

FIGURE 15-1:
An example of an essay's first page.

Ending the right way: The closing

Your closing (see Chapter 5) is your last opportunity to make a good presentation impression. Formatting at the end of the closing includes a hard–page break following the last line of the closing. The hard–page break forces the bibliography to begin at the top of the next page. Without a hard–page break, your bibliography will begin in the middle of a page, not the look you want to leave your professor with after reading your essay.

Preparing for Grading: Formatting

After navigating the opening formatting of the title page, your essay is ready for cruise control. Keep formatting flowing at a steady pace that doesn't attract attention of your professor. After the title page, flawless formatting is seen and not heard. You want it to remain that way until the final mark of punctuation. These sections delve deeper into the ins and outs of formatting.

Engaging your reader: Page appearance

Following the first page, the body (see Chapter 5) of the essay continues on a new page. APA requires the title repeated at the top of the second page. When most professors begin reading the second page, they're engaged with your content and not repetition of your title.

But if your professor follows a style rigidly, the top of the second page looks like Figure 15-2:

FIGURE 15-2: An example of the top of a second page.

> **Driverless Vehicles: Risk or Reality?**
>
> The text of the essay begins with an indentation on this line and continues to the bottom of this page. Use your imagination for one-inch margins of all four sides of this page.

(c) John Wiley & Sons, Inc.

REMEMBER

Formatting after the title page continues with 12-point Times New Roman font. Double spaced and framed within one-inch margins.

Organizing your essay: Level headings

The organization of some writing projects, usually longer essays and reaction papers (see Chapter 16), require levels of subheadings. Table 15-1 breaks down APA's recommended five-levels of headings.

REMEMBER

Similar to an outline, headings require two or more subheadings. Also, a heading may have no subheadings.

TABLE 15-1   **Formatting Headings**

Heading Level	How to Format
Level 1	**Centered, Bold, Title Case Heading** New paragraphs begin here, indented and double spaced from the heading.
Level 2	**Flush Left, Bold, Title Case Heading** New paragraphs begin here, indented and double spaced from the heading.
Level 3	***Flush Left, Bold Italic, Title Case Heading*** New paragraphs begin here, indented and double spaced from the heading.
Level 4	**Indented, Bold, Title Case, End Punctuation.** Text begins on the same line immediately after the end punctuation and continues to develop the paragraph.
Level 5	***Indented, Bold Italic, Title Case, End Punctuation.*** Text begins on the same line immediately after the end punctuation and continues to develop the paragraph.

Including large bits of info: Lists

Page formatting also includes lists, an organizational strategy for writing large quantities of similar information. Lists may be introduced with bullets, letters, numbers, or steps. I use bulleted lists throughout this book and occasionally numbered lists for steps.

Including optional parts: Front and back materials

College writing projects are addicted to addons. They like the added attention.

Here's a look at optional parts required by some professors (refer to Chapter 12 for more information unless otherwise directed):

>> **Title page:** If not required, consider adding a title page that offers a professional appearance to writing projects.

>> **Abstract or executive summary:** Although not used with essays, abstracts are commonly required with research projects (see Chapter 16), and executive summaries are commonly required with business reports.

>> **Table of contents:** They aren't commonly used with essays, but they add organization and readability to research papers and larger projects.

>> **Reference:** If sources are required, a reference (bibliography or works cited) is required immediately following the last page of text. References are required to follow formatting of the documentation style.

>> **Appendix:** Appendices may be required with any writing project.

Submitting your essay

You completed your writing project, and your grade will be determined by how accurately you complete a seemingly unimportant item — your to-do list that identifies the major requirements listed in the assignment. When you analyze assignments (see Chapter 12), meticulously create your list of requirements to be submitted with your assignment.

REMEMBER

Your to-do list for submission requirements is the control center of your writing project. It controls your grade by identifying what you're required to submit. If you forget to submit a requirement, you fail to earn credit for it. In addition, when professors identify one neglected requirement, they look for more — and usually find them.

Here are examples of requirements that students frequently neglect to fulfill:

>> Reference to one of the required readings

>> Required documentation style

>> Front and back optional parts such as a table of contents, appendix, or glossary

>> An outside-the-classroom requirement such as an observation, visit to a museum, or on-campus lecture attendance

Eagle-Eyeing the Editing

After all is read and done, editing (see Chapters 11 and 14) is never done. Editing, frequently used synonymously with proofreading, is your last interaction with text.

As editor-in-chief, you're the dictator in charge of your page. But you're not a rule maker, you're a rule follower. You're the final person responsible for your editing, which is time to call for back up.

Six eyes are better than four, and four eyes are better than two. Editing requires collecting eyeballs to review your paper. Collaborate with your peers to edit each other's papers. Call on the professionals at the writing center to edit your paper with you. The following sections share some editing strategies and common errors to avoid.

Strategizing editing

Editing is a tedious mechanical skill. It's like checking for loose rivets on a Boeing 737, missing one can cause a crash and burn. The edit you miss may cause a crash of your essay, such as misspelling your professor's name or misspelling a word in the title.

Editing requires more focus than writing because you're looking for specifics such as an error as small as a period or extra space. Because of the concentration required, many writers edit in 20-to 30-minute time frames, and they focus on one or two issues such as punctuation.

Here's a list of editing strategies:

>> **Read text aloud.** Reading text aloud adds the sense of hearing to your editing, in addition to the sense of sight.

>> **Edit backward from end to beginning.** Editing backwards eliminates editing for meaning and focuses exclusively on word editing.

>> **Edit with a ruler.** Editing with a ruler while reading in sequence helps the eye focus exclusively on one line of text.

>> **Edit with a ruler from the end to the beginning.** Editing backward with a ruler eliminates editing for meaning and helps the eye focus exclusively on one line of words.

>> **Track your patterns of editing issues.** Keep a list of patterns of errors for future study — for example listing edits in the categories of possessives, commas, agreement, formatting, and so forth.

>> **Edit with an enlarged font.** Because most people learn spelling by identifying word configurations or shapes (letter ascenders and descenders), an enlarged front helps exaggerate word shapes.

If you enlarge font size for editing, be sure to change back to 12-point Times New Roman before submitting your paper.

Identifying and avoiding common errors

Editing is knowing rules and recognizing when they're violated (see Chapter 11), which is a different skill than knowing when to apply them. Table 15-2 shows categories of common college edits.

TABLE 15-2   ## Common College Essay Edits

Editing Topics	Classification of Edits
Grammar	Agreement, pronoun use, fragments, run-ons, coma splices, and tense consistency
Punctuation	End punctuation, commas, conjunctions, semicolons, colons, titles, dates, numerical references, quotations, parenthesis, brackets, ellipsis, and clauses
Spelling	Proper nouns, titles, headings, plurals, possessives, contractions, hyphenated words, and homonyms
Usage	Commonly confused pairs and trios, such as affect and effect, and there, their, and they're

Editing errors aren't created equal. The most egregious errors I've seen in college papers include misspelling the professor's or student's name, misspelling a word in the title, and an error in the year of the date.

Here are the top five editing errors I have seen on college students' papers.

>> Omitted comma following an introductory clause

>> Omitted comma in a compound sentence

>> Misuse of affect and effect

>> Misuse of "its" and "too"

>> Misuse of "fewer" and "less"

Truth Be Told: Verifying Information

Fact checking is as important to a writer as reliable transportation is to a college student. Without reliable information, your writing will never reach its destination.

Your professor fears fake facts and misinformation, and you should also. You don't get a second chance to make a good first impression, and you don't get a second chance to correct misinformation.

REMEMBER

The academic community lacks tolerance of misinformation. If you submit misinformation on one paper, your professor will question your accuracy on subsequent papers.

Here's a look at categories of information that may need verification of spelling and factual accuracy (see Chapter 11):

>> **Proper nouns:** Names (including titles and prefixes), geographical references, historical events, trade names, source names, and names of racial and ethnic groups

>> **Punctuation:** Major works of art with italics and minor works or art with quotation marks

>> **Mathematical references:** Dates, ages, years, numerical quantities, lifespans, and percentages

>> **Digital references:** URLs, DOIs, and hyperlinks

TECHNICAL STUFF

Fact checking of this book included verifying the following: spelling titles and authors of books referenced, accuracy of words in quotations, spelling and accuracy of names, and accuracy of author references in style models in Chapter 9.

REMEMBER

Bias (see Chapter 10) and hidden agendas remain a challenge for college students to investigate. For example, if a researcher shows unfavorable results toward an organization or industry, students lack resources to investigate if the researcher is motivated financially or politically. As a student, demonstrate reasonable diligence to verify facts. Pursue accuracy of current events similarly. Verifying facts also remains a challenge for professional news agencies today.

Figuring Out What's Missing

Your title page and formatting are completed. You reached your word count, documented your sources, included your reading, checked spelling and punctuation. One question remains — what's missing?

Here's a list of what I frequently see missing:

>> **Submission file format:** Most professors today are requiring assignment submissions electronically, either email or uploaded into a cloud storage box. Verify the file format required for submission, such as Word or a PDF. A PDF is less likely to lose formatting when emailed, compared to Word. Email your assignment to yourself to test file stability. Then email your assignment to your professor as an attachment, and label your file with your last name and a brief name of the assignment.

REMEMBER

You may think your professor is unreasonable about an unidentifiable filename that can be changed in a minute. You're correct, your professor can change your filename in a minute. But if 30 students among a professor's total students require a change in filename, and another 30 require a change in file format, your professor has spent an additional hour grading the essays. And 60 college students learned that they don't need to attend to details because someone will attend to details for them.

REMEMBER

Versions of Word vary. Ask your professors the name of the word processing format they require for assignment submission. Many professors provide assignment feedback with Word Markup, software used to comment on your assignments. Markup is compatible with the Microsoft Office version of Word. Markup isn't compatible with other versions of Word such as Google Word.

>> **Submission address:** Don't assume assignments are required to be emailed to your professor's email address. Many professors prefer not to overload their office email with 60 or 80 assignments, and require assignment submission to an alternate email, a course management email, or a cloud email. Read your syllabus first before asking your professor.

>> **Annotated reference page:** When annotated reference pages (see Chapter 7) are required, students frequently omit the annotation. The omission is unintentional because summaries and purposes of sources are required during the research process.

>> **Titles:** An essay or writing project without a title (see Chapter 5) is like opening a blank menu at a restaurant. Professors have no idea with they're getting.

Also consider the following as likely to be missing from submitting:

>> An inconspicuous requirement such as referencing a class lecture or course reading

>> Omission of an optional section such as table of contents or appendix

>> An out-of-class requirement such as an observation or survey

Looking Forward: Literacy Improvement Plan

If your writing grade has remained stagnant between a C and B, it's time to call in the heavyweights — the books, the ones produced with the hard covers because they were expected to survive chronic book abuse.

The plans that follow offer immediate improvement for your reading and writing. The plan required the same commitment and determination you demonstrated to buy and read this book.

Improving your reading

You're familiar with the reading-writing connection (see Chapter 2) and its two-for-one properties. When you practice one, you develop the other.

It's college decision time for your literacy. How determined are you to discover how good a student you can be? If you're motivated by educating yourself, your path is through turning pages. If you're motivated by lifestyle, Cs get degrees, but As get the dollars.

Here's a reading improvement plan:

>> **Set an annual book goal.** Set a goal to read a number of books beyond what's required. Decide on a goal to read books that exceed your required books. These books represent your personal reading improvement books. Not having time isn't an excuse. People make time for activities they want to do. Make time around your academic requirements. Everyone has mindless activities that can add hours to their reading budget. Read a respectable number of books for a college student. If your number is fewer than five, it speaks volumes, the volumes you should be reading.

REMEMBER

Remember that people who carry goal cards (or goal photos) reach their goals at a rate of 90 percent. In addition to the goal card of your graduation date, carry a goal of the number of books you're challenging yourself to read annually.

>> **Set a quality-control goal:** Read at least two classics by authors you read in high school or college. Read at least one book on a bestseller list.

>> **Establish an annual leisure reading goal.** Read one or two books on a topic of your choice.

>> **Analyze your reading.** Read your classics and bestseller for a sense of style, sentence structure, and storytelling. Observe sentence variety, direction of branching sentences, and nouns and verbs (see Chapters 9 and 11). Compare styles. Compare your writing with their style. What did you learn about yourself as a writer?

TECHNICAL STUFF

Here's a little research project. Go to your friends who are all about the As. Ask them how many books they read annually, in addition to books they read for courses.

Improving your writing

Adopt the mindset that writing — like thinking, problem solving, and many other successes in life — requires concentration and effort to develop proficiency. Writing is also a teachable and learnable skill at which millions of college graduates have succeeded and millions more who will graduate in the future will also succeed. You're not training to make an Olympic team, you're training to write an essay that earns a respectable grade in your Writing 101 course.

I'm offering you a back-to-basics, evidence-based writing improvement plan that has been successful for millions who celebrated their degrees. Here's a look:

>> **Read books.** Make book reading part of your academic and personal life. Begin with ten minutes of book reading a day.

>> **Write regularly.** Write in conjunction with your studying. Summarize class notes. Create lists of information for tests.

>> **Read for assignment background.** Read background material (see Chapter 12) on assignments you're required to write.

>> **Practice thesis writing.** Develop proficiency writing the most important sentence of academic writers, the thesis statement (see Chapter 5).

>> **Schedule writing.** Plan a writing schedule (see Chapter 12) for your assignments.

>> **Organize ideas.** Organize your ideas into the opening, body, and closing of your writing (see Chapter 5). Organize the evidence in the body paragraphs (see Chapter 7).

>> **Practice writing topic sentences.** The second most important sentences you write are topic sentences (see Chapter 8). Read them, practice them, revise them, and rewrite them.

>> **Follow the writing process.** The writing process (refer to the nearby sidebar) isn't for dummies, it's for nerds who want to write A essays and other successful college writing projects.

>> **Revise.** Professional writers, Ernest Hemingway and his friends, profess that the most important writing process is revising (see Chapter 14).

>> **Write specifics.** Write with detail, including anecdotes (see Chapter 5) and action verbs and specific nouns (see Chapter 9).

THE WRITING PROCESS PRODUCES RESULTS

Many college students neglect following the writing process because they think it requires more time than writing by inspiration. The evidence-based writing process saves you time because it generates content moving you from idea generation through revised final product. It eliminates waiting for inspiration and provides systematic recurring stages to move you from brainstorming to final revised product.

The writing process eliminates the need for inspiration because it provides strategies for creating inspiration, such as brainstorming. Here's a quick overview of the writing processes, which I detail throughout the book:

- **Pre-writing:** Pre-writing or brainstorming generates ideas and your previous knowledge of your topic (see Chapter 12). Freewriting shows you what you didn't know you knew. It includes background reading and organizing information.

- **Drafting:** Writing a first draft isn't such a challenge when you have information to write about.

- **Revising:** Chapter 14 identifies legendary writers who believe that revising is more important than writing. Revising continues throughout the other processes.

- **Presentation:** This chapter explains how to prepare your assignment for submission.

If you're a believer in the writing process, continue using the processes and refine your strategies for prewriting and revising. If you're not committed to the writing process, and you're not earning B and better writing grades, you're not focusing on what you can do to help yourself.

» Connecting across courses

» Building with the essay

» Reading, writing, and reacting

Chapter 16

Reaching Out: Writing across Courses

You have an essay due Tuesday, a math test Wednesday, a hundred pages to read for economics Thursday, a presentation in philosophy Friday — and you were just assigned a reaction paper in psychology for Monday. Sound familiar? Welcome to the world of higher education where assignments pile higher and higher.

But you planned (take a look at Chapter 12) for the overload and you're helping yourself with learning the multiplication theory of knowledge, what you learn in one course applies to other courses.

This chapter explains writing papers for other courses: essays, reaction papers, reports, and research papers. It also introduces you to the dreaded "review." Time to boot up.

Talking Discourse: Content Communities

Here's a simplification to make yourself smarter. It's a three-step *For Dummies* version:

1. **Input information.**

2. **Process information.**

   This "get smarter" step is to create insights from reading that results in outputs for writing.

3. **Output information.**

The major you're studying isn't an isolated subject. It's part of a community of other disciplines, opportunities to connect your major with related topics. For example, if you're majoring in business, marketing is closely related to your field and a closely related source of similar knowledge. Knowledge in one area is multiplied by knowledge in a related area.

The two areas of study that follow, the humanities and social and behavioral sciences, exemplify opportunities for multiplication of information. They represent opportunities to connect your writing to similar fields and create new insights for your reader.

Some courses are listed as both humanities and social and behavioral sciences. The designation depends on the teaching approach — from a cultural perspective (humanities) or from a behavioral perspective (social and behavioral sciences).

Humanities

If you're interested in what makes you who you are, the humanities are for you. Humanities is the story of the human race and what makes human beings human. They teach us who we were, who we are, and who we will be. Humanities are the foundation of a purposeful life.

The importance of humanities includes the following:

>> Encourages critical and analytical thinking

>> Introduces new insights in areas such as the arts, politics, communication, and ancient civilization

>> Helps understanding others through their culture, customs, traditions, and language

>> Encourages ethical thinking

>> Increases cultural and social sensitivity

Knowledge of the humanities adds human experiences to your thinking and writing. They are the stories of imagination and inspiration. The humanities are the common denominator among writing audiences.

Courses related to the humanities include the following:

>> Ancient languages

>> Archaeology

>> Art appreciation

>> Communications

>> Digital communications

>> Gender studies

>> History

>> Journalism

>> Literature

>> Media studies

>> Modern languages

>> Music history

>> Philosophy

>> Political science

>> Religion

Essay topics in the humanities include the following:

>> What makes life meaningful?

>> What do ethics add to life?

>> What are the most fragile qualities of being human?

Social and behavioral sciences

If you're a people watcher, you may find a home in the social and behavioral sciences. These fields examine how people behave and react. They study the activities and interactions of people. They include a broad understanding of human behavior and studies behaviors of groups and individuals.

Social and behavioral sciences include the following:

» Anthropology

» Archaeology

» Criminology

» Economics

» Education

» History

» Law

» Linguistics

» Performing arts

» Political science

» Psychology

» Sociology

Knowledge of social and behavioral sciences adds human behavior experiences to our thinking and writing. It helps writers create human characters.

Essay topics in the social and behavioral sciences include the following:

» Identify the role of performing arts in education.

» Argue the economics of a college education.

» What motivates employees in the workplace?

Exploring Genre: Writing in the Disciplines

Essays are like pizza dough. Regardless of how you reshape it, stretch it, or reorganize it, it always maintains its original cohesive structure. Your original structure for almost all your college writing projects is the essay.

But as you're discovering, your writing requirements are stretched into writing for other courses. You're writing essays for courses such as economics, philosophy, and psychology. You're also writing reaction papers and reports for those same courses. You're stretched.

These sections explain language distinctive to various courses and writing assignments that are extensions of your comp essays, such as content-specific essays, reaction papers, reports, literature reviews, and research papers.

Recognizing content conventions

The type of writing you complete for each course is distinctive to each course. Your professor may explain this by saying writing is discipline specific, meaning that each subject area contains its distinctive writing features. Those differences are called *conventions*.

Writing without discipline-specific conventions is like dressing formally to participate in a recreational activity. You captured the look, but you prepared for a different audience and purpose.

One writing convention common to all disciplines is language.

REMEMBER

Language has multiple meanings. In addition to a general meaning, it has a specific content meaning. For example, the word "medium" has a general meaning and also meaning in art and math. Language has meaning specific to its content use. Table 16-1 shows language common to different subjects.

TABLE 16-1 **Language Specific to Different Subjects**

Art	Business	Literature	Psychology	Science
composition	earnings	figures of speech	case study	genetics
form	executive summary	foreshadowing	clinical	molecule
medium	marketing	literary analysis	double-blind study	particle
still life	portfolio	point of view	phobia	periodic chart
texture	supply chain	plot	trials	scientific method

TIP

Your professor may use these terms:

>> **Writing across the curriculum (WAC):** WAC refers to assignments in your courses.

>> **Writing in the disciplines (WID):** WID refers to the conventions of writing in different subjects.

You may also see the abbreviation *writing intensive (WI)*, a common abbreviation used to identify writing intensive courses that are frequently required for graduation.

Table 16-2 shows examples of content conventions common to various disciplines.

TABLE 16-2 **Common Content Conventions**

Discipline	Writing Conventions
Art	Elevation drawing, 3D, accelerated perspective
Computer science	Names of computer languages, specific hardware and software, technology terminology
Economics	Financial data, government reports, economic indicators
Math	Proofs and explanations, equations, symbols
Psychology	Case studies, clinical trials, research studies
Science	Lab reports, experimentation results, tables and charts

Writing conventions common to all disciplines include ethical responsibility (look at Chapter 13), credible sources (flip to Chapter 7), critical analysis (check out Chapter 5), sound argumentation (see Chapter 7), and respectful language (refer to Chapter 10).

Extending the comp essay

Many college students become proficient playing a musical instrument and developing knowledge of reading music and understanding melody. Writing for your 101 course is like playing one musical instrument. Writing for your other courses is like playing in multiple sections of the philharmonic.

Advantages of writing in your other courses includes the following:

>> Helps learn new language and content

>> Analyzes and synthesizes information

>> Identifies common elements among courses

Molding essay parts

Your Writing 101 essay is like the starter dough of all your college writing projects, including the essays you write in other courses. The starter elements common to almost all writing projects include the following:

>> Organization of an opening, body, and closing (see Chapter 5)

>> Frameworks such as narrative, persuasive, cause and effect, and so forth (refer to Chapter 5)

>> A thesis-controlling statement that forecasts development of the writing (check out Chapter 6)

>> Evidence that supports the thesis (flip to Chapter 7)

>> Elements of style that create reader interest (head to Chapter 9)

>> Language that addresses an audience and identifies a specific purpose (see Chapter 6)

>> Analysis (see Chapter 5) and synthesis of information (go to Chapter 7)

Basic essay elements common to all essays include topic sentences, coherence, and transitions (refer to Chapter 8).

Writing essays in your other courses

Professors who assign writing in non-English courses frequently use the expression, "Content is king." The expression translates into writing in content courses must be content driven. For example, psychology professors accept responsibility to teach you psychology, which supersedes learning about writing, reading, and researching.

TIP

When you're assigned an essay outside your 101 course, focus on evidence that shows you understand course content. Table 16-3 lists essays topics common to courses frequently required by first-year college students:

REMEMBER

These topics aren't thesis statements (see Chapter 6) and lack an argument.

TABLE 16-3   Common Essay Topics for First-Year Courses

Course	Topics
Computer science	The relationship between computer science and educational opportunity
	The role of government regulation and the Internet.
	Ethical responsibility and data mining
Economics	The most important principle of economics
	Ethical responsibilities of one-percent earners
	The ideal unemployment rate
Philosophy	The relationship between thoughts and language
	The role of ethics in higher education
	Humans rights and animal rights
Psychology	Howard Gardner's theory of multiple intelligences
	The psychology of money across four age generations
	Gender roles and family structure

Identifying the Other Types of Papers You May Write in College

Your course professors may require you to write different types of papers besides the kind of essay you write in Writing 101. These sections focus on those types and offer some pointers to help you get started.

Reacting to something: Reaction papers

Reaction papers are the younger siblings of essays. They admire the organization and stature of the essay, but reaction papers know they'll never have the status of their own course like their older sibling.

REMEMBER

From your perspective, reaction papers are easier to write than essays because they don't require researched evidence to support an argument. The argument in a reaction paper is more condensed than the argument in an essay.

Why so many reaction papers? Professors love them. Here's why:

>> They can be assigned in a few words, "Read . . . and react to it, for Monday."

>> They apply to a wide variety of genres beyond reacting to text: audio and video clips, podcasts, movies, live performances, lectures, class discussions, student presentations, television shows, artifacts, and more.

>> They apply to any course and any topic.

>> They generate class discussion centered on student perspectives.

>> They require critical reading and analytical writing.

If you can write a B essay in your first-year writing course, you can write an A reaction paper. Also, reaction papers are graded by professors who grade less on writing skills and more on course content. Writing reaction papers demonstrates your proficiencies in your two most important academic skills, reading and writing.

Guidelines for writing reaction papers include the following two-part process:

Part 1: Focusing on the source

Provide the following information about the source:

>> Begin with an engaging title, first sentence, and opening.

>> Reference the source's author, title, date, and publication source.

>> Identify the importance of the source.

>> Write a brief summary of the highlights of the source.

Part 2: React

React to the source addressing the following:

>> Form a position on the source such as agreeing, disagreeing, questioning, qualifying, or associating.

Outlier positions earn more points than traditional positions (flip to Chapter 12).

>> Support your reaction with partial quotes from the source (look to Chapter 7).

>> Regularly use the phrases "such as" and "for example."

>> Connect reactions to additional content, especially content related to the course the paper is assigned in and other courses you're enrolled in.

>> End with a "so what" and broader application of the position (see Chapter 5).

REMEMBER

Apply the following writing guidelines specific to writing reaction papers:

>> Seamlessly combine the third person and the first person. Prefer the third person in Part 1 and the first person in Part 2 (look at Chapter 6).

>> Summarize in Part 1 and analyze (refer to Chapter 5) and synthesize (see Chapter 7) in Part 2.

>> Reference an outside source in Part 2 to exceed your professor's expectations.

>> Prioritize reactions you chose to respond to, but don't exceed more than two.

Focusing on information: Reports

Reports have been part of your life since your first report card in first grade, and they'll continue throughout your academic life. Your most recent report was your last grade transcript. Your essay-writing life ends when you graduate; your report-writing life may continue throughout your career.

You have more experience as a reader of reports than as a writer. You've been reading reports such as academic reports, performance reports, financial reports, health reports, dental reports, vehicle reports, and hopefully not too many accident reports.

The common denominator in reports is that they're focused on information that usually results in a decision. The purpose of reports is to answer questions. Table 16-4 shows questions that determine the type of reports.

TABLE 16-4   **Question and Report Type**

Question Report Answers	Type of Report
How am I doing in school?	Academic report
What's the condition of our building?	Architectural report
Can I afford new housing?	Credit report
How are my teeth?	Dental report
How am I doing at work?	Employee evaluation report
How am I budgeting my resources?	Financial report
How are company's sales?	Sales report

Here's a look at questions to ask before writing a report:

>> Who's the audience? Is it internal or external? Who will read it up the organizational ladder (check out Chapter 6)?

>> What's its purpose (go to Chapter 6)?

>> What's the structural organization (see Chapter 5)?

>> Will it include optional parts such as tables, figures, graphs, and an appendix (explained in Chapter 12)?

>> Does it include a recommendation?

>> How will it be formatted (as shown in Chapter 15)?

>> What documentation style is required (look at Chapter 7)?

Evaluating research: Literature reviews

You haven't experienced college academics until you've been assigned what is pretentiously know as "the review." But it's much more challenging than a review because it isn't a review; it's a synthesis (see Chapter 7).

Not to worry. As an undergraduate, you're assigned the "light version" of a review. When you're a graduate student, you'll be assigned a full semester's requirement to research a topic in your field, analyze it, synthesize it, and write a document with a beginning, middle, and ending — with an essay on your research sandwiched in.

REMEMBER

But your undergraduate degree first. Literature reviews, minus the major document, are frequently assigned as a stand-alone review on a topic in your field. The purpose is to analyze current research and demonstrate your knowledge of issues related to your topic. It's an informative assignment and may include analysis of career opportunities in your field. Reviews satisfy an academic curiosity.

Here's a four-step process for writing a stand-alone review of literature:

Step 1: Search a topic

Select a topic, create keyword terms, and search for studies, especially those identified as landmark, pivotal, or seminal. Those terms represent hall of fame studies. Identify 15 to 18 studies.

Step 2: Read and analyze the literature

Read each piece of literature and identify specifics such as the following (Chapter 7 can help):

>> Credibility of the author and source

>> Major argument and supporting evidence

>> Key concepts of the argument

>> Strengths and limitations of the study

Step 3: Identify patterns in the argument

From all sources, identify patterns in the argument such as the following:

>> How each researcher's position aligns with other researchers

>> Each researcher's contribution to the topic

>> Recurring themes

>> Outlier themes

>> Significantly omitted themes

>> Contradictory themes

Step 4: Write the review

Review the research and write your review addressing the following:

>> Analysis of the topic and its importance (refer to Chapter 5)

>> Limitations of the topic

>> Highlights of findings

>> Analysis and synthesis the findings

Writing more in-depth: Research papers

If an essay is a road trip, a research paper is two weeks at an all-inclusive — in the tropics, with two dozen close friends, eligible for course credit, paid by an anonymous benefactor.

Back to reality, each essay you write provides experiences for writing a research paper. Transferable skills include analyzing the assignment, researching, focusing a topic, supporting a thesis, drafting and documenting, revising and rewriting, and preparing for presentation.

The number of research papers you write is determined by your field of study. You'll write more for majors in the humanities and social sciences and fewer in fields such as math, science, and engineering.

Here's a five-step process for writing research papers that your professor will reward you for.

Step 1: Analyze

Analyze the assignment and meet with your professor if you have questions. Choose a topic that addresses the assignment, and complete a writing schedule that includes revising and editing. Identify the documentation style. Perform background reading to familiarize yourself with the topic (refer to Chapter 12).

Step 2: Research

Research and evaluate sources (see Chapter 7). A reference librarian can save you time. Evaluate sources for credibility and create a bibliography as you identify sources.

Step 3: Organize

Organize research into an outline that includes an opening, body, and closing (as in Chapter 5). Create an outline for the body that includes evidence that argues the thesis.

Step 4: Write

Write a draft from the outline, with the goal of completing the draft (see Chapter 12). Complete documentation as you write. Strategically position summary, paraphrase, and quotations (refer to Chapter 7). Give the draft a rest, and then revise (check out Chapter 14).

Step 5: Present

After the final edit, prepare your paper for presentation (see Chapter 15).

Finding Advantages: Content Resources

You've grown up with information on demand, and it became easier with the births of Siri and Alexa when information became available for the asking. For example, you can ask for topic ideas for your next philosophy essay, and you can ask her for college resources to help you write. If you ask if they're having a good day, they'll tell you everything is copasetic.

But they have limits and they're unaware of information that immediately surrounds you. This section reminds you of information for your writing that's closer than a click, information that will help you connect sources of information and add insight to your writing.

Identifying course content resources

Your largest source of information to input into your writing is your course work. It's a steady flow of new ideas that's in your head every day, and if you process that information, you can establish connections between course information and your writing topics. Your content resources include the following:

>> Assignments

>> Class discussions

>> Course management platform

>> Course-related databases

>> Library

>> Peers

>> Professor

>> Readings

Examples of specifics available in course content resources include the following:

>> Links to your college library's databases and reference librarian

>> Links to full academic resources in all disciplines of your university

>> Links to academic citation styles

>> Department and university core values for writing

>> Professor availability to answer questions

Relying on mass media resources

Mass media resources are massive. Media includes outlets such as websites, podcasts, TED Talks, YouTube channels, Twitter, and college online resources. Content includes famous speeches, historical documents, and artifacts. It's an ocean full of information and an asset to your writing — your challenge is to connect the drops.

Examples of specific pieces of information available from mass media include the following:

>> Highlights of almost any book

>> Tour of museums such as the Hermitage or Louvre

>> Inauguration speeches by U.S. Presidents

>> Background on almost any topic on Wikipedia

Making connections with content

Course connections are the brain-processing step where you create new insights from stagnant information. (Refer to the section, "Talking Discourse: Content Communities," earlier in this chapter where I discuss the three-step process that makes you smarter.) For example, you apply philosophical questions to an economics assignment like, Are approvals of student loans an ethical practice?

Here are sample questions to ask to build connections between writing topics and course content (your answers develop insights):

>> How is the structure of a piece of writing similar to the structure of a democratic government?

>> What is similar about the innovations of Leonardo da Vinci and Steve Jobs?

>> What book have you read recently that offers insight into a burning life question?

>> Do the disadvantages of computer-dependent societies outweigh the advantages?

>> What are similarities between musical composition and blood flow?

>> What are similarities between philosophy and psychology?

Looking at current events

Current events are another unlimited and ever-changing source of information to connect with your writing. Today's current events are tomorrow's history.

The importance of current events includes the following:

>> Tells what's new in your field of study

>> Tells new events in parts of the world you can't spell

>> Creates additional interest in reading

>> Provides unlimited resources for adding connections to your writing

Resources for accessing what's happening daily include asking Siri and Alexa and subscribing to podcasts, You Tube channels, and newsfeeds.

Seeing Is Believing: Model Excerpts

Mastering how to write in content areas also includes reading in those areas. The following examples show models of writing in content areas common to first-year college students.

Psychology

A major purpose for writing in psychology is writing to communicate information about a psychological study, theory, or a topic. A challenge of writing in psychology is simplifying terminology for non-psychology audiences.

Here's an example of writing in psychology:

> Recent reports in educational psychology show that the physical structure of the classroom contributes "a calming effect" on behavior of students with emotional disabilities. Dorchester's "Causes of calmness" identifies the following conditions that contribute to soothing students: comfortable soft chairs in place of hard-plastic desks, wall decorations with student photographs, light pastel colors, and low volume speakers. The lack of a clock was also recommended.

Finance

The purpose of writing college finance includes communicating information and supporting information about finances.

Here's an example of writing in finance:

> Birtwell's "Learning Financial Literacy" showed that children's experiencing handling money contributes to the practice of sound financial literacy as adults. She described the correlation between organizing a lemonade stand as a child and financial literacy as an adult. The study showed that childhood experiences that contribute to financial literacy included payment for chores that exceeded contribution to the household, saving money, keeping a financial diary, and talking with adults about money.

The arts

Writing in the arts serves multiple purposes, the most common being interpretation and analysis of works of art. Another common approach to writing in the arts is comparison and contrast.

Here's an example of writing in the arts:

> The focal point of the painting is lady in the red coat with the white umbrella. She is walking down a tree-lined wet sidewalk followed by a handful of adults and children. The tilt in her umbrella is balanced by a cream handbag on the arm opposite the umbrella tilt. The square painting is also balanced with a tiny red shop against a dark cloud backdrop. The painting is a formal depiction of people walking in the rain.

Political science

Political science answers the how and why question, such as: How does a two-party system contribute to the principles of a democratic society? Political science integrates related disciplines such as economics, law, history, criminology, and sociology.

Here's an example of writing in political science:

> The term system of the U.S. President and Congress results in annual inefficiencies such as full-term campaigning, focusing on special interest needs to secure political support, and using resources that distract from serving constitutes. A change from the traditional election cycle includes one six-year term for the President and Congress. The major advantage of the change is the near-elimination of re-campaign financing, allowing more focus on serving constituents.

5

The Part of Tens

IN THIS PART . . .

Examine readily available resources to help improve your writing.

Discover ten advantages for nonnative English-speaking writers.

Chapter 17

Ten (or So) Resources for Improving College Writing

Writing projects are like problems waiting to be resolved, and frequently solving the problem requires finding the appropriate resource. The resources to solve problems are as close as your phone, and as far away as a walk to your professor's office. These resources may not be as popular as a lifetime meal plan at your favorite pizza shop, but you'll be well fed with writing knowledge.

In this chapter I familiarize you with resources available on most campuses, resources that require your initiative, resources available online, and resources as old as the printing press — hard copy books.

Use Office Hours

Professors dedicate a few hours weekly for students to stop in at their convenience and ask questions or review assignments. Surprisingly, very few students take advantage of meeting one-on-one with their professor, the person most knowledgeable about how to improve your writing and person who awards your grade. Professor time during office house is similar to a class size of one. You have the highest GPA in the class.

TIP

Prepare for your office hours visit by reviewing your writing and creating questions you want answered, such as the following:

>> Does the thesis address the question in the assignment?

>> Does the evidence support the argument?

>> Is documentation accurate?

>> Do any paragraphs drift from the thesis?

A specific question is a starting point for discussing your writing, rather than walking in and saying, "Can you take a look at this, please?" Have a hard copy of your writing, far more professor-friendly than displaying your essay on your laptop. Don't consider asking your professor to read your essay on your phone. Take notes while your professor talks about your essay, and refresh your notes as soon as you leave the office.

REMEMBER

Office hours are the best educational value you can receive for your tuition dollars. Send your professor a follow up thank-you email and return as often as needed.

Maximize Accessible Campus Resources

Other campus resources are more readily available and similarly compliment your classroom instruction. Here's a look at readily accessible resources:

>> **Writing center:** Your campus writing center offers trained tutors to help you with any writing issue. Hours are usually eight to ten hours daily, and many offer anytime online feedback. Person-to-person help is more effective than online help. You can maximize your session by bringing your assignment sheet, a draft of your writing assignment, and a list of your questions. Ask your questions from the top down — from the structural level to the word level. Take notes during the session.

>> **Tutoring:** Most campuses offer tutoring programs that usually include students and teaching assistants trained to help you. Some students schedule a writing tutor at the beginning of the semester, knowing that a tutor is a time-saver and source of writing feedback. Similar to writing center sessions, person-to-person sessions are more effective than online sessions. Prepare for tutoring sessions similar to preparing for writing center sessions.

>> **Academic support center:** Most campuses offer an academic support center to help you with general academic support such as time management, note taking, study skills, reading, and writing.

>> **Technology center:** Your academic life depends on a healthy technology life. Most campuses offer technology support that includes help with passwords, connectivity, database access, online course access, and much more. Many centers also repair your personal computer or tablet that you use for school. Many centers also offer weekly technology training sessions. These services are available as part of your tuition.

Maximize Other Campus Resources

Your campus is a tower of knowledge. Additional resources are available to help you with your writing, but you need to seek them out. They include the following:

>> **Other professors:** Think of your school's faculty as the brain center of your university. Most professors will enthusiastically offer you scheduled time to share expertise with you that may apply to your essay.

>> **Librarians:** When your assignment says research, think reference librarian. They not only save you research time, but they also can frequently anticipate your questions because they've helped other students with similar needs. Librarians' expertise includes knowledge with your on-campus databases and the skills to navigate them.

>> **Course websites:** Explore course websites to identify available resources, frequently related to assignments. In addition to the expected syllabus, assignments, and weekly class schedule, look for riches such as handouts, models of previous student assignments, links to supplementary resources, and recommended readings.

>> **Department online resources:** Many departments offer you resources to help with specific department courses, especially writing-related courses. A team of professors who teach those courses, possibly including your professor, frequently provide these materials. You may also find department policies and core values that apply to your writing projects.

Form Study Teams

Any four of you are smarter than any one of you. If you follow the math and form small study teams, you'll experience the benefit of multi-expertise and feedback on your writing. The benefits of small writing teams include

>> Clarifying concerns about the course and assignments

>> Hearing explanations in the language of your peers

>> Observing a variety of approaches to assignments

>> Offering and receiving feedback

The two major advantages of small study teams are accountability to your peers and academic socialization from your peers.

TIP

Form small teams by asking peers in your class if they're interested in meeting for an hour twice a month. Agree on a time and location. Colleges usually provide a number of locations where small groups can go to study. A leader will emerge, you, who accepts responsibility for logistics and establishing a meeting agenda. Have team members submit questions that are answered during the meeting. Sample questions include the following:

>> How are you approaching the assignment?

>> What was the most difficult part of the assignment?

Study Writing Reference Books

To improve your writing skills, go to the experts, the expert authors who write the best-selling reference books that are consumed daily by ambitious writers of all levels. Here's a list of popular books consumed by writers:

>> *The Elements of Style* by William Strunk and E.B. White (Harcourt, Brace & Howe)

>> *They Say I Say: The Moves That Matter in Academic Writing* by Gerald Graff and Cathy Birkenstein (W.W. Norton)

>> *The Art of Nonfiction* by Ayn Rand (Plume)

>> *The Glamour of Grammar* by Roy Peter Clark (Little, Brown)

- *On Writing Well* by William Zinsser (Harper Collins)
- *English Grammar For Dummies* by Geraldine Woods (John Wiley & Sons, Inc.)
- *A Dictionary of Modern English Usage* by H.W. Fowler (Oxford University Press)
- *Semicolon* by Cecelia Watson (Harper Collins)

Practice Exclusive Revising

Writers learn more about writing when they revise than when they write (see Chapter 14). An advantage of revising writing other than your own is that you see other writers' attempts to clarify information. The advantage of revising a peer's essay is that you're familiar with organization, structure, and development (see Chapter 5). You're surrounded with materials for revising: your past essays, friends' essays, and online essays.

Revise from printed copies, more brain-friendly than electronic copies. Practice different levels of revising on different essays; focus on isolated revising strategies such as the title and first sentence, sentences for middle paragraphs, the last sentence, evidence paragraphs, action verbs and specific nouns, and eliminating unnecessary words, source references, and transitions.

Use Online College Resources

Online writing centers and labs have developed into powerhouses of resources for college writers. In recent years, their specialized information has become public for the world to share — at no tuition cost. The similarities of resources show commonalities of writing resources valued in higher education. Here's a list of online college resources representative of the best available:

- **Harvard University Writing Center:** The oldest university in the United States (1636), Harvard University houses one of the best college websites for helping students with their writing. An extension of the Harvard University Writing Program, the online writing center offers resources for helping college students with essays and other college writing projects.

- **Yale University Writing Center:** I can't say Harvard without saying Yale — but students of those academic powers can. Yale online writing offers annotated handouts for your essay and college writing needs.

- **Purdue OWL (Online Writing Lab):** A power among online writing resources, Purdue is a go-to resource for many high school and college students. If the topic is connected to writing, Purdue has a handout, as well as resources for your documenting and formatting questions (APA, MLA, or Chicago/Turabian).

- **The Writing Center, University of North Carolina:** The UNC Writing Center provides well-designed handouts for your research and essay writing as well as handouts for writing in disciplines such as art history, business, communication studies, political science, and sociology.

- **The Excelsior College OWL:** This OWL specializes in online videos to help you with your essay and other college writing needs.

- **Writing@CSU (Colorado State University):** The CSU Writing Center specializes in writing guides for essays and other college writing projects. They also provide resources for writing faculty.

Create a Writing Improvement Plan

As a college student, writing is central to your academic success. Your academic achievements to date correlate with your writing success. Take a step back, assess the state of your writing, and list your goals for improvement. Use topics listed in the index of this book as your guide.

TIP

Create a personal writing plan that identifies your writing strengths, evaluates your liabilities, and lists your goals for improvement. Identify your strengths from positive feedback on past assignments and skills. Don't underestimate skills that flow intuitively such as planning, focusing on nouns, verbs, sentence structure, sentence variation, commas, end punctuation, paragraph structure, organization, and spelling, and editing (see Chapter 11). And read more books.

Listing liabilities may include college level skills you've recently been introduced to and that need practice such as synthesizing (see Chapter 7), engaging sources (Chapter 7), closings (see Chapter 5), documenting (see Chapter 7), and connecting evidence to thesis (see Chapter 7). You'll practice these skills throughout your college writing.

Formulate your goals from skills that develop writing style (see Chapter 9), such as word and sentence rhythm and figures of speech. Your writing goals may include exploring writing resources listed in the chapter.

Practice Reading and Writing Skills

If you want to learn to play the guitar, practice playing the guitar. If you want to develop your reading and writing skills, increase your daily literacy requirement. You can accomplish anything you make a commitment to, including increasing your reading and writing skills — and improving your GPA.

Your study schedule most likely maximizes your available hours for reading and writing, but you can increase the efficiency of those hours by improving literacy strategies. Here are examples:

>> Determine whether the thesis addresses the question in the assignment (see Chapter 12).

>> Read with a purpose identified at the beginning of your reading session.

>> After completing a section of reading, summarize it with one sentence.

>> Connect your reading ideas with similar ideas in your writing and course discussions.

>> Reference your academic reading in your academic writing.

>> Reference your reading and writing topics in your classroom discussions.

>> Read as a writer evaluating reader elements such as organization (see Chapter 5).

Chapter **18**

Ten Tips for Nonnative English-Speaking College Writers

f you're a nonnative English–speaking college writer, you know the challenge of learning a new language and culture that encapsulates it. You also recognize the importance of practice to improve skills. The challenge includes deciphering illogical nuances such as idioms. Aren't you just tickled pink?

These ten practice tips can yield quick improvements in your writing. They're practices designed to help you with your college writing projects, especially your essays.

Read and Read Some More

Reading is the second most challenging literacy skill required for learning English as an additional language. Writing is the most challenging. Reading and writing are complementary skills; when you practice one, you also develop the other.

TIP

Practice your reading by studying essays. Gather a dozen essays from students in your classes by printing copies, which are more brain-friendly than electronic copies, and read through each essay as you would normally read. Then read each one aloud and record yourself on your phone. The recording helps you hear the words pronounced, similar to how you hear them in your inner ear when you read silently.

As you read, identify the elements that follow by highlighting and annotating them (see Chapter 12). Record one observation for each, such as how you address those elements in your own essays. Read from the point of view of a writer studying how to write an essay:

>> **Structure:** Three major essay sections: opening, body, and closing (see Chapter 5)

>> **Thesis:** The sentence that identifies the argument and purpose of the essay, usually found in the opening paragraph (see Chapter 6)

>> **Evidence:** Three or four reasons that support the thesis (see Chapter 7)

>> **Topic sentences:** The first sentence in the body paragraphs that introduce evidence (see Chapter 5)

>> **Framework:** Organization such as persuasive, cause and effect, and compare and contrast (see Chapter 5)

Practice Writing

Practice writing essay elements similar to the approach to practicing reading and practicing thesis statements. Use the essay models to create sentences for each of the following:

>> Sentences that identify the essay purpose (see Chapter 6)

>> Sentences that identify language specific to the essay audience (see Chapter 6)

>> Sentences that reference sources introducing each study (see Chapter 5)

>> Sentences that give background information on the topic, usually located in the second paragraph in the essay (see Chapter 12)

>> Sentences that open and close essays (see Chapter 5)

Look for sentences that connect each piece of evidence to the thesis, usually located near the end of body paragraphs. Practice writing similar evidence–thesis connecting sentences. Write sentences that identify one strength and weakness of each essay. Doing so helps you evaluate essays. Record each sentence and listen to its sound.

You can additionally practice writing to learn information by writing sentences summarizing class notes from your courses and preparing for tests.

Write Nouns and Verbs

Focus your writing using the two most important parts of speech in English: nouns and verbs (see Chapter 9). Nouns name people, places, objects, and ideas. Verbs are action words in sentences.

Try the following strategies for improving nouns and verbs:

>> Before beginning a piece of writing, list nouns and verbs you expect to appear in the writing. For example, if you're writing on a college topic, anticipate verbs such as *register, enroll, socialize, study, research, attend, read,* and *write.* Anticipate nouns such as *library, computer lab, writing center, recreation center,* and *business office.*

>> From the essays you gather, circle nouns and underline verbs. Also notice the combination of nouns and verbs at the beginning of most sentences. These nouns and verbs are used to express the subject-action verb sentence pattern, which represents the doer of the action (subject) and the action performed by the subject (verb).

>> List verbs and nouns on topics you're familiar with, such as travel, music, food, social media, or an activity.

>> Write sentences using your listed nouns and verbs.

>> Record your sentences and listen to them.

Think nouns and verbs when you're composing sentences. Write with more nouns and verbs than adjective and adverbs.

Prevent Plagiarism

If you're unfamiliar with academic formalities of Western culture, you'll be frustrated by academic-honesty guidelines preventing plagiarism. But you can understand plagiarism by practicing key sentences that help avoid plagiarism (see Chapter 13). Chapter 7 discusses crediting sources.

Here are a couple of practice writing activities that help prevent plagiarism:

>> **Practice writing the sentences that credit your sources, sometimes called *attribution sentences.*** Begin by writing the author's last name (in the possessive form) as the first word of the sentence. Follow the author's name with the verb argues followed by a few words summarizing the source. Read a few practice articles on any topic and practice writing attribution sentences.

>> **Practice source engagement sentences.** Their purpose is to combine your personal comment with what the author says.

For more information on documenting sources, see my book titled *APA Style & Citations For Dummies* (John Wiley & Sons, Inc.).

Practice Structural Revising

In addition to your language editing, revising (see Chapter 14) adds an additional layer of complexity to your writing. Revising also offers you two opportunities to organize your writing: your first draft and your revised draft.

TIP

After completing a draft of your essay, circle your opening and closing sentences, and then circle the middle sentences that remain. You circled the structural elements of your essay. Each section contains distinctive information that doesn't logically apply to another section. For example, the body (middle) section contains the evidence. The body contains almost all the research and usually all the documentation.

As I describe in Chapter 5, write the body section first, after you create the thesis statement (see Chapter 6). The body section also includes the argument, the evidence that supports the thesis. As you write the first body draft, ensure that information relevant to the body remains in that section. If body information filters into the opening or closing, your professor will write a comment such as "lacks logic" or "lacks flow."

Earn Non-Essay Grade Points

Your course grade includes a percentage of points for your portfolio (approximately 60 to 65 percent) and the remainder percentage (35 to 40 percent) for your non-essay writing requirements. Jump on those non-essay points that include requirements such as the following:

>> **Attendance as participation points:** Some professors include attendance as part of participation points. Their thinking is that you can't participate in class if you're not in class. Regardless of the reasoning, attend every class and earn every point.

>> **Participation:** College classrooms are a welcoming environment for students to contribute their opinions. Professors remember students who contribute to classroom discussions. Participate in classroom discussions and earn the points.

>> **Homework:** Throughout the semester you may be assigned homework such as writing a response to a reading, punctuating sentences, or participating in a team presentation. Complete those assignments and earn the points.

>> **Deadlines:** Record assignment due dates on a planning calendar. Meet every deadline because they're easy points.

Befriend the Writing Center

Your campus writing center provides resources for your writing needs. Most centers have specialists who can help you as an nonnative English language learner, and their services are available as part of your tuition.

REMEMBER

Specialists can help you with documentation and annotation. They can identify patterns of errors and locations of confusion. They specialize in helping you with feedback and revising. Furthermore, no other service on campus assists student academics more than the writing center. Refer to Chapter 17 for more information.

If you have the determination to succeed, they can help you. Give them a good effort, and they'll improve your writing grades.

Ask Artificial Intelligence

Don't underestimate Siri's or Alexa's value to you as an English language learner. She can access information on almost any topic. Here are examples of how AI can help you:

>> **Spelling:** Ask her to spell any word you can pronounce.

>> **Meanings:** Ask her for a word meaning, and she'll give you three levels of meanings.

>> **Synonyms:** She knows words with similar meanings.

>> **Antonyms:** And she can give you opposites.

>> **Organization:** Ask her to enter an event, and you'll find it in your calendar.

>> **Reminders:** When you need a reminder, such as revise inactive verbs, ask your favorite AI, and she's on it.

>> **Resources:** If you're looking for information or need to check a quotation, your AI has you covered.

Your favorite AI can provide much more, but don't let her be a distraction.

Practice Freewriting Daily

Freewriting (see Chapter 12) represents another writing practice activity. Practice one ten-minute freewriting daily. It's as easy as writing off the top of your head, and some of the topics can help you with your studying.

Here's a list of topics to freewrite about:

>> An interesting topic you learned about in one of your classes

>> Information you need to study for an upcoming test

>> Questions you have about a course topic

>> The answer to one of those questions

>> What you find interesting about American culture

>> What if . . .

>> Similarities between two topics you studied

>> The response you get to asking AI her favorite topic

Don't forget to ask your AI to remind you to freewrite daily.

Master Idioms

No one knows better than you the difficulty of learning English idioms. They lack logical meaning, but they're critical to understanding spoken English. Fortunately, many are avoided in writing because they're overused expressions. You may have identified a few idioms in this chapter.

Here are a few idioms related to education:

>> **Ace a test:** Earn an A.

>> **Brainstorm:** A discussion for the purpose of generating ideas.

>> **Cover a lot of ground:** Complete a lot of work, such as content a professor covers in the classroom.

>> **Crack a book:** Open a book to read it.

>> **Draw a blank:** Unable to respond to a question.

>> **Old school:** An outdated method of thinking.

>> **One school of thought:** One philosophy, one method of thinking.

Don't forget to ask your AI about idioms that stump you.

Chapter **19**

Ten (or So) Tips for Repairing Broken Essays: DIY

've read and evaluated more than 10,000 writing projects over five decades teaching. From that experience, I offer you this piece of advice: A broken writing project, especially an essay, begins with a broken thesis statement. A broken thesis statement is like beginning a road trip with a broken vehicle — only bad things can happen. This chapter identifies issues that result in major point failures and explains how you can address them.

Fulfilling Requirements First

Start assignments in grade-building mode. Create a checklist of requirements from your syllabus and assignment sheet. Check the syllabus (take a look at Chapter 2) for language such as, "The first essay requires you to address university core values, and the second essay requires you to address department core values."

TIP

Review requirements on the assignment sheet (flip to Chapter 12) — the first two are usually audience and purpose. Check for a secondary audience. Look for bulleted requirements such as the following:

>> Reference the readings of . . ..

>> Include a reference from a class discussion.

>> Include an appendix (see Chapter 15) with a diary entry describing your revising process.

>> Annotate your bibliography (look at Chapter 7).

Each bulleted item may include additional requirements. Take advantage of all professor feedback (see Chapter 14) opportunities. Review your checklist before writing, during writing, and before submitting your assignment.

Looking Large for Major Issues

If your professor asks for a major revision (look at Chapter 14) of your essay, the essay issue is usually structural, a serious problem in the opening, middle, or closing (check Chapter 5). The major issue that appears in the opening includes a thesis statement that lacks focus and an arguable issue.

After reviewing the thesis, look for major issues in the middle paragraphs, such as weak or underdeveloped evidence, insufficient, or a lack of connecting evidence to the thesis.

Additionally identify any major issues by addressing the following questions:

>> Does the essay fulfill all requirements (check out Chapter 12)?

>> Does the opening and closing avoid strategies common to high school writing such as a dictionary definition and a summary?

>> Do sources have academic credibility (see Chapter 7)?

>> Do the middle paragraphs (see Chapter 5) read like a college essay and not a high school essay?

>> Are all sources credited?

Pleasing Your Professor

Never forget that your professor assigns your grade and controls your path to graduation. Although your college grades are performance grades, make sure you avoid any unacademic behaviors that could unintentionally affect your professor's assessment of you.

Addressing Professor Comments

Before you can address a problem, you need to understand the problem and the words your professor writes to identify it. Professors usually comment from the structural level down.

REMEMBER

Comments identifying structural problems include "needs focus," "needs organization," and "needs structure." These and similar organizational comments suggest lack of a clearly structured opening, middle, and closing (flip to Chapter 5). These comments also suggest a weak thesis (see Chapter 6). A comment such as "needs development" suggests weak evidence supporting the thesis. Comments such as "needs stronger evidence" suggests lack of quality sources supporting the thesis. These issues are easily correctable, assuming you dedicate time and thinking to it.

Your professor may suggest paragraph and sentence issues with comments such as "lacks flow," meaning paragraphs lack a logical flow (see Chapter 8) of ideas. Comments suggesting you should visit the writing center include "improve sentence structure," "needs clarity of ideas," and "choppy sentences." A comment such as "spelling," "punctuation," or "grammar" (shown in Chapter 11) tells you that you have a pattern of such errors and also need support. When your essay is submitted again, your professor will read to see how well you addressed comments.

Opening and Closing Strong

With the exception of writing majors, your professor has lower expectations for strong openings and closings — you have an opportunity to exceed your professor's expectations. (Quality opening and closings are low priority with most college writers, and many writers are satisfied with achieving a good paragraph indentation.)

The following suggestions can help you as you write your openings and closings (refer to Chapter 5):

>> Capitalize on the opportunity to use opening and closing strategy common to professional writers.

>> Study openings and closings from your reading.

A sign that your openings are successful is when they elicit a reaction from your readers, such as from your peers when openings are read aloud in the classroom. A strong closing leaves your professor with a sense of optimism when finalizing your grade.

Clarifying the Repair Problem

Before you can repair a problem, clarify with your professor the extent of the problem. Ask your professor to explain the issue and how to approach repairing it. If your professor is unavailable, go to the writing center for clarification. Or go to the writing center for more clarification on what your professor says.

Repairing a broken essay is usually more efficient than beginning another essay, assuming you have good evidence from your original essay. Beginning another essay requires additional researching of sources. If you decide to write another essay, write it with the supervision of a tutor in the writing center.

Presenting Perfectly

Presentation of your college projects is points for the taking — assuming you follow the details. Your professors design submission procedures to expedite their handling of assignments. For example, they may ask you to submit your assignment to an alternate email address so that they can separate it from class email, or they may ask for a PDF so that formatting isn't compromised.

WARNING

Avoid a cavalier attitude toward submitting your assignments. Your professors have reasons for their methods, sometimes as simple as the assignment not getting misfiled. Just do it as required and follow the details. Chapter 15 offers more information on presentation and submitting assignments.

Avoiding Failure to Credit Sources

The academic community values academic integrity and sources are the sacred vessels of that value. Misuse of sources — plagiarism — may result in dismissal from school.

Crediting sources begins with selection of the appropriate source. Use an acceptable source. Commonly used sources for essays include *secondary sources*, documents discussing a primary source. See Chapter 7 for an overview of crediting sources.

Regardless of the source, the academic community demands accurate crediting and recognition of that source. For formal source documentation, review the stylebook required by your professor, usually APA or MLA. One of the costly errors you can make in college is intentionally or unintentionally misusing sources. Credit all information in your essay that you reference from a source.

Index

fragile qualifiers, revising, 298–299
fragments, 158–159
frameworks, revising, 289
freewriting, 250–251, 348–349
front materials, 305–306
"functional needs," 197
'further,' 232

G

gap year, 29
gender nonconforming, 202
gender orientation, referencing, 201–204
gender stereotypes, avoiding, 203
genderfluid, 202
gender-neutral language, 192
genderqueer, 202
generalization fallacy, 144
genre, 42, 318–322
Giampalmi, Joe (author)
    APA Style & Citations For Dummies, 83, 86–87, 117, 143
Give it five brainstorming strategy, 251
The Glamour of Grammar (Clark), 338
glossary, 260
goals
    for essay portfolios, 66–67
    for writing, 265
'good and well,' 222
grade point average (GPA), 29
grading
    essay portfolios, 67
    essays, 100
grading section, on a syllabus, 30
Graff, Gerald (author)
    They Say I Say: The Moves That Matter in Academic Writing, 338
grammar
    about, 207–208
    adjectives, 148, 190, 222, 296–297
    adverbs, 149, 171, 222, 296–297
    approaching, 233
    common usage errors, 232–233
    comparisons, 198, 221

conjunctions, 149, 156, 214–217
improving page accuracy, 234–236
nouns, 166, 171–172, 228–229, 296–297, 345
parallel structure, 217–218
placing description, 218–219
prepositional phrases, 149, 212–214
pronouns, 148, 208–212
punctuation, 222–231
similar-sounding words, 233–234
terminology for, 149
verb forms, 219–221
growth mindset, 80

H

Harvard commas, 224
Harvard University Writing Center, 339
headings, 228, 229, 304–305
help availability section, on a syllabus, 32
Hemingway, Ernest (writer), 166, 282
hidden agendas, fact checking and, 309
hidden verbs, 170
high school teachers, compared with college professors, 13–14
high school writing, compared with college writing, 11
holistic scoring, 100
honor codes, 274
humanities, 316–317
hyperbole, 187
hyphenation, 231

I

icons, explained, 4
idioms, 349
ignoring counterpoints fallacy, 144
illogical tense shifts, 111–112
illustration, in middle paragraph, 91
impairment, 199
imperative sentences, 151, 152
'in order that,' 216

inactive verbs, 169
inclusion
    of cover letters in essay portfolios, 69–71
    showing, 198–201
incomplete sentences, 148–159
indefinite pronouns, 209
indenturing sentences, 159–163
independent clause, 149
independent clause-dependent clause, 157
independent study, 29
'insure,' 232
intensifiers, 156
intentional fragments, 156
interjection, 149
interpreting professor feedback, 285
Interrogate it strategy, 251–252
interrogative pronouns, 209
interrogative sentences, 151, 152
introductions, revising, 290–291
introductory comma, 176
inverted pyramid format, 91
irony, 187
irregular possessives, 231
irregular verbs, 219–220
irrelevance
    avoiding, 203
    in references, 193
Isaacson, Walter (author)
    Einstein: His Life and Universe, 82
    Steve Jobs: The Exclusive Biography, 85
italics, 229

J

journals, 71–72

K

Kahneman, Daniel
    Thinking, Fast and Slow, 293
key words, 155
knowledge, showing, 25

P

page, appearance of, 304–305

paragraphs
  about, 147–148
  coherence, 163–164
  developing, 161–163
  revising, 293–296
  structure of, 159–163
  topic sentences, 160–161
  varying lengths of, 162–163

parallel references, 203

parallel structure, following, 217–218

paraphrasing, to use sources, 132

parentheses (()), 227

participation section, on a syllabus, 31

partnerships, discovering new, 32–34

parts of speech, identifying, 148–149

part-time student, defined, 29

pass/fail, 27

passive voice, 167–168

past participle, 220–221

past tense, 112, 113

patchwriting, 276

patronizing language, avoiding, 197–198

patterns, varying, 173–179

pedagogy, 27

peer feedback, 43, 283–286

people-first language, 192

perfectionism
  channeling, 267–268
  delays and, 267

performance, level of, 52–53

persistence, growth mindset and, 80

person
  about, 116–117
  in transitional strategies, 163

personal commentary, writing for, 51

personal genre course, 41

personal narratives, 81

personal observation, in middle paragraph, 91

personal pronouns, 209

personality points, 53

personification, 187

persuasive essay/writing
  about, 38, 83–84, 239
  analyzing assignments, 242–245
  assignment requirements, 245–248
  background reading for, 248–249
  brainstorming strategies, 249–252
  optional assignment sections, 257–260
  organizing your, 240–241
  reading and recording, 252–255
  selecting topics for, 255–257
  team projects, 261–262

photographs, as extended sources, 127

Pink, Daniel (author)
  To Sell is Human: The Surprising Truth About Moving Others, 83

placing description, 218–219

plagiarism
  about, 273
  academic integrity, 273–275
  avoiding, 276–277
  consequences of, 275–276
  history of, 275
  nonnative English students and, 277–278
  preventing, 346
  researching, 275–276

plagiarism-detection technology, as strategy for avoiding plagiarism, 277

planning
  essay portfolios, 62–66
  revising, 300

play on words, in titles, 99

plurals, 235

poignant questions, in titles, 100

point emphasis, 155–156

point of view, 116–117

policies, on a syllabus, 31–32

political science, writing for, 331

polygender, 202

positioning
  prepositional phrases, 212–214
  of sentences, 155
  topic sentences, 161

possessive case, 211

possessive pronouns, 209

possessives, 230–231

practicing
  reading skills, 341
  structural revising, 346
  writing, 344–345
  writing skills, 341

predicate nominative, 210

preparing
  e-portfolios, 72–74
  persuasive essays, 241

preposition, 149

prepositional phrases
  about, 149
  positioning, 212–214

prepositional phrase-subject (understood)-compound verb, 157

prepositional phrase-subject-verb, 157

prepositions
  about, 212–213
  ending sentences with, 213–214

prerequisite, 27

present participle, 221

present tense, 112, 113

presentation and formatting
  about, 301, 304, 313
  back materials, 305–306
  closing, 303
  determining what's missing, 309–310
  editing, 306–308
  of essay portfolios, 72
  first page, 302
  first paragraph, 303
  first sentence, 303
  front materials, 305–306
  identifying common errors, 308
  importance of, 354
  literacy improvement plan, 311–313
  page appearance, 304–305
  strategizing editing, 307
  submitting essays, 306
  titles, 302
  verifying information, 308–309

About the Author

Dr. Joe Giampalmi, a lifetime learner and teacher, has more than half a century classroom teaching experience from middle school to graduate school and consulting classroom experience from K to 12. He taught at Nether Providence Middle School (Wallingford, Penn.), Sun Valley High School (Aston, Penn.), and on the collegiate level at Neumann University, Immaculata University, Widener University, Delaware County Community College, and recently Rowan University for two decades.

His publications include five books (the recent *APA Style & Citations For Dummies*), a dozen articles for national magazines, and a 34-year twice-monthly newspaper column. He received numerous academic awards and was named to a number of area halls of fame.

He earned his B.A. and M.Ed. from Widener University and Ed.D from Temple University. He writes from Florida's Gulf Coast and Center City Philadelphia. He's inspired by warm weather, whispering palms, and white-sand beaches.

Dedication

Joe, Jeff, Lisa. You were raised by first-generation college graduates, and you in turn raised (and are in the process of) the third generation of college graduates. So proud of your generosity and what you accomplished — high-level leadership success in business and education, and a nonprofit that raised more than a million dollars for breast cancer in honor of your mother.

And to other first-generation college students in the process of earning degrees and changing direction of their families for future generations. Degrees make a difference; commitment earns degrees.

Forever thankful for the daily enjoyment of life and academic support, Carole Anne. Thank you for your availability to read chapters within hours' notice.

Author's Acknowledgments

This is the book that's been inside me a lifetime. The ideas matured during my two decades teaching at Rowan University where I was immersed in a writing process culture. My teaching of writing was supplemented with newspaper writing at Delco News Network. The combination worked well.

Thank you . . .

Margot Hutchison, my literary agent, and Bill Gladstone, founder of Waterside Productions.

John Wiley & Sons, Inc. executive editor Lindsay Lefevere, project manager and editor Chad Sievers, and editor Vicki Adang. Lindsay wisely suggested the Writing 101 chapter (Chapter 3). Vicki's insight improved the flow of the table of contents. Chad is the most knowledgeable language person I ever met. No one knows the *For Dummies* audience like Chad.

Proofreaders daughter Lisa (her fifth book proofreading), wife Carole, and West Chester University adjuncts Christine Cuozzo and Michelle Guinam. Thank you, Chrissy and Michelle, for feedback on what to emphasize and what to further develop. Lisa, a pleasure working with you professionally. Together we share more than 80 years classroom teaching.

Jack and Bonnie, younger siblings whose children continued the degrees. Mom and Dad, how did you know to raise me with the assumption I would go to college?

John Mooney (St. James High School), my most influential English teacher. Joe Logue, my coach at St. James, much of my success is his teaching the belief that any accomplishment is possible.

Former students at Nether Providence, Sun Valley, and Rowan University, who deserved the best from me.

Colleagues at Rowan University's Department of Writing Arts.

Former newspaper editors Dottie Reynolds, Chris Parker, and Peg DeGrassa at Delco News Network. Thank you for the start of my writing career.

Publisher's Acknowledgments

Executive Editor: Lindsay Lefevere
Project Manager and Editor: Chad R. Sievers
Technical Editor: Amber Chenoweth, Ph.D.

Production Editor: © valentinrussanov/ Getty Images
Cover Image: Pradesh Kumar